I0147948

Praise for Previous Books by Rick McIntyre

"[Rick McIntyre is the] chief historian for the most famous wolf population in the world."
WASHINGTON POST

"Yellowstone's resident wolf guru Rick McIntyre has been many things to many people: an expert tracker for the park's biologists, an indefatigable roadside interpreter for visitors, and an invaluable consultant to countless chronicles of the park's wolves... But he is first and foremost a storyteller."
NATE BLAKESLEE, *New York Times* best-selling author of *American Wolf*

"Rick's writing is so vivid, so powerful, that I feel I have been right there with him among the wolves of Yellowstone."
DR. JANE GOODALL, DBE, founder of the Jane Goodall Institute and UN Messenger of Peace

"What thrilling stories about the Yellowstone wolves! The daily observations by Rick McIntyre are unprecedented in their detail and bring the personalities alive. The wolves are intelligent, feeling beings who... learn over a lifetime what their role in the pack is or ought to be."
FRANS DE WAAL, author of *Mama's Last Hug*

"McIntyre's vivid accounts of Yellowstone wolves are reminiscent of Ernest Thompson Seton's animal tales, but these wolves are real and their skillfully told stories offer invaluable insights for researchers and readers alike."
BERND HEINRICH, professor emeritus of biology at the University of Vermont and author of *Mind of the Raven*

"Rick McIntyre has observed wild wolves more than any person ever. It is the way he sees wolves—as fellow social beings with stories to share—that makes his books so powerful. Through that lens, we glimpse our own hopes and dreams."

ED BANGS, former US Fish and Wildlife Service wolf recovery coordinator for the Northern Rockies

"Few people have ever observed wildlife as closely as Rick McIntyre, or written biographies of individual animals with as much clarity and wisdom."

BEN GOLDFARB, author of *Crossings*

"[McIntyre's] greatest strength is the quiet respect and wonder with which he regards his subjects, a quality clearly informed by decades of careful watching."

PUBLISHERS WEEKLY

"Like Thomas McNamee, David Mech, Barry Lopez, and other literary naturalists with an interest in wolf behavior, McIntyre writes with both elegance and flair, making complex biology and ethology a pleasure to read."

KIRKUS starred review

"No one has ever had the insight and intuitive understanding of wolves that Rick McIntyre brings to the page, because no one has ever had enough experience with the lifetimes of wild wolves to write their individual biographies. McIntyre is a phenomenon. His series of wolf books is unprecedented in writing about the natural world."

CARL SAFINA, *New York Times* best-selling author of *Becoming Wild*

"No one has put in the hours watching wolves that McIntyre has. No one has his in-depth knowledge of individuals, the landscape, neighboring packs, and other wildlife. Using all this knowledge, he puts together stories of lead wolves in a way that has never been done before."
DOUGLAS W. SMITH, former senior wildlife biologist and project leader for the Yellowstone Gray Wolf Restoration Project

"Rick McIntyre writes about wolves with the reverence they are owed. His detailed descriptions of the interwoven lives, deaths, deadly feuds, and romantic liaisons of Yellowstone's wolves are Homeric in nature. And his intimate portrayals of individual wolves' personalities and the sometimes humorous, sometimes tragic circumstances of their lives reveal them as kin to us, each of their days subject to fortune or fate as are our own."
AMAROQ WEISS, senior wolf advocate with the Center for Biological Diversity

Books by Rick McIntyre

Denali National Park: An Island in Time

Grizzly Cub: Five Years in the Life of a Bear

*A Society of Wolves:
National Parks and the Battle Over the Wolf*

*War Against the Wolf:
America's Campaign to Exterminate the Wolf*

*The Rise of Wolf 8:
Witnessing the Triumph of Yellowstone's Underdog*

*The Reign of Wolf 21:
The Saga of Yellowstone's Legendary Druid Pack*

*The Redemption of Wolf 302:
From Renegade to Yellowstone Alpha Male*

*The Alpha Female Wolf:
The Fierce Legacy of Yellowstone's 06*

*Thinking Like a Wolf:
Lessons From the Yellowstone Packs*

*The Unlikely Hero:
The Story of Wolf 8* (with David A. Poulsen)

*A Time of Legends:
The Story of Two Fearless Wolves—
and One Rebel* (with David A. Poulsen)

*Queen of the Wolves:
The Legendary 06 Female* (with David A. Poulsen)

RICK McINTYRE

My Life With Wolves

How I Became the Storyteller for the Yellowstone Packs

GREYSTONE BOOKS
Vancouver/Berkeley/London

26 27 28 29 30 5 4 3 2 1

Greystone Books Ltd.
greystonebooks.com

Cataloguing data available from Library and Archives Canada
ISBN 978-1-77840-121-3 (cloth)
ISBN 978-1-77840-122-0 (epub)

Editing by Jane Billinghurst
Copyediting by Brian Lynch
Proofreading by Meg Yamamoto
Maps and illustrations by Kira Cassidy
Jacket design by DSGN Dept.
Jacket photograph by Keith R. Crowley/ZUMA Wire/ZUMAPRESS.com
Text design by Fiona Siu

Printed and bound in Canada on FSC® certified paper at Friesens. The FSC® label means that materials used for the product have been responsibly sourced.

Greystone Books thanks the Canada Council for the Arts, the British Columbia Arts Council, the Province of British Columbia through the Book Publishing Tax Credit, and the Government of Canada for supporting our publishing activities.

EU Safety Information: Easy Access System Europe, Mustamäe tee 50, 10621 Tallinn, Estonia, gpsr.requests@easproject.com.

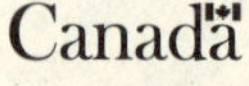

Canada Council for the Arts
Conseil des arts du Canada

Greystone Books gratefully acknowledges the xʷməθkʷəy̓əm (Musqueam), Sḵwx̱wú7mesh (Squamish), and səlilwətaɬ (Tsleil-Waututh) peoples on whose land our Vancouver head office is located.

Oh, the Places You'll Go!

BOOK BY DR. SEUSS

Two roads diverged in a wood, and I—
I took the one less traveled by,
And that has made all the difference.

ROBERT FROST, "THE ROAD NOT TAKEN"

CONTENTS

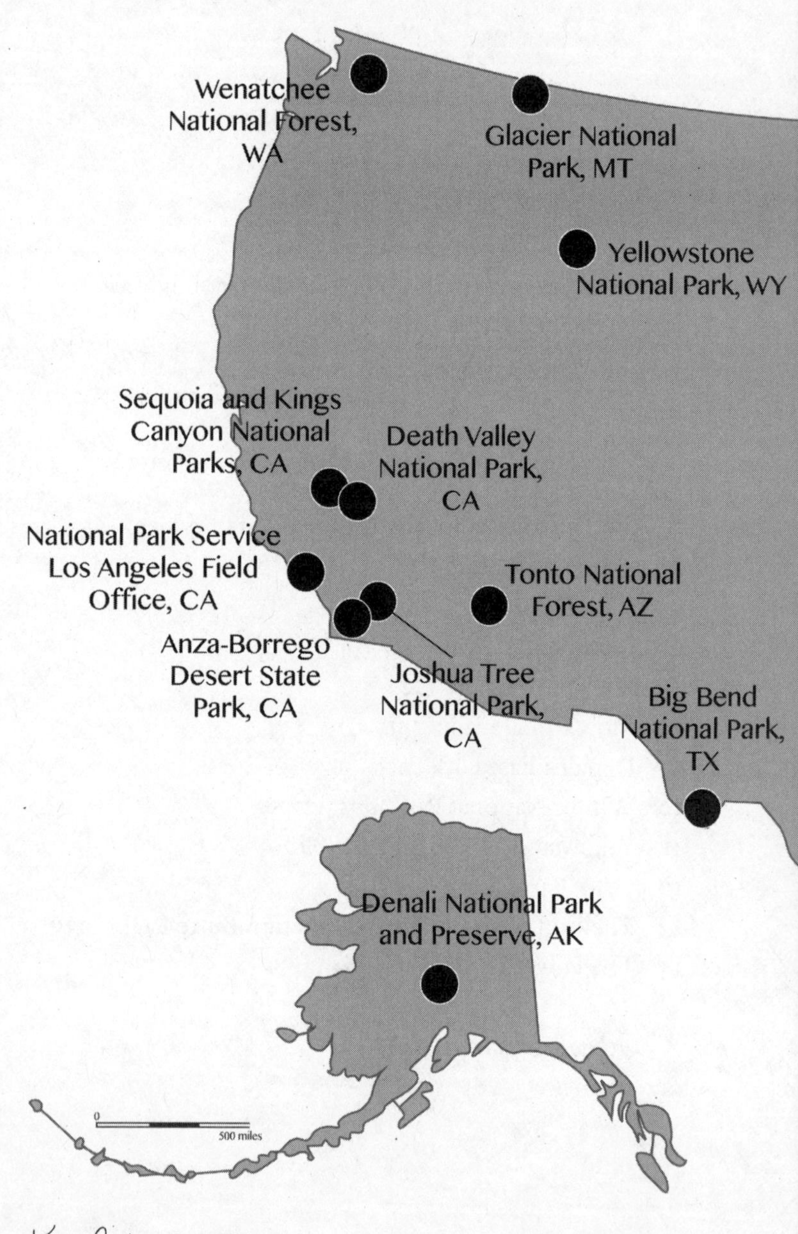
Wenatchee
National Forest,
WA
Glacier National
Park, MT
Yellowstone
National Park, WY
Sequoia and Kings
Canyon National
Parks, CA
Death Valley
National Park,
CA
National Park Service
Los Angeles Field
Office, CA
Tonto National
Forest, AZ
Anza-Borrego
Desert State
Park, CA
Joshua Tree
National Park,
CA
Big Bend
National Park,
TX
Denali National Park
and Preserve, AK
0
500 miles

National Parks, Forests, and Other Areas Rick McIntyre Has Worked Since 1968

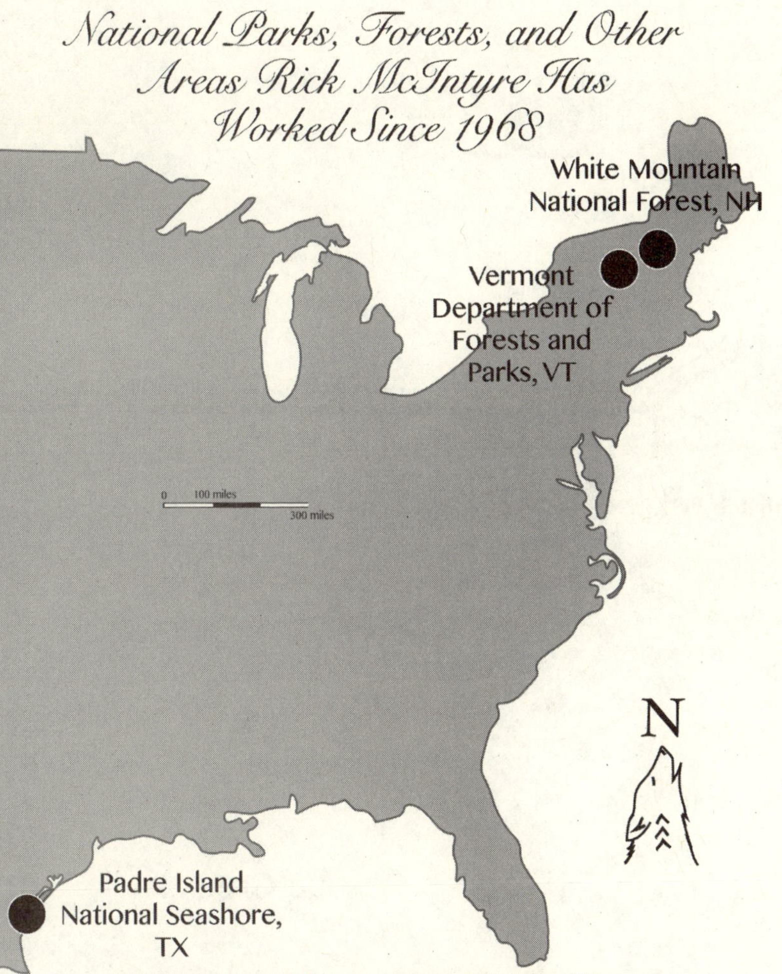

White Mountain National Forest (summers 1968, 1969, 1970)
Wenatchee National Forest (late summer 1970)
Vermont Department of Forests and Parks (winter/spring 1975)
Sequoia and Kings Canyon National Parks (summer 1975)
Anza-Borrego Desert State Park (winters 1975/76 and 1976/77)
Denali National Park and Preserve (summers 1976 to 1990)
Tonto National Forest (winter 1977/78)
National Park Service Los Angeles Field Office (fall 1978)
Padre Island National Seashore (winter 1978/79)
Death Valley National Park (winters 1979/80 to 1985/86)
Joshua Tree National Park (winters 1986/87 to 1991/92)
Glacier National Park (summers 1991 to 1993)
Big Bend National Park (winter 1993/94 to 1998/99)
Yellowstone National Park (summers 1994 to 1998, year-round 1999 to 2018, retired and continued to study wolves 2018 to present)

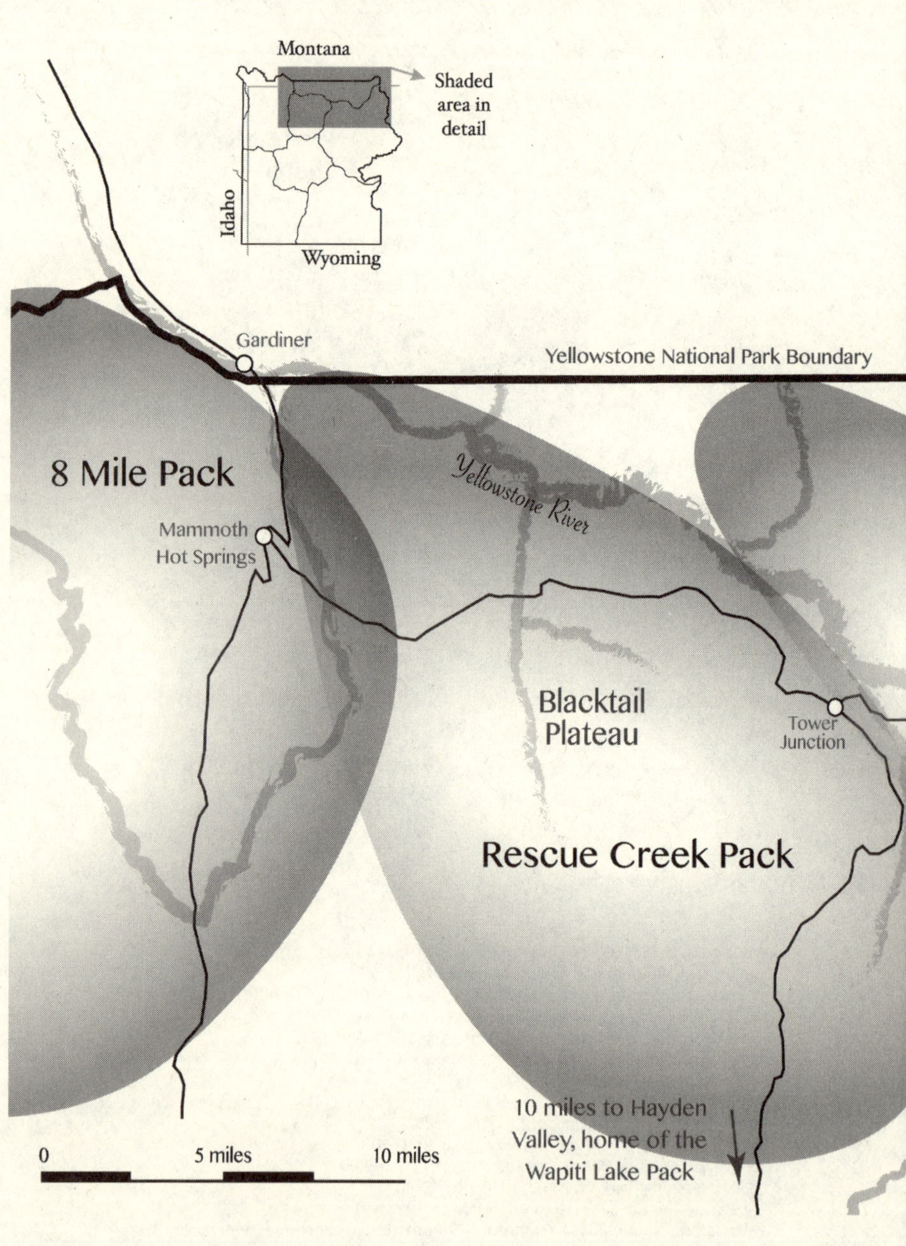
Montana
Shaded area in detail
Idaho
Wyoming
Gardiner
Yellowstone National Park Boundary
8 Mile Pack
Yellowstone River
Mammoth Hot Springs
Blacktail Plateau
Tower Junction
Rescue Creek Pack
10 miles to Hayden Valley, home of the Wapiti Lake Pack
0
5 miles
10 miles

Select Yellowstone Wolf Pack Territories 2025

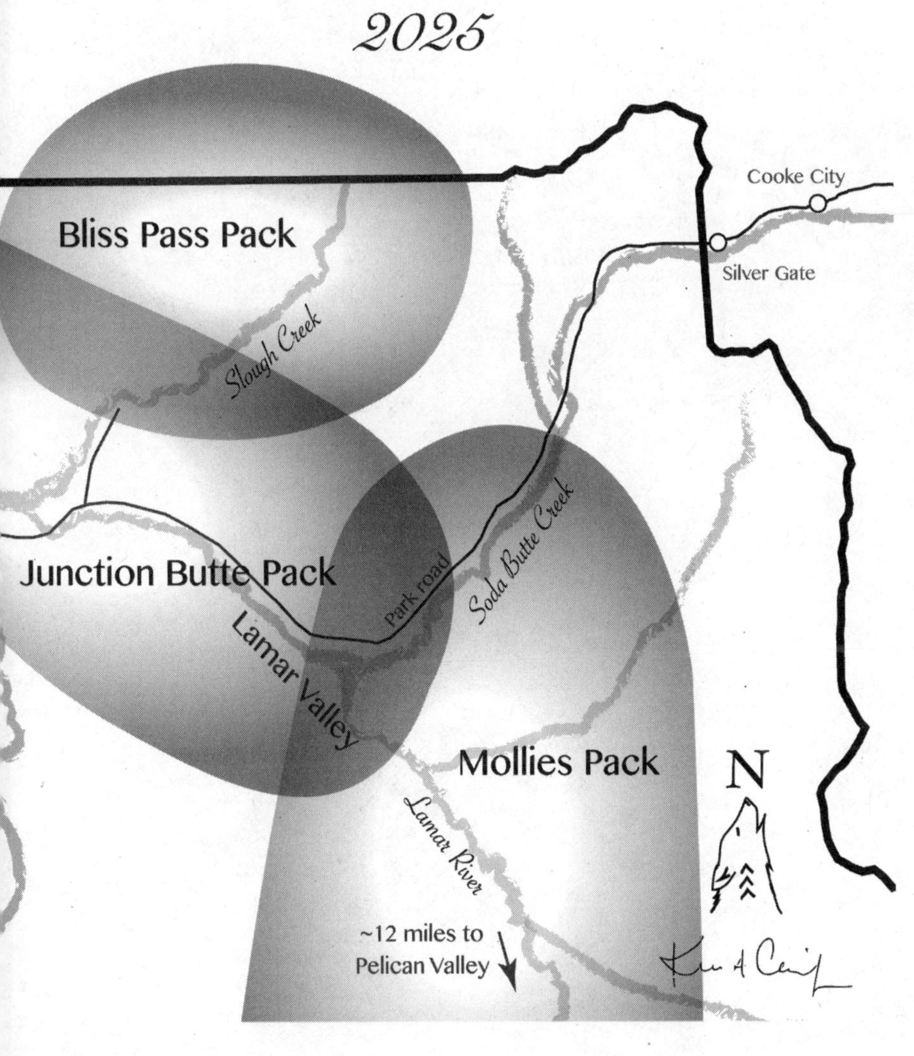

907's Family Tree

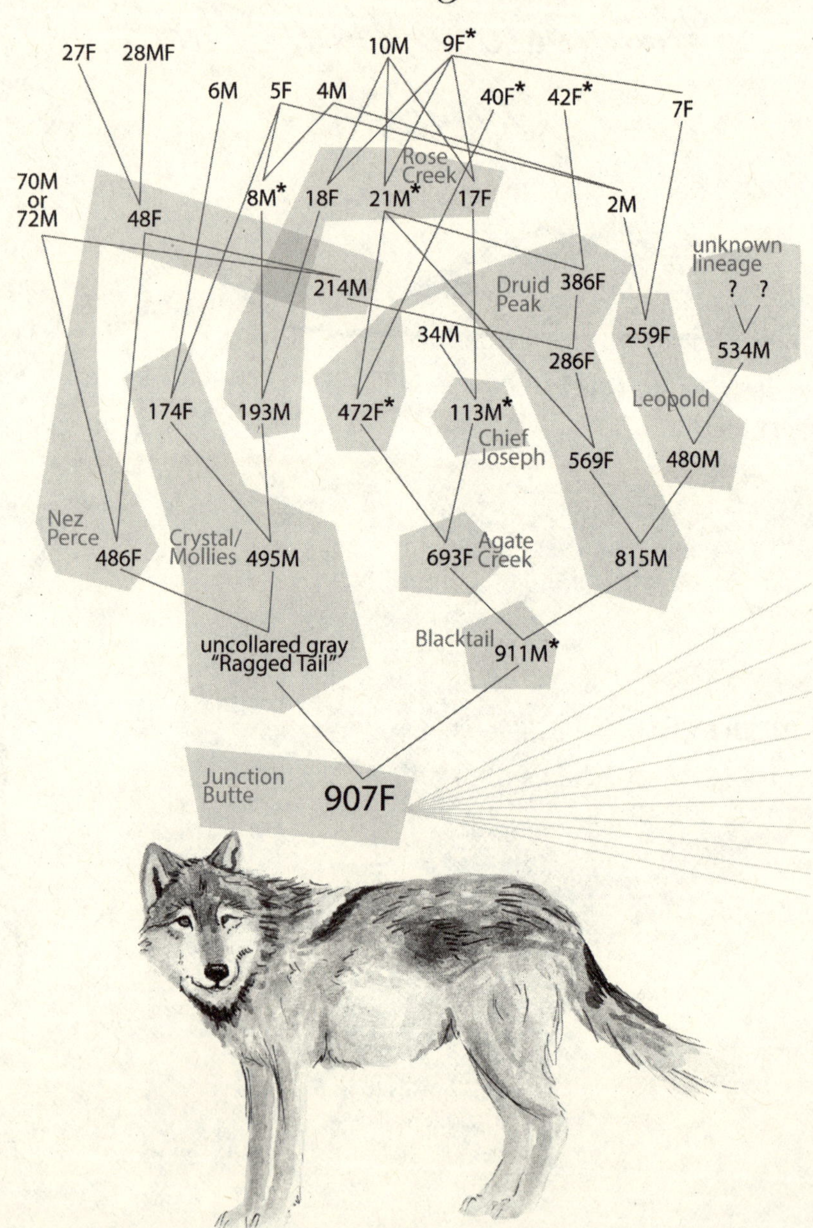

Wolves without a shaded pack of birth were born in Canada or northwest Montana and brought to Yellowstone during the reintroduction in 1995 or 1996.

*I cover the stories of these important wolves in my book series, The Alpha Wolves of Yellowstone.

907's Pregnancies
(all in Junction Butte)

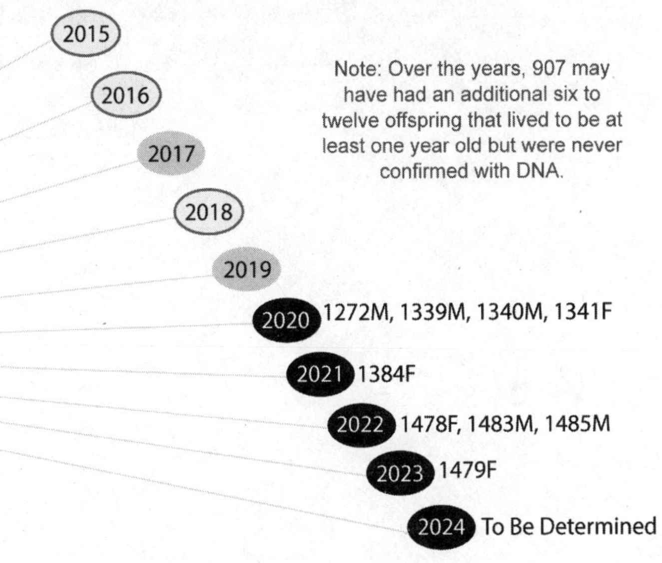

Key

Unknown if any of her pups survived.

Pups died before emerging from den.

Pup(s) survived.

Wolf numbers after ovals are offspring confirmed with DNA.

INTRODUCTION

DECEMBER 22, 2024, started off like many of the nearly ten thousand days I had spent in Yellowstone National Park researching wolves. I found the Junction Butte wolf pack bedded down at Slough Creek, a mile south of their traditional den site. I had studied this family for twelve and a half years, ever since it had been formed in the spring of 2012. Before that, I had watched their ancestors all the way back to 1995.

At their peak in 2020, the Junctions had numbered thirty-five. A few weeks ago, there had been fourteen wolves in the group, but now there were only six: eleven-and-a-half-year-old alpha female 907, three young female adults, and two black pups. The missing pack members, including the alpha male, had likely been shot when they left the park in recent days in search of elk. 907 had brought the surviving pack members back to the core of their territory at Slough Creek.

An invading group of sixteen Rescue Creek wolves suddenly appeared and charged at the greatly diminished pack. 907 immediately ran off to the north and the other five Junction wolves followed her. The Rescue wolves chased them and soon all the wolves went out of sight a few miles to the north. Over the next four days, I would see the ramifications of the pursuit I had just witnessed, another chapter in the ongoing saga of the Yellowstone wolves.

The wolves of Yellowstone have allowed me to witness the joys, disappointments, and often heart-stopping dramas of their lives day after day, year after year, and generation after generation for thirty years. This is both my story—and theirs.

1

Formative Years

I WAS BORN IN the city of Lowell, Massachusetts, in August 1949. I grew up with my older brother, Alan, and my parents in a nearby rural town called Billerica, which is close to the famous historical communities of Concord and Lexington, where early battles of the Revolutionary War took place in 1775. The Concord River flowed through part of our town, and we lived on Concord Road.

As a kid, I was pretty self-reliant. On my first day of school, I got on the bus in front of our house, spent the day in the first-grade classroom, then, when school ended, followed the other kids to the buses. I did not understand that the buses were going to different neighborhoods and got on the nearest one. When I realized it was not going to my section of town, I asked the driver to stop, and he dropped me off without asking any questions. I looked around, visualized which roads I needed to walk along to get to my house, and an hour or so later arrived home. My mother did not notice that I had not arrived on the bus or ask why I was so late.

I had a general sense that it was my responsibility to look after myself. One day when I was about six, all the guys in our neighborhood were in our yard and a teenager named Phil told me to fight a boy named Tommy Proia. Tommy was a year older than me and a big tough kid. Despite being so young, I knew that to earn the respect of the other guys I had to agree to the match. Phil had used the word *fight*, but because we all watched a local professional wrestling show on the television, our neighborhood style was to wrestle rather than box.

Tommy and I stood up and went at it. Right away I could tell that Tommy was going easy on me. He was a good kid and was not going to hurt or humiliate me. We wrestled for a few minutes, then he put me in a headlock. Our rules were that you could win by pinning your opponent for a count of three or by getting him to give up. After a few minutes of struggling, I said, “I give,” and Tommy let me go.

That fight was one of the most influential events of my life. I learned how important it is to step up if you have a challenge, regardless of how you think you might do. Failure or defeat does not matter if you have the courage to take on the challenge. From that day in the 1950s to right now, I have lived my life on that basis, taking on many risks and difficult tasks, and the lesson has served me well.

AFTER THAT FIGHT, Tommy and I became best friends. My brother and I, Tommy, his two older brothers, and other guys from the neighborhood would get together every day after school and in the summer to play games, fish in ponds, and walk around the woods and fields in the neighborhood.

I was the youngest boy in the gang, but I soon discovered I had a superpower. The other guys were very afraid of poison ivy, which was plentiful in our area, but I was immune to its toxic chemical. I would show off by picking some leaves and holding them up. Even chewing leaves had no effect on me. Later, when I heard that a person could lose their immunity, I was smart enough to stop handling it.

I would catch and release sunfish and perch in the local ponds, but my biggest interest was the turtles that swam there. We had a fishing net at home, and I figured out how to use it to catch turtles. After looking each one over, I would let it go. One day Tommy and I were looking for fish and turtles in a small creek. He saw something in the water and reached in to see what it was. It was a muskrat leghold trap, but luckily it did not spring shut on his hand. We threw it away, for we had no tolerance for people who killed animals for profit or sport.

Other than goldfish and a parakeet, my family had no pets. We tried adopting a stray cat, but the first evening we had it, it leaped up onto the parakeet cage and tried to get at the bird. We decided not to keep the cat.

Our house was modest, and there were several families in our neighborhood who owned houses much larger than ours. We regarded those people as being rich, but even though they had more money than our family and the Proias, we did not think of them as being better than us in any way.

The Galvins lived across the street. They had come to America from Lithuania and had become well-off after starting a successful business. Even though she lived in a big house, Bessie Galvin was down-to-earth and friendly to us kids. We were welcome to come over anytime and see her pheasants and chickens. Being typical boys, we always wanted to be there when Bessie grabbed a chicken to cook for dinner. She would chop off its head with an axe, then it would run around headless for a while.

Shepy was one of Bessie's dogs. Every morning, Shepy would leave the house to roam the local woods and fields. He came back home when he felt like it. One day I followed him as he explored. It was a big adventure for me. When I look back, I can see how following Shepy helped prepare me for my time watching and following wolves in Yellowstone as they roamed through the meadows and valleys that were their home. When I was a boy, the closest I got to having a dog was hanging out with the Galvins' dog Shepy.

IN THE FIRST or second grade, all the kids in our elementary school were brought into the auditorium to hear a talk given by a member of one of the tribes that had lived in our part of New England for many centuries. He went through all the treaties the US government had made with Native tribes and how our side had broken nearly every one of them. Listening to him gave me a lifelong empathy for Native people and also a sense of how a talk can change people's attitudes and impact their lives.

The kids in my generation were known as baby boomers because of the surge in births in the years after World War II. That big increase in the number of children coincided with television becoming available to most American families. It was normal for kids to watch cartoons on Saturday mornings and western shows in the evenings. My dad must have seen that I liked watching pro wrestling on television. Sometimes he would come into the living room and we would wrestle on the rug. He always let me pin him. I knew that was just pretend, but it meant a lot to me to have that time with him. My father and I also played catch in our yard. That was why it was so emotional for me decades later to watch the scene at the end of the movie *Field of Dreams* where Kevin Costner's dad comes back to play catch with him.

Like most dads in the 1950s, my father found it hard to show his emotions. I never remember hearing him say he loved me. But those times when we wrestled and played catch spoke more than words could. Many decades later in Yellowstone, I saw a father wolf, wolf 21, wrestling with his pups and letting them pin him to the ground. Watching the family at play confirmed my feeling that wolf families and human families show very similar behaviors.

I HAVE ALWAYS enjoyed books, and as a young kid, I read comic books. At first that was Donald Duck, Uncle Scrooge, and other Disney comics, then I graduated to Superman stories. I remember going to the town library in Billerica every week. I took out books on dinosaurs and, later, science fiction and H. P. Lovecraft stories that were usually set in nearby rural New England towns. One science fiction story stuck with me. Aliens from space gave earthlings small devices that were so compelling to watch we became addicted to them and did not fight back when those aliens took over our planet. That was a pretty good prediction of how addictive smartphones would be in modern times.

I also really enjoyed movies. Starting when I was about six years old, the other guys and I would take the bus into the nearby city of Lowell to see movies at the Strand and

RKO Keith theaters. I liked the ones with monsters in them best, especially dinosaurs. I watched the original 1933 *King Kong* and the 1956 *Godzilla* on television dozens of times, and all the 1950s movies about how atomic radiation caused ants, scorpions, grasshoppers, and even shrews to grow into gigantic creatures.

Next to *King Kong*, my favorite movie was *20 Million Miles to Earth*. It featured a dinosaur-like animal that astronauts captured on Venus and brought back to Earth. Like Kong, the creature escaped captivity, went on a rampage, and ended up being killed. That was the downside to all those movies: the innocent main character, the one I was rooting for, always ended up dead.

One monster movie, however, was different: *Gorgo.* It came out in 1961 and was about a dinosaur that was captured in the sea near England. Gorgo ended up in a London amusement park, where crowds of people paid to see him. It turned out that Gorgo was a baby. His mother showed up, destroyed parts of London as she made her way to her baby, and freed Gorgo, then both went back into the sea. That seemed like a much better ending to me.

I also watched the 1962 Disney live-action movie *The Legend of Lobo*, which was based on a massively popular 1898 short story called "Lobo, the King of Currumpaw" by naturalist Ernest Thompson Seton, and I read Jack London's books *White Fang* and *The Call of the Wild.* All those stories had sympathetic wolf characters.

Looking back, I believe the empathy I felt for all those misunderstood creatures on the page and on the screen prepared me for my later studies of wild wolves, animals that have been hated and killed just like the main characters in the stories that captured my imagination as a child.

Music was another part of popular culture of the times that I particularly enjoyed and enjoy to this day. I was too young to remember what many regard as the first rock and roll hit record, "Rock Around the Clock." It came out in 1954 and went on to sell 25 million copies. Bill Haley did not have the classic handsome appearance of a rock star, but two years later, along came a guy who did: Elvis Presley.

Presley used to sneak into Black churches to watch the preachers go all out emotionally, and he listened to the choirs sing like their lives depended on the music. People would fall into trances, jump around, roll on the ground, and speak in tongues. In 1956, Presley's "Hound Dog" became a smash hit. The original version was sung by Black artist Big Mama Thornton. Later in life, I would know a Yellowstone wolf called 302 who was very much like the irresponsible bad boyfriend in Big Mama's version of that song.

I THOUGHT I would live in rural Billerica forever, but that was not to be. My dad worked as an engineer for AT&T in the town of Framingham, about an hour's drive away. In the summer of 1959, after I finished fourth grade, we moved into one of hundreds of identical ranch-style homes in a suburban development in that town. My father died a few months later. He was only fifty-two.

A few years earlier, my dad had had a heart attack. Back then doctors could not do much to prevent a second attack. He came home for lunch one day feeling tired. After eating, he lay down on the living room couch and had a second heart attack that killed him. Many decades later, I would have my own heart problems, but thanks to modern medicine and a quintuple bypass operation, I had a total recovery.

I was ten years old at the time of my father's death. In those times, no one knew what to say to a young boy when his father died, so none of my relatives, neighbors, or teachers ever mentioned his death to me. I was already pretty independent, and I think not having a father figure or male role model gave me even more confidence that I could figure things out on my own.

My dad must have had a good life insurance policy, for we never seemed to want for anything after his death. My mother later worked part-time in the bakery section of the local supermarket, but that salary would not have been enough to support her, my older brother, and me. She also had enough money to pay off the mortgage and, later, to cover college tuition for both her sons.

I quicky made friends in my new neighborhood and those guys were pretty much like my friends in Billerica. We had a big reservoir behind our backyards, where I could fish and catch turtles. I borrowed some of my mother's red nail polish to mark each turtle I caught. Some I would release where I had caught them and others I would release well away from the capture site. I then tried to keep track of which ones stayed put and which went back to their original home. That was my first attempt at wildlife research.

One of the guys figured out how to make a raft supported by two car inner tubes, and we all copied his design. One day we were out on our rafts when we spotted a huge snapping turtle. We had heard rumors of snapping turtles attacking kids and pulling them underwater to drown. To us the turtle was a monster lurking in the water, waiting for its chance to kill us.

A boy on one of the rafts had a bow and arrow, and he shot the turtle. We dragged it to the shore, where another guy killed it. Technically, I was not involved in harming the turtle, but I was part of the group and had done nothing to stop the killing. In the following days, I got depressed over my part in that incident. The snapping turtle looked dangerous, but it had done us no harm. We should have left it alone.

Sometime after the turtle killing, there was another incident, this time involving a gun. My dad had a single-shot .22 rifle. He died before showing me how to shoot it. I got interested in the gun and bought some ammunition. I loaded the rifle and took a walk out in the woods. A gull flew over, and without thinking, I aimed in its direction and pulled the trigger. Fortunately, I missed. I immediately berated myself for doing such a stupid thing. Like the snapping turtle, the gull had done me no harm.

Those incidents and my sympathy for the animal characters in books and monster movies combined to give me a strong sense of looking at things from the perspective of the innocent creature who was just trying to survive. I wanted to be respectful of animals' right to live their lives without interference.

IN FIFTH AND sixth grades, my best friend was Doug. We bonded over our love of dinosaurs and a comic book series called *Turok: Son of Stone* about two Native Americans who discovered a valley where dinosaurs still lived.

One day Doug came over to my house and we got on separate rafts. We paddled over to a forested peninsula in the reservoir and got ready to camp out for the night. It rained a few hours later, and since we did not have a tent, we decided to get into the rafts and paddle back home. That was a big mistake, for in the dark Doug's raft capsized and he fell into the water.

Working together, we somehow got him back on his raft, but he was now soaking wet and cold. We made it back to my house, where my mother got some of my clothes and gave them to Doug, then put us to bed. I now look back at that near-death rafting adventure and realize it could have been an incident out of Mark Twain's *Huckleberry Finn*. I never said anything to the guys at school about rescuing Doug, as that would have diminished his tough guy persona and been embarrassing for him.

In sixth grade, something happened that threatened to destroy my friendship with Doug. Our teacher wanted to show us the proper way to behave at dances, so she took us to the gym, put on some music, and taught us boys how to ask girls to dance as well as how to correctly hold them while dancing. That involved chastely putting your right hand on her lower back and using your left hand to hold her right hand in the air at shoulder level. Then she told the boys to choose a partner and practice dancing.

My mistake was to go to the prettiest girl in the school, Carolyn, and ask her to dance. She accepted and we danced once, then walked away from each other, mostly because I had no idea how to talk to a girl.

I soon realized I had a big problem. Doug "liked" Carolyn, meaning he wanted to be her boyfriend. He had never asked her to be his girlfriend. It was just something in his twelve-year-old mind. There was a code among the guys: you did not ask a friend's pretend girlfriend to dance, and I had just done that. It was dead serious stuff for boys our age.

We were let out for recess after the dance lesson and that was when the trouble began. To keep respect from the other guys in the school, Doug had to do something about the guy who had asked his girlfriend to dance, and that was me. Otherwise, he would lose his street cred. I understood that and did not blame him, for in that context, I was the one at fault.

He came over and said we would have to fight. I immediately knew I was going to have to accept his challenge or lose face. By that time, all 250 kids in the schoolyard, from first to sixth grade, had run over and were surrounding Doug and me. It was our version of *Fight Club* decades before that movie came out.

Like Tommy Proia, Doug was a tough Italian kid and a good fighter. A few weeks earlier, he had gotten into a fight with another kid everyone regarded as a tough guy and had easily destroyed him with a series of punches to both ears. That other kid ran off crying, the worst possible thing a boy could do. I knew I had a problem. Doug was a talented striker while I was just a wrestler. I had never hit anyone in my life and have maintained that record to this day.

We came together and I expected to get hit in the face right away, but Doug held off on using his fists. Instead, he played to my wrestling strengths. He tried to get me in a hold, but I blocked him, then I attempted the same thing on him and was also blocked.

At that point, I realized two things. Doug was not trying to beat me and he had started the fight when recess was almost over. In a minute or so, the bell would ring and we would have to go back to class. Doug and I continued to try to get holds on each other, then the bell rang and it was over. Officially, the fight was a draw, but I knew he could have won if he had wanted to. After that, he and I went back to being best friends and he never mentioned the incident with the girl to me again.

We both came out of that incident with the respect of the guys in the playground. Doug did what he had to do during those times: confront the guy who had danced with his girlfriend. And I did not back down when he challenged me to a fight. But I knew the truth: Doug had taken it easy on me, just like Tommy had years earlier.

Somehow I had managed to remain calm, despite the stress of being surrounded by the entire school in the playground as I was about to fight a more talented opponent. As with my earlier match with Tommy, that conflict with Doug confirmed to me that in tough situations you figure out the right thing to do and then do it, regardless of how difficult it may seem.

Those experiences, along with the incident where Doug almost drowned, helped me have confidence when I had to deal with challenges later in life. They instilled in me what became a lifelong optimistic attitude that enabled me to take on a lot of risks and gave me a willingness to try new things.

After my fight with Doug, I often had wrestling matches with local guys, but they were all friendly competitions. I won most of them by pinning the other boy or by him quitting when I put him in a hold he could not get out of.

I later found out that the type of wrestling we used in the rural towns where I grew up was a remnant of a form known as grappling. The primary differences between that and amateur or Olympic-style wrestling are that grappling allows submission holds that force an opponent to give up and pinning in a grappling match requires a count of three rather than a one count. As mentioned earlier, in our towns you signified you had lost by saying the words "I give."

Both George Washington and Abraham Lincoln were champion grappling wrestlers. Lincoln often competed at county fairs and was regarded as unbeatable. As for Washington, one day during the Revolutionary War when there was no chance of encountering the British army, he gathered his troops and offered to take on any challengers. A series of seven men, both officers and enlisted soldiers, took him up on his challenge and were quicky beaten by the future president, one after the other.

After reading about Washington's triumph, I had a daydream about going back in time so I could have matches with Abe and George. Both were taller than me (Washington was six-foot-three and Lincoln measured six-foot-four) and weighed more. Based on what we know about their skill level, I would likely lose both matchups, but it would be a great set of experiences.

Decades later I read an autobiography by a pro wrestling champion named Lou Thesz. In his era, from the 1930s to the early 1960s, most matches were preplanned as to who would win. But Thesz was a real grappler and could legitimately beat the best athletes in the world. When Lou showed up for an event, he would ask the promoter if he wanted a real contest or a performance, which meant putting on a show for the audience, and he would wrestle the match accordingly. On reading that part of his book, I realized that is what Doug and I did in the schoolyard: we put on a performance for the other kids.

Thesz also wrote: "Wrestling teaches self-reliance regardless of whether or not the wrestler wins or loses. He alone is responsible for the outcome and seldom loses the same way twice. I have never known a good wrestler who did not succeed in life simply because the first thing we learn is tenacity." While writing this book, I had my ten thousandth day in the field in Yellowstone. I guess that qualifies as tenacity.

IN THE FALL of 1960, when I was in sixth grade, I acquired a neighborhood paper route. I collected the newspaper money from my customers every week, then went to the distributor's office to pay what I owed for the papers. What was left over was my profit. A few weeks after getting my paper route, I told my mother that now I was making my own money, I no longer needed an allowance. My allowance had been one dollar per week, which was enough back then to see movies on the weekend and buy candy and drinks.

There was a dodgy family I delivered papers to. Their house was run-down, and one day, without any notice, they vanished. They owed me a few dollars, a significant amount of money for a kid at that time. If they did not pay me, I would have to pay my distributor with my own money.

A few weeks later, my mother and I drove to a supermarket on the far side of town. I was walking around the neighborhood while she shopped when I spotted the car that belonged to that family. I walked up to the house it was parked by and knocked on the front door. The father opened it and seemed shocked to see me. I looked him in the eye and calmly said, "I'm collecting," my standard line when I asked people to pay their bills. He stared at me for a moment, then pulled out his wallet and paid me. I never told my mother what I had done.

At the start of that school year, some of the families in our neighborhood, including my mother's, were told that their kids no longer qualified to take the town bus to school, because we did not live far enough away. So that school year, including the winter months, I walked the two miles from my house to school in the morning, then back again in the afternoon.

There was a candy store across the street from our school, but the kids were forbidden to visit it during recesses and were required to get on buses immediately after classes were over. Since I was walking, I could go to that store on the way home. I began to buy extra candy and sell it at cost as a favor to the kids who had no access to that store. Soon the neighborhood boys, without any encouragement from me, were bidding against each other for the candy and I was making five to ten times what I paid for it. All that ended when several mothers went to my mother and complained.

IN THE EARLY 1960S, during my junior high school years, all of us read *Mad* magazine and loved the way the writers and artists satirized American life and pointed out the hypocrisy of politicians and other authority figures. I can now look back and see how that magazine prepared us for the social and political revolutions of the late 1960s. *The Twilight Zone* was my favorite TV show in junior high and I loved the clever twists in the weekly stories.

While I was going to junior high, my mother started her part-time job in the bakery. It was unusual to have a mother who worked. The norm was for mothers to stay home and be housewives, which meant cleaning the house, doing laundry, and preparing meals. None of my friends' mothers worked and we all said that when we got married, we would not let our wives work, as it would be a bad reflection on us. We were clueless about what the women would think or say about that and only thought about how the issue would affect our egos.

About that time, I found out that a paleontologist named Raymond Alf was living and working in a nearby town. To study dinosaurs was my dream profession, so I wrote him a letter asking if we could meet so he could tell me how I could become a paleontologist like him. He responded by return mail and invited my mother and me to visit him. He and his wife were very gracious, and a few weeks later they visited us at our house. I never did become a paleontologist, but based on the kind example of Dr. Alf, I answer every letter and email kids send me and agree to meet with all of them when their families bring them to Yellowstone.

My interest in dinosaurs led me to read several books by Roy Chapman Andrews. He was director of the American Museum of Natural History in New York City and famous for discovering the first fossilized dinosaur eggs during an expedition in Mongolia. I fantasized about working at that museum and going on expeditions to remote areas.

I never did get a job at the museum, but decades later I did give a couple of presentations there, one on grizzly bears and another on wolves. Chapman was also an early president of the Explorers Club. When I was invited to be a member of the Explorers Club in 2022, I did some research and discovered Chapman carried a whip on his belt when he was in remote, bandit-infested areas. Many people think Chapman's adventures in the early 1900s were the inspiration for the movie character Indiana Jones. Chapman's whip ended up being donated to the club's collection.

Around that time, there was a new hit television cartoon show called *Yogi Bear* about two bears who lived in the fictional Jellystone National Park. The bears always got in trouble with Ranger Smith. That was my earliest understanding that there was a place called Yellowstone and that the people who worked there were called rangers.

IN JUNIOR HIGH, Doug was putting all his energy into playing soccer and I was not much interested in that, so we drifted apart. I hung out with guys in my neighborhood, but they were increasingly getting into stealing and drinking. It was hard to do, but I decided to stop seeing them. Soon after that, I got involved with another group of guys and one of them set off a stink bomb in a movie theater men's room. Because I was with those guys, I got in trouble. Two policemen came to our home and told my mother that I was hanging out with a bad crowd. Fortunately, I did not particularly like those boys, so it was no problem to agree to avoid them.

In fall 1963, I started at a local Catholic high school. Although my mother was Episcopalian, my dad had been

Catholic. When they met in the early 1940s, Catholics were not supposed to marry outside their religion, so it was a bit of a scandal when they announced they were engaged.

My mother tried to visit one of my father's sisters to introduce herself. She knocked on that sister's door several times. There was no response, but my mother happened to look through a window and saw the woman hiding near the door. After Dad died, my mother drove my older brother and me to church every Sunday and later picked us up after Mass and Sunday school were over. She never said anything negative about the Catholic religion.

We often visited my mother's brother Walter and his wife, Stella. I always was fascinated when my uncle talked about growing up in Boston decades earlier. That was when descendants of the English upper and middle classes ruled the city and had a strong bias against the Irish. Uncle Walter said it was very common to see signs in the windows of restaurants and bars that said, "No Irish allowed."

But the Irish figured out how to turn that around. Many men joined the Boston Police Department, and they eventually became the most powerful faction in the organization. At the same time, Irish politicians took over the city government. Then the Kennedy family went into politics and their son John F. Kennedy was elected president in 1960. I always felt a kinship with Irish boys because of my Scottish ancestry and our shared history of constantly fighting the English.

My father's ancestors left the Scottish Highlands in the early 1800s. That was during a terrible period known as the Highland Clearances. Rich English families allied with the king had been given large tracts of land in Scotland. Poor

Scottish families were allowed to sharecrop on small plots of land but had to give a large share of their produce to the overseer. The overseer would sell that produce and send the money to the landowners in England. It was bare subsistence for the poor people, much like the sharecropper system in the American South in the old days.

When a new breed of sheep was created that could stay outdoors year-round, even in the severe Highland winters, the overseers realized that far more money could be generated by getting rid of the poor sharecroppers and replacing them with sheep. What commonly happened was families were ordered off the land by the local sheriff and told to march to the seacoast, where they would board ships. Some ships took those families to Australia and others sailed to southern US states such as North Carolina.

My McIntyre ancestors ended up in Nova Scotia, which means "New Scotland." One rose to become the Catholic bishop of Nova Scotia. Around 1900 some of the clan moved to the Boston area, and my father was born in the nearby city of Lowell in 1906.

In contrast, my mother's family, the Dunlops, immigrated from northern Scotland directly to Boston. Many of the men were experienced mechanics and easily found well-paying jobs in their new city. My mother was born in Boston in 1908. She was one of eight kids and my father came from a similarly large family.

One member of our clan was Duncan Ban MacIntyre (1724–1812), a famous Gaelic bard who lived his entire life in Scotland. MacIntyre primarily composed and recited verses about nature and heroic human characters. When I read about him, I realized that my books are also about heroic characters, but the heroes I write about are wolves rather than people.

MY CATHOLIC HIGH school was very different from the neighborhood schools I had attended up until then. The teachers were nuns who wore elaborate black-and-white habits, and a priest taught religion. Unlike the students in the town's two public high schools, the students who attended the Catholic high school were expected to go on to get a higher degree.

In elementary school and junior high, I always had plenty of friends. But in my first year at that high school, I did not fit in well. Many of the guys had gone to a Catholic junior high and already knew each other. A lot of them played on the school's football team. I was not good at football. We were required to wear coats, ties, and dress pants. The other guys knew how to dress well and I did not.

After school during my freshman year, I worked in the town library. The job was mainly putting books on the shelves after readers returned them. I always liked libraries, so I enjoyed the job.

We went through two huge events that school year. In November 1963, President John Kennedy was assassinated in Dallas, Texas. The shooting shook the country to its core. But then, just a few weeks later, something came along that changed everything. I remember being in my room one evening, listening to a Boston AM station. The disc jockey said a friend had sent him a record by a new band in England. I was not very interested and wanted the DJ to play something familiar. But after hearing "I Want to Hold Your Hand" by the Beatles, I knew I had never heard anything like it—not because of the lyrics, which were very simple, but because of the infectious sound and enthusiasm of the band. The gloominess of the assassination was wiped out by the joy and optimism of that song.

Within a week or two, Beatlemania took over the country. Their hold on the public imagination was solidified when the band came to America and made three appearances on the popular Ed Sullivan TV show in early 1964. That summer their upbeat movie *A Hard Day's Night* came out and further enhanced everyone's love for the guys in the band and their music. All the boys in our school started dressing like the band members and began letting their hair grow long. The Beatles and what was known as the British Invasion helped me fit in better and have more friends, as we all were going through the same cultural revolution.

The British Invasion bands flooded America with hit songs. They included the Rolling Stones, the Animals, who did "House of the Rising Sun," and Them, who had a hit with "Baby Please Don't Go." I did not know it back then, but I eventually realized the Stones and the other two bands were blues-based groups. I read the credits on the Stones' albums and bought records by Black artists they covered, like Bo Diddley. That prepared me for blues-influenced music that came out later in the 1960s by artists like Jimi Hendrix, Janis Joplin, Cream, and Led Zeppelin. That is still my favorite music.

Many years after that, I heard my all-time favorite joke. It was on *Saturday Night Live* in the late 1970s. In their

"Weekend Update" fake news segment, the cast member set up the punch line by reminding viewers that the *Voyager* spacecraft had been launched into outer space on a mission to find intelligent life. A recording was in the capsule with speeches by politicians and examples of our culture. That included music from Beethoven, Brahms, and the seminal rock and roll song "Johnny B. Goode" by Chuck Berry. After those lines, the cast member excitedly announced that we had gotten a four-word message from an alien race that had listened to the recording: "Send more Chuck Berry!"

MY BEST FRIEND in high school was my cousin Eddie Glynn. He was eighteen months older than me and his mother was my dad's sister. The Glynns had a summer home at Hampton Beach, New Hampshire, and I spent several weeks there every year. To make extra money, Eddie and I collected Coke bottles and turned them in for the two-cent deposit. We also sold newspapers on the streets. At his house, we played board games and badminton. At the beach, we bodysurfed the waves. When we were older, we ran a few miles on the beach, played tennis at a local court, and golfed at a par 3 range.

Eddie's mother and father were both schoolteachers, and in the summer months Eddie's father managed a movie theater at Hampton Beach. His boss owned two theaters: the Casino and the Surf. Eddie was hired as an usher in one of those theaters, and starting when I was fifteen, I got my own usher job in the other theater.

Eddie and I worked split shifts. That meant we got up early and swept out both theaters and cleaned the restrooms.

In the evenings, we helped people get to their seats in the dark and herded folks out of the first show so we could seat the crowd for the later show. I had to do crowd control on those jobs, which included stopping guys from trying to get in to see the movie for free. Being comfortable controlling crowds was a skill I would use when I worked as a bouncer in college and when I became a park ranger later in life.

I befriended our projectionists, and they taught me how to run 35mm movie projectors. I remember that we frequently showed Warner Bros. Road Runner cartoons before the movies. They were always about Wile E. Coyote's comically failed attempts to capture and eat the Road Runner. Every scene was set in a mythical desert, country that was totally foreign to me. I did not know it then, but I was destined to spend many of my early years as a park ranger in desert areas such as Death Valley.

One morning when we were cleaning one of the theaters, we found a wallet with a lot of money in it. It belonged to the son of a man who owned much of Hampton Beach. Eddie and I were both honest guys, so we returned the wallet and money to the family. We never got a reward or even a thank-you. It made us realize that some rich people can be jerks when dealing with regular folks who have a code of always trying to do the right thing.

I will always have great appreciation for all those times I stayed with the Glynns at their beach house as well as for my lifelong friendship with Eddie, who died a few years ago. Writing about him has made me realize that he was the best person I have ever known and the best friend I ever had.

THOSE OF US who lived through the early 1960s will never forget the horrifying news footage of peaceful Black people and white supporters marching to demand equal treatment and being viciously beaten by police and attacked by German shepherd dogs trained by police departments. The marchers showed unimaginable courage, as they knew the police would assault them, but they were not going to back down on equal rights. Those scenes forever put my generation on the side of demanding that everyone be treated fairly, regardless of race or any other issue, and these are values I hold to this day.

In my early high school years, I thought I would become a politician after finishing my education. I read many books written by politicians, I visited the Massachusetts State House in Boston, and I subscribed to the *Congressional Record*. But in my junior year something happened that changed all that. It was an American literature class, and our textbook included an excerpt from the 1854 book *Walden; or Life in the Woods* by Henry David Thoreau, who had lived in the nearby town of Concord. After reading that excerpt, I got his book and rushed through it. I had never read anything by a writer who liked walking in the woods and watching animals like I did. It got me thinking about how I could live a life like Thoreau's.

By then I had gotten my driver's license, and my mother let me borrow the family car and drive to Concord. I visited Walden Pond, where they have a replica of Thoreau's tiny cabin. Then I walked around the pond and through the surrounding woods, country that was identical to the woods I had tramped around in just a few miles away in Billerica and Framingham.

I also went to Ralph Waldo Emerson's home in downtown Concord. At times Thoreau had worked for Emerson and lived with his family, sleeping in a spare bedroom. That room had some of Thoreau's books and notebooks on display, along with his survey equipment. I later took a surveying class in college and did surveying work that was probably not much different from what it was in the time of Thoreau. In that American literature class, we also read Robert Frost's poem "The Road Not Taken." Frost was another New Englander who, like Thoreau, lived close to nature and wrote about finding your own path in life, a path less traveled by other people. That is exactly what I did.

We did not have a wrestling team in my high school, so instead I ran for the track team in my junior year. I was a fast runner among the neighborhood guys but soon realized that I was not as good as the talented runners on the team. I decided my goals were to go to every practice and run every race, no matter how well I did, to cheer on the other guys in their races, and to finish the season.

As I reviewed my early years for this section, I realized how deeply I regret several occasions when I treated other people in a cruel manner. Once in Billerica and again later in Framingham, I pushed boys who were not on my level of physical ability. In high school, I knew a girl who was overweight. We were friendly to each other, but one day for some reason I cannot fathom, I used a mean word to call attention to her size. Maybe I had just seen a TV show where a character got a laugh by saying something similar to such a girl. I wish I could go back and redo those incidents.

I don't know if I am qualified to give anyone advice, but let me say to young people: never pick on or bully another human being. First, it is wrong, and second, you will regret it for the rest of your life. Instead, say a kind word to kids that have challenging issues in their lives. I keep these thoughts with me to this day as I stand by the side of the road in Yellowstone, making it possible for people, especially young kids, to see wolves. I am happy that I can do my part in helping people fulfill their dreams, no matter who they are or what challenges they may be facing in life.

WHEN I GOT back to school for my senior year, I sent off for college catalogs and tried to figure out where to go and what to major in. Harvard University was just twenty miles away, and back then local high school students did not think it was a big deal to apply to Harvard or other private Ivy League colleges. I ended up deciding I wanted to go to the University of Massachusetts in Amherst, which was a ninety-mile drive west from our town. I got accepted and picked forestry as my major because it sounded like the best option if I wanted to live a life like Thoreau's.

That winter I worked at Jordan Marsh, a huge department store at the local shopping mall. First I was a stock boy in the women's nylon stockings section, where I learned all the colors and sizes of stockings, then I was promoted to more general shelf stocking. I worked with a great group of guys from all walks of life. They were like the boys I knew in elementary and junior high, just regular guys. That contrasted with the students in the Catholic high school who came from families that were better off financially.

Toward the end of my senior year, I tried to get a summer forestry job with the state of Massachusetts, but you had to be eighteen, and my eighteenth birthday was not until late August. I ended up working for a guy in a neighboring town, mostly doing lawn work but sometimes cutting down trees in people's yards. The hours were long, but the pay was good.

In August of that year, 1967, Eddie set me up on a blind date at Hampton. I had not had a great deal of experience with girls. There was that ill-fated dance class when I was twelve and one date the previous summer, when I had gotten up the courage to ask a girl at Hampton to go out with me. We had gone to a James Bond movie at one of the theaters where Eddie and I worked. Then we got some hamburgers and ate them on a bench by the boardwalk. After that, we kissed a few times and that felt pretty good.

This time, I opted to buy tickets for my date and me to go to a ballroom where the Doors were going to play. Their debut album had just come out and this was their first national tour. I had that album and really liked it. Their music was different from anything else out at the time and their album quickly became a huge hit. "Light My Fire" was the number one song all over the country.

Back then, bands who had a hit record or two were often booked to play in ballrooms. Except when a group played a hit song, people would usually dance to their music rather than watch them play. All of us danced to the Doors' first few songs, then stood and watched them play "Light My Fire." After that hit, we went back to dancing as they started up other songs.

I sensed their singer, Jim Morrison, was getting upset. To me, the audience was behaving normally. Ballrooms were for dancing, after all. I watched as Morrison turned around to his band mates and said something to them, then they started playing the first notes of their next song. As before, several hundred people started to dance. But after about twenty seconds, the crowd gave up because it was impossible to dance to the beat of that song. That was only part of the issue. The lyrics were about a character who wanted to kill his father and do terrible things to his mother. It was a twelve-minute song called "The End," but it seemed to go on forever and the crowd was getting hostile.

I stood there with everyone else and soon figured out what was going on. Jim Morrison did not care at all if you liked his singing or his songs, but he could not stand it if you disrespected him by dancing while he was performing. You had to pay attention to him. Years later, when I was doing thousands of talks in front of large audiences in National Parks and other venues, I often thought of how Morrison behaved that evening. The lessons I took from that experience were: don't take yourself too seriously, respect your audience, and never be arrogant.

Life Lessons From Wolves
Courage

Early on in my life, I learned that if you have courage, you can overcome even seemingly insurmountable obstacles. This lesson has helped me move forward in my own life, and I saw the value of courage clearly in one of the first wolves I got to know in Yellowstone National Park many years later.

As a pup, Yellowstone wolf 8 was bullied and picked on by his three bigger brothers. It looked like he was unlikely to accomplish anything significant in life. When he was a yearling, 8 came across mother wolf 9 whose mate had been illegally shot and killed. She was struggling to raise eight pups by herself. 8 made friends with the pups and the mother wolf accepted him into the pack as her mate. That meant he was now an alpha male. Despite his young age and lack of experience, 8 stepped up to take on that responsibility as well as the task of helping to raise and train the eight pups. Later, when his adopted family was about to be attacked by a rival pack, 8 charged at their alpha male, who was much bigger than him, somehow won the battle, and saved his family.

I deliberately used the words *stepped up* to describe what 8 did when facing a challenge, because that is what I often had to do in my own life: when I helped save my best friend from drowning, when I wrestled bigger and more experienced boys than me, when I knocked on the door of the sketchy man who owed me money for newspapers, when I had to fight a guy in college who was assaulting a girl, and, later in life, when I raised the funding for my Yellowstone Park Service position.

I tell wolf 8's story in *The Rise of Wolf 8: Witnessing the Triumph of Yellowstone's Underdog.*

2

College and the US Forest Service

MY MOTHER DROVE me to Amherst at the start of the 1967 fall semester and dropped me off. At that time, there were about twenty thousand students at what we called UMass. I fit in much better in college than I did in my early high school years. I really liked the fact that with so many students, you could always meet new people. I also liked the wide array of events on campus, including movies, speakers, talks, and concerts.

I gradually figured out how to talk to girls and take them out on dates. I did not have a car, so we mostly went to events on campus. If there was a new movie in town, we would walk the one mile to the theater. One time when I got back home, I called Carolyn, the girl I had asked to dance in the sixth grade, and asked her out. She politely turned me down by saying her boyfriend would not like that.

My degree would be in the sciences, so I had to take geology, physics, and chemistry, all of which were hard for me. But by then I had learned how to pass exams, and I got through those tough courses with C grades.

My first forestry class was dendrology. We went out into the woods to learn the common and scientific names of the local trees and shrubs. On my first test, I got a score of 4 percent because I had not yet learned how to spell their Latin names. Another early class was wood technology, where we were taught how to identify wood used in furniture made from local tree species. The one class I had on wildlife offered no information on animal behavior or on the intrinsic value of having a diverse array of species in an ecosystem.

In my later classes, I realized my major was based on managing forests to produce the greatest amount of wood for industries such as home construction and furniture manufacturing. The value of leaving some trees or even an entire forest to grow naturally without cutting the trees down for human use was never considered. I recall how one of my forestry professors often went on rants about the preservationist management philosophy of National Parks. In lectures he would say something like "You tell me, what good does it do anyone to let a tree in Sequoia National Park grow old, die, and rot away when it could have been cut into lumber and used to build homes for people?"

I had friends majoring in both wildlife and fisheries management, and their professors seemed to take a similar approach. The wildlife classes were oriented to managing species such as deer for utilitarian purposes, which meant maximizing the number of deer for hunters. Fisheries classes stressed producing high numbers of fish in hatcheries, then releasing them into streams just before fishing season so anglers could catch them. Most of the forestry and wildlife professors grew up in the Depression and they abhorred any hint of waste. That translated to only valuing natural resources such as trees, wildlife, and fish for what they could do for humans. Despite that, I have to say that all my professors were good people who meant well.

The most important moment of my college career took place toward the end of my freshman year. Here is how I remember that incident. I ran up the stairs of the forestry building to the second floor as fast as I could, raced down the corridor, then turned right and rushed toward a professor's office. Looking up, I was devastated to see that someone was already waiting for the professor to arrive.

The reason for my despair was that I had seen a sign posted on a bulletin board on the first floor that announced the US Forest Service was going to allow that professor to choose forestry majors to fill two summer jobs. One was in the White Mountain National Forest in New Hampshire and the other was in the Allegheny National Forest in Western Pennsylvania. My friend and fellow forestry major Steve was already standing at the professor's door. Because he was first in line, Steve would have his choice of the two Forest Service jobs.

The White Mountain position was my dream job, as I had already started to hike the mountain trails there. I desperately wanted that slot, but Steve was there ahead of me, and I figured he wanted that job just as much as I did. The professor arrived and asked Steve which job he preferred. I was shocked when he chose Pennsylvania. It turned out he had relatives in that area and wanted to be near them. Then the professor turned to me and said, "Well, you got the New Hampshire job if you want it." That was probably the happiest moment of my life up to that point.

Soon after that, our country experienced two tragic events. The first was the assassination of Martin Luther King Jr. in April 1968, the day after he speculated he might not live to see true racial equality in our country in his "I've Been to the Mountaintop" speech. The second was the fatal shooting of presidential candidate Robert Kennedy two months later. Both men were heroes to my generation. Those were dark days for our country.

WHEN THE SPRING semester was over, I went home and got ready to spend the summer in New Hampshire. My mother bought me a used car, a 1964 Chevy Nova, and I drove up to Gorham, New Hampshire, where I reported for duty at the Forest Service district office. I had a beard at the time and was told they were not allowed. I could keep my mustache.

I was eighteen and felt sure I was on my way to a career with the United States Forest Service. I bought my uniform shirts and was given Forest Service patches to sew on the upper left sleeves. As I had never done any sewing before, it took me a long time to sew on the first patch. When I was done, I realized I had sewn it through both sides of the sleeve. I had to tear out the stitches and start all over again.

I was assigned a bunk in the crew quarters building in Dolly Copp Campground and met the five guys who would be my roommates for the summer. We were all crammed in one bedroom with three sets of bunk beds. Each of us had just one drawer for storing our clothes and other possessions, but that seemed normal to us after living in college dorm rooms. The restroom had one toilet, one sink, and one shower stall. There was a small kitchen with a table. We agreed that we would alternate cooking dinners for one another. None of us knew much about cooking, and I mostly boiled hot dogs for the guys when it was my night to cook.

The following morning, I drove back to the district office to meet the rangers and other staff and fill out paperwork, including a pledge to support and defend the US Constitution from all enemies foreign and domestic. I have now worked for the federal government for many decades in many different jobs. I signed that pledge forty-two times before starting my position in Yellowstone in 1994, and I always took it seriously.

I found out I would be on a three-man crew doing what the agency called crop tree release. In that part of New Hampshire, the forests were mostly hardwood trees. Birch and maple were the most valuable species for the local sawmills because the wood was used in furniture making, and those sawmills were a major source of jobs for people in the area. Aspen trees were considered worthless.

Our summer job consisted of going through our New England hardwood forests and looking for places where aspens were growing next to more commercial species. We would then kill the aspens by taking our axes and girdling the trees, meaning we chopped through the bark all around the trunk. That severs the cambium layer inside the bark and prevents water and nutrients from reaching the upper part of the tree. We were issued hard hats, axes, and hockey shin guards in case an axe bounced off a tree and went toward our lower legs, something that occasionally happened.

My coworkers, Bob and Joe (not his real name), were both forestry majors at the University of New Hampshire. Joe had grown up in Gorham, while Bob came from a nearby town. The three of us would take our pickup to our assigned section of the National Forest, unload our equipment and backpacks, then spread out and walk through alternating strips of the forest looking for aspen to girdle.

The local guys had a couple of issues with me. The first strike against me was that I had failed a test on driving a standard-shift truck. It seemed like everyone in the area drove a pickup, but I had never driven a stick shift. That meant no driving for me that summer on the job. The second strike against me was that I was from Massachusetts. The guys from New Hampshire thought Massachusetts people were way too liberal.

My crewmate Joe repeatedly made derogatory racial remarks about Black people to get a rise out of me. I came close to settling things between us with a fight but decided to try a different strategy. I concentrated on treating him well and doing favors for him, such as carrying some of his equipment when we later fought a fire in the mountains. That worked and soon he stopped trying to bait me. We got along all right for the rest of the season.

I later concluded that he had grown up among people who had a racial bias and was mainly repeating things he had heard them saying. My experience that summer taught me that if you are going to work closely with someone, you have to figure out how to get along and get the work done regardless of the differences and issues involved.

After we had gotten used to our job, our supervisor called us into the office and told us that from then on, instead of girdling the trees, we were going to kill them with chemicals. They gave us gallon jugs filled with a toxic mixture. The new method was to chop shallow indentations around the trunk of a tree, then squirt the chemicals into the cut.

Being forestry students, we were proud of our axe work and did not like switching from traditional girdling to herbicide use, but those were our new instructions. We quickly found out that it was nearly impossible to keep that chemical from spilling on us. After a few days, we rebelled, and surprisingly our supervisor let us have our way. I later suspected that the chemical was Agent Orange, which was being used in Vietnam to defoliate forests. It was subsequently proven to cause cancer, and many vets had terrible health problems after they were exposed to it. I am grateful we rebelled but worry the chemicals we used might have had some effect on me.

EVER SINCE THE local fire department came to our elementary school and put on a demonstration of their equipment, I had thought it would be cool to be a firefighter. In this job, I got to be a firefighter for real when a small lightning fire started in the high-elevation conifer forest in our district.

Our crew, along with other staff, were assigned to hike up there and put it out. That involved first making a fire line around the burning material. We cleared the brush just past the burning area, then dug down to mineral soil. Once the fire line was completed, the flames could not spread past it.

That was the first time I used a firefighting tool called a Pulaski, which has an axe on one side of the business end and a hoe on the other side. It was invented by Ed Pulaski, a Forest Service ranger, in the early 1900s. It was the perfect tool, as we could use it to chop down a tree or scrape out a fire line in the dirt. Such a fire line has no burnable material and will stop the spread of most fires.

There was no water up there, so a plane dropped several loads of five-gallon containers to us in thick pouches. One of them got caught in a tree and we really needed that water. Since I had climbed so many trees when I was a kid, it was easy for me to go up that tree and toss down the water. We left the mountain after other workers certified the fire was out.

A few evenings later, back at our crew quarters, one of us happened to look up to where the fire had been in the mountains and saw flames. It turned out that there were still some live embers in what New Englanders call duff. That is slowly decomposing plant material that can be a foot or so deep. Those embers had set the area on fire again.

We called that report in and early the next morning hiked back up to the fire. I was the last man at the site a few days later and had the responsibility of reporting whether the fire was out. It was a relatively small fire, so I took off my gloves and felt through every square inch of the burned area for hot spots in the duff. I tore up my hands, but I had to be thorough. After a few hours, I radioed the office to report that the fire was completely out.

That summer our crew was sent to help with three rescues on Mount Washington. At 6,288 feet, it is the highest mountain in the northeastern states and it often experiences severe weather, including the highest wind speed ever recorded in the Northern and Western Hemispheres: 231 miles per hour. We usually ended up carrying the injured party down the mountain in a litter. On one rescue, that was a 230-pound, six-foot-six-inch marine. He was a heavy load. Over 130 hikers have died on Mount Washington since the mid-1800s, making it the deadliest peak in the country. Most of the fatalities were novice hikers who neglected to bring proper equipment and clothing.

On some of my days off, I worked for the company that managed the narrow private road that goes up Mount Washington. On a typical day, I was assigned to help manage the parking lot at the top. Sometimes people got freaked out by driving up the steep, winding road, and I got to drive them back down. I would hitch a ride back up on one of the company's tour buses.

When I was not working, I hiked local mountain trails, many of them part of the Appalachian Trail, a 2,200-mile route that starts in Georgia and ends at the summit of Mount Katahdin in Maine. I would spend the night in Adirondack shelters constructed by the Forest Service. An Adirondack shelter looks like a small cabin with three sides and a roof. The front is open to the elements. During the three summers I worked in that National Forest, I met friendly hikers from every imaginable background and profession in those shelters.

Back in the late 1960s, there were forty-six peaks in New Hampshire certified as being over four thousand feet. I eventually climbed all of them. Later, mostly with friends from UMass, I added winter climbs of some of the highest peaks in New York, Maine, and Vermont.

Mountain climbing was not my only extracurricular activity that summer. I often drove to a dance hall in Vermont after work, danced with the girls there, drove back to our crew quarters, and got up early the next morning and went to work. It was a crazy thing to do.

WHEN THE SEASON ended in early September, I went back to college for my sophomore year. I got to keep my car in a campus lot, and that put me in a great situation for the rest of my college years. I could drive my friends to movie theaters and to dances at the two women's colleges in our area: Smith and Mount Holyoke. I dated girls from both of those schools.

When I had a date back then, I would show up at the girl's dorm in a coat and tie and with a small present. As we walked out to my car, I would step ahead of her, open the passenger-side door for her, then close it once she was seated. On arriving at our destination, I would rush around to her door and open it for her. I hear guys don't do those things anymore.

That fall semester, I worked part-time at a McDonald's for a few months. At the end of my evening shift, I could take home any hamburgers that had not sold. I passed them out to my dorm friends and that made me a big hit. The job taught me to have sympathy for people who have to work in those positions.

At the beginning of my sophomore year, I made the mistake of not attending a meeting to elect the representatives and officers of our dorm's governing council, only to find that I had been elected vice president and social chairman. It was not a choice I would have made, but I decided to make the best of it.

I discovered that we had a good amount of money to stage events, and I came up with a surefire plan. I contacted the social chairman in one of the nearby girls' dorms to let them know that I had friends who were musicians in rock bands. I proposed that I would supply the music if the girls' dorm would host the dance, guaranteeing that a lot of guys would show up. Every dance I promoted that year attracted a huge turnout, and we made a lot of money for both dorms.

Since I was in charge of the events, I had to deal with any problems that came up. That meant I was the bouncer if there was trouble. At one dance, a drunken guy assaulted one of the girls. When I rushed over and yelled at him to leave her alone, the guy came at me with several of his friends. When he took a swing at me, I ducked just enough that it was only a glancing blow. I then moved forward and put him in a headlock, the wrestling hold Tommy had used on me years earlier.

The buddies who had run over to back him up hesitated. I had friends near me, so I felt protected if those guys tried something. After a half minute or so, I let go of the guy and pushed him away. He threatened me for a few moments, then left with his friends. I turned around and told the band to continue. They started their next song, and the dance resumed.

Years later in Yellowstone, I met one of Mick Jagger's bodyguards, a very big man who was about six-foot-six, much taller than me. After we became friends, I mentioned I had worked as a bouncer at dances. Not knowing that I organized and planned the dances and had to deal with any problems that came up, he said, "They must have hired you based on your intelligence rather than your size."

During several of my years in college, I also worked part-time for the university's police department as a security guard during the midnight to 3 a.m. shift. At first that was in my men's dorm, then I switched to working in a nearby women's dorm. That was a livelier situation, because I had to deal with a lot of drunken guys who wanted to break in to the dorm and find girls. I always managed to stop them.

In the fall of my sophomore year, I had a roommate, a big guy who was a member of a Hells Angels–type motorcycle gang. He had a side gig as a drug dealer. When I was studying in my half of our small room, I would hear him make calls on our shared phone, demanding his customers pay their drug bills.

I could tell when one of them made excuses about being unable to pay because I would hear my roommate make detailed threats about what type of violence he would visit on them. Then he would slam down the phone, turn to me, instantly change his demeanor to a normal, friendly person, and ask if I wanted to go get something to eat.

I figured it was best to always do whatever he suggested. Because of that and the fact that I never owed him any money, I never had a problem with him. After about a month, I came back from classes to find that his side of the room was totally cleared out. I never knew what happened to him but often thought he might be buried somewhere in a shallow grave for not paying his supplier.

COLLEGE WAS WHERE I got my start as a photographer, a skill I honed over the years until I was regularly getting wildlife photographs published in books—over two hundred of them—and in magazines such as *National Geographic*. A guy on my floor was the photo editor at our college newspaper, the *Daily Collegian*, and he talked me into signing up as a news photographer. I had never used a 35mm camera before but was given one for my first assignment, which was to get photos of the women's equestrian team. I showed up without any idea of how the controls on the camera worked. I used every possible combination of aperture setting and shutter speed, then developed the film in the paper's darkroom. Luckily, a few shots turned out okay, and one was published in the next day's paper.

For the rest of my college years, I continued to be a photographer for the paper and gradually learned to be a decent shooter. I covered football and basketball games, concerts, rallies, demonstrations, and general life on campus. During that era, Julius Erving played on our basketball team. He later became a famous professional player. One of my newspaper shots was of him seemingly floating three feet above the basketball court with the ball in his hands.

Back in those years, I hated getting up in the early morning for classes. I developed a pattern of coming back to my dorm room and getting extra sleep when I had a substantial break between classes. That schedule worked really well for me then and I reverted to it later when I had to get up well before dawn to study wolves in Yellowstone.

One day I was with some friends in the Student Union cafeteria when I saw a guy from my high school. He must have just transferred from a junior college. He had been a popular athlete in high school and part of the in crowd, but here he was alone and no one other than me knew he had once been a big shot. I was not in the popular crowd in our high school, but now I had plenty of friends and was accomplishing a lot in life. All in all, I was happy with the way my life was going.

UMASS WAS BIG enough to attract top music acts, and I went to most of the shows. I saw B. B. King, Jefferson Airplane, and Simon and Garfunkel. I took a date to a show that featured a group called the Association. They had several top 40 hits, including "Cherish" and "Never My Love," but for me their music was too bland. My date wanted to see them, but I went to see the opening act: the Yardbirds. They were a seminal blues-based British group who had earlier had legendary lead guitarists Eric Clapton and Jeff Beck in the band. Some of their hit songs were "For Your Love" and "Over Under Sideways Down," but they also covered great blues songs such as Bo Diddley's "I'm a Man," Howlin' Wolf's "Smokestack Lightning," and Tiny Bradshaw's "The Train Kept A-Rollin'."

Both Clapton and Beck had left and been replaced by a guitar player who had primarily worked as a recording session gun for hire. His name was Jimmy Page and people in the know said he was about to become the next big thing. After the band played their hit songs, Page took over and started doing unbelievable things with his guitar on a song called "Dazed and Confused." The climax was when he took out a violin bow and used it to make sounds that topped all that he had just done. The date of that show was April 6, 1968. Soon after that, Page formed the band Led Zeppelin, and their first public performance was five months after I saw him. "Dazed" was on their debut album, which came out in early 1969.

Then there was Janis Joplin. Her group, Big Brother and the Holding Company, was part of what had become the hugely influential San Francisco sound. Janis's two hit songs, "Piece of My Heart" and "Ball and Chain," played constantly on campus jukeboxes. I saw her band in October 1968. I later learned that the writer and singer of the original version of "Ball and Chain" was Big Mama Thornton, the same artist who had such an influence on Elvis Presley.

Janis Joplin was the best blues singer I have ever heard and was far better in person than on records. When she sang the blues, she meant it, for she had lived a very hard life. More than just lyrics, the words to those songs were her life story. Janis was emotionally fragile, partly owing to being severely bullied in high school. As a guy, I felt a nearly irrepressible impulse to jump onstage, hug her, and tell her everything was going to be all right.

Decades later I think a lot about Janis Joplin. What I took from her show was the importance of putting emotion into a performance. She sang the blues, and I tell stories about wolves, stories that are full of emotion, tragedy, and heroism. When a lone wolf howls, what I hear is an animal singing the blues. I often think how great it would be if Janis were still alive and I could take her out to hear the wolves howl. I am sure she would feel a connection with them.

MY GENERATION WAS frequently in heated conflict with older generations over Vietnam, the military draft, civil rights, and other profound issues. The first demonstration I went to in college was in support of women's right to have access to contraceptives. It had been organized by a doctor who had been arrested for holding up a birth control pill at a lecture.

A Vietnam vet named Tom who lived on our floor told us about the horrors of going on patrols in the jungle. Being short, he often was picked to crawl into tunnel systems dug by Vietcong soldiers. Many of the tunnels were booby-trapped, so it was an extremely dangerous mission. By that time, it was well known that the leaders of the South Vietnam government, the regime we were fighting to support, were mostly corrupt. Tom repeatedly told us that it was a stupid, unnecessary war and encouraged us to do whatever we had to do to avoid being sent there.

For many of us, the greatest hero was Muhammad Ali, partly because he was the world heavyweight boxing champion, but mostly because of his opposition to the war and his refusal to be drafted into the army. He paid a high price for that: his boxing license and championship were taken away from him in April 1967 and he was sentenced to five years in prison. Here is what Ali said that year about refusing to be drafted, as recorded in a 1980 documentary by the public affairs television program *Like It Is*:

> My conscience won't let me go shoot my brother, or some darker people, or some poor, hungry people in the mud for big, powerful America, and shoot them. For what? They

> never called me [the N-word], they never lynched me, they never put no dogs on me. They never robbed me of my nationality, or raped and killed my mother and father… How can I shoot them poor people? Just take me to jail.

Around the time of Ali's conviction, an estimated one thousand noncombatant Vietnamese were being killed by our armed forces every week, mostly by aerial bombing, and one hundred American soldiers were dying weekly in combat there. Ali won his case against the draft before the Supreme Court and later won back the championship in a famous match in Africa against George Foreman. That epic story is told in the 1996 documentary *When We Were Kings*. The film also does a great job of showing why Ali was so loved by poor people throughout the world.

IN THE SPRING of 1969, I had to take a three-week surveying class. I learned how to use a compass and how to pace out a traditional form of measurement called a chain. A chain is sixty-six feet long, and we all practiced walking that distance while counting our paces. When Thoreau worked as a surveyor in the mid-1800s in the Massachusetts woods, he used the same methods. The timing of that class was perfect, for when I got back to our district, I was told that our crew would be doing National Forest border work that summer. We would look up deeds from the early 1900s that documented tracts of land sold to the US Forest Service, gather information on the border lines, then go into the field.

Our crew would start at a corner marker, which was a post with a pile of rocks at the base to hold it in place. After that, we used the surveying information on the old deeds in combination with a compass to walk the border line. On the way, we stopped at random trees, used our axes to cut off a small patch of bark, then brushed red paint on that spot to mark the line.

At corner markers that were in disrepair, we would either chop down a nearby tree or find a suitable log to replace any posts that were rotting, then we would add a layer of red paint to the posts. The paint always got smeared on our hands and sometimes on our faces. When we came out of the thick forest and crossed trails with our hard hats and axes, faces red, paint cans in hand, startled hikers often looked at us like we were alien beings.

I worked on several fires that summer. On one of them, I was put in charge of the compass work. The fire was spotted from the air, and the pilot gave us compass directions. After I tied a red ribbon on a tree along the trail, we hiked a few miles through the thick forest and I used my compass to take us right to the fire. It was small and easy to put out. Then I had the responsibility of navigating the way back through the dense trees. That made me a bit nervous, but I had that recent training at college. We made it back to the trail within a few feet of the ribbon.

THE BIGGEST INTERNATIONAL event that year was the moon landing on Sunday, July 20. I drove down to Hampton Beach and watched the astronauts climb out of the capsule and walk on the moon on TV at the Glynns' house.

Woodstock took place about a month later in upstate New York. I really wanted to go but I would likely have lost my

Forest Service job if I missed work. Woodstock seemed to prove that our generation could come together and accomplish great things, but events later that year challenged our optimism. In December 1969, a college student was murdered by members of the Hells Angels while the Rolling Stones performed at the Altamont music festival in California. A few months before that, followers of Charles Manson had murdered several people in California. And the Vietnam War was still in full swing.

That same year, the movie *Easy Rider* came out. You could say the Beatles' 1964 movie *A Hard Day's Night* had presented the world and the people in it as fun, upbeat, and optimistic. You left the theater feeling good about yourself and felt you could accomplish anything you set your mind to. The America depicted in *Easy Rider* just five years later was the opposite of that. It was a dark and violent place where well-meaning young people could be killed for no reason at any moment. All three of the main characters, who were frequently high on various drugs, were murdered by the end of the film. America seemed to be at war with itself.

One of the final lines in *Easy Rider*, spoken by Peter Fonda, summed up the young filmmakers' take on the 1960s generation: "We blew it." Was that right? Did we blow it? In his book *The Greater Generation: In Defense of the Baby Boom Legacy*, Leonard Steinhorn argued that my generation deserved great credit for making the reality of America closer to the promise of America. We made progress on civil rights, women's rights, and environmental protections, and the 1973 passage of the Endangered Species Act eventually led to the reintroduction of wolves to Yellowstone National

Park. We may not have been the Greatest Generation, but we accomplished a lot of good things.

Perhaps the single most critical moment for guys of my generation took place on December 1, 1969, in my junior year. The Selective Service System had converted the military draft into a lottery system, and that evening they randomly picked birthday dates. The stakes were potentially life or death because draftees would almost certainly be sent into combat in Vietnam. That year 543,000 American troops were stationed there.

I was in my dorm room that night and every guy on campus listened to the college radio station's live coverage of the lottery drawing. The initial date picked was September 14, meaning men born on that day would be the first to be drafted. It was almost equivalent to a death sentence. I remember hearing one man scream. He must have been born on that day.

When my date came up, it was 141. The following year, 1970, the draft went up to number 215. I was scheduled to graduate in the spring of 1971, so that would be the year my student deferment would expire. Back then there were many counseling operations where we could get advice on how to avoid getting drafted. Some options were legal and others were morally questionable. Guys from wealthy families often got a doctor to write a letter stating that the son, who was perfectly healthy, had medical problems that would exempt him from the draft. My friends and I did not consider that an honorable way to get out of the draft.

In the spring of 1970, the Vietnam War was extended to Cambodia, and that set off mass demonstrations around the country. Four students were killed and another nine wounded by National Guard soldiers at Kent State University in Ohio, and at a Mississippi college two students were killed and twelve were wounded. College students all around the country reacted by going on strike. That included our school. Classes were canceled, except for forestry majors. Our conservative professors were not going to let us get away with anything, so we had to go to their classes or flunk.

The more violent and radical students at UMass threatened to blow up a building, something that was happening at other colleges. They announced that Memorial Hall, a beloved symbol of the school, would be their target. I was in the nonviolent wing of anti-war activists. We announced we would take turns staying in Memorial Hall until the bomb threat was over. I had the late shift and spent many nights there. We finally prevailed and the radicals backed off. Those of us in the nonviolent faction wore white armbands with a dove symbol to represent peace. Somewhere, I still have that in my belongings in case I ever need it again.

Thoreau had been a role model to me for his nature writing. Now he was my hero for his opposition to an unnecessary war against Mexico. He wrote the essay "On the Duty of Civil Disobedience" after spending a night in jail in 1846 for refusing to pay his taxes as a protest against that war. I appeared twice before my local draft board and voiced my objection to the war and to the draft. The board was composed of older men from the World War II generation and they had no sympathy for college-age men who said it was an unjustified war. Both times they declared me legally eligible to be drafted when I graduated.

AROUND THAT TIME, there was a lot of talk about Marvel superheroes among college students. I had read Superman comics when I was younger but knew little about the new Marvel characters. Our campus bookstore carried Marvel comics, so I bought one that featured a superhero team called the Fantastic Four. I was immediately hooked on the story, which featured a fascinating adversary called Galactus, who came to Earth to drain the planet of all its energy.

Galactus explained to the Fantastic Four that he needed that energy to survive. He told them he had nothing against earthlings, but he was so far above them in cosmic significance and power that they were like ants to him. He was just doing what he needed to do to survive, and stated, "I bear no malice toward any living thing." It was a far more sophisticated story than the earlier Superman comics I had read.

Galactus had an aide called the Silver Surfer. Eventually, the Silver Surfer rebelled against his master and helped the Fantastic Four save the planet. For years after that, I followed Marvel characters, especially the Fantastic Four, Galactus, and the Silver Surfer. I later realized that the Galactus character, who was treated sympathetically and was not presented as evil, served as a metaphor for predators like wolves who were just trying to survive.

At a comic book convention in the 1970s, I got to meet Jack Kirby, the cocreator of most of the famous Marvel characters. Jack did the artwork and Stan Lee wrote the dialogue. I still have the illustration of the Silver Surfer that Jack signed for me.

I also heard a talk given by Jerry Siegel, the cocreator of Superman in the late 1930s. He explained that as Adolf Hitler was threatening to dominate Europe and the free world, he thought, "If only there was someone who could do something about that." He and his partner Joe Shuster then came up with the Superman character. Years later I read an article that said they based Superman on a sixteenth-century story about a rabbi who created a hero made of stone to protect Jewish people from oppression.

One year my roommate Don's family visited him, and his little brother came along. I remember seeing him sitting in our dorm room, reading superhero comic books. That was Peter Laird, and he later attended the University of Massachusetts as an art major. After college, he and his friend created a team of superheroes that seemed to have no hope of ever catching on. They were called the Teenage Mutant Ninja Turtles. The two guys did pretty well with those characters.

IN THE SPRING of my junior year, I was looking forward to getting back to the New Hampshire mountains because I was in line to be our district's backcountry ranger. In the two previous years, I had hiked nearly all the trails in our area, so I was well prepared for the job. I had also been on a lot of rescues and fires.

I called my supervisor Steve Chandler to ask when I needed to report for duty. I could tell right away that something was wrong. Steve seemed to be somewhat embarrassed to tell me that they had already given the backcountry ranger job to someone else, a new guy I had never heard of. Then Steve said something that changed my life. They wanted me to take over the naturalist programs in the district's Dolly

Copp Campground. For the first time, I would be interacting with the public and wearing a badge on my uniform. He explained that I would be giving evening slideshows, leading nature walks, conducting children's nature programs, and leading a convoy of vehicles to a local fish hatchery.

The term *naturalist* usually means a person who is familiar with a wide range of subjects that relate to the natural world. These would be things like wildlife, geology, and botany. Charles Darwin called himself a naturalist. He was trained as a geologist but soon broadened his interests. After I left the Forest Service, I was employed as a naturalist for the first half of my career with the National Park Service. Being in positions for so long that required such a broad background made it easier for me to write books for regular people than if I'd had a career specializing in a narrow area.

In past years, the Forest Service had hired high school science teachers to do the naturalist programs, including the evening slideshows. I had attended some of their programs and found them to be academic rather than inspiring, but their programs were the only examples I had for this new job.

I decided to prepare a slideshow on the US Forest Service's multiple use management philosophy, which allowed timber harvesting, hunting, and fishing in National Forests, and in some areas grazing and mining. At that time, I was all for the multiple use of National Forests because this was the philosophy taught to me by my forestry professors. I wrote an outline, loaded up a tray with around fifty slides from the file at our district office, set up a slide projector in the big log building where I would be doing my shows, and practiced my talk over and over again.

The evening came for my first talk and the building was jammed with around two hundred people. Scared to death, I walked to the front of the room, turned, and faced the audience. I made some announcements about upcoming programs, then turned out the lights. Then I walked back to sit behind the projector, where I had hidden my detailed outline. There was just enough light from the projector bulb to allow me to read it. This meant I was looking at the projector and screen rather than the audience, but I was so worried about remembering all my points that I did it anyway.

I presented that program every week that summer. My audiences were always receptive and encouraging. I began to feel more comfortable with my material, and I soon switched from sitting behind the projector to standing at the front of the room. That meant I was facing the audience, where I should have been from the beginning. Getting the confidence to do that made everything else much easier. I could modify what I said or add new comments when I wanted. The people in attendance were reacting much more positively and that motivated me to continue to improve.

Later, I compared my experience of doing talks that summer to a class on public speaking I had taken earlier in college. In that class, we prepared and gave several talks but presented each talk only once. I now knew the key to getting better at giving talks was to do the same program over and over. That gets you to the point where you stop worrying about what you are supposed to say and instead concentrate on how you are connecting with your audience.

I had never worked with kids, so the children's program was another thing I was nervous about. I was given Smokey

Bear fire safety comic books, which I passed out to the kids at the start of my talk. I got up in front of the room for that first program and went over all the material in the comic book, then held up a Smokey Bear badge. I announced that the kids were going to take a test on what they had learned and all who passed would get a badge.

I waited until every kid finished the test, then quickly tabulated who got enough right answers to pass. Right after that, one by one, I announced the names of the kids who passed and gave them their Smokey Bear badges. After the last kid got their badge and left the building, I looked out and saw that about twenty other boys and girls were still sitting in their chairs. Some were crying. I was too inexperienced to understand what was going on, so I asked the nearest boy why he was crying. He said he really wanted that badge and didn't get one. All the other kids still in the room nodded their heads in agreement.

That was when it hit me: I had a crisis on my hands and had to quickly figure out what to do. An idea came to me. I told those kids we would go through all the questions and answers, then they could take the test again. After I told them the answers, they all passed the second test, and I gave them their badges.

The easiest program for me was the fish hatchery trip. People drove their cars to a designated spot in the campground, then they followed me to a state fish hatchery in a convoy. Once we got there, I handed my people over to the fisheries biologists, who gave them a slideshow on native fish in the New England area, then walked them around the hatchery grounds. All I had to do was be part of the group.

The third time we did that trip, there was an emergency. A worker ran up to me and said beavers had chewed through a section of the hatchery and a lot of fish were escaping. All the staff would have to concentrate on repairing the damage. I expected him to say the tour would have to be canceled. Instead, he told me that I would have to do it. That was a problem because I had not paid much attention on the previous tours. The slideshow came first, and a few shots into the program people were asking the names of the fish in the pictures. I had to admit I did not know. I talked about the few things I recalled from earlier tours, then took them outside to see the fish. Somehow, I got through that stressful tour and took my people home. From then on, I paid much more attention to the guy doing the slideshow and took detailed notes.

Led Zeppelin's second album had come out the previous winter and we were all mesmerized by Jimmy Page's guitar solo on "Whole Lotta Love." There was a record player in our crew quarters, so we often put on that album at top volume, then sat outside and listened to it. We played "Whole Lotta Love" over and over again. Luckily, we were far enough away from the campsites that we never got any complaints.

That summer I turned twenty-one. I was finally figuring out how to do my naturalist job, and I felt like I was beginning to grow up.

IN THE US Forest Service, every National Forest is divided up into districts, usually around five or six. The boss of each of those units is called the district ranger. Our district ranger was a big, tough ex-marine who looked a lot like John Wayne.

Everyone regarded him as a man you would never want to cross.

One day when I was scheduled to do my children's program in the auditorium, I walked in to find trash scattered all over the floor. Much of it was food. I remembered that the district ranger had put on a party for his friends the previous evening. I had to conclude he expected me to clean up after him. I had no choice because it was my responsibility to have the room ready for my show. It took some time, but I eventually got the room in acceptable shape and later did my talk.

I wrote a notc to my supervisor, explaining what had happened. The next time I went to his office, I expected him to thank me for cleaning up the mess. Instead, he was totally stressed out. He had passed the note on to the district ranger, who had gotten angry, cursed me in the colorful language that marines are experts in using, then threw my note in the trash.

I stuck to my guns and responded that the district ranger was in the wrong and needed to be called on it. My supervisor did not want to say that to the big boss. He nervously suggested I leave before he came back. I did take off and soon put the incident out of my mind. In the coming days, the district ranger and I did not cross paths, so I let the issue go.

Then, late one night, when I was sleeping alone in our crew quarters, there was a banging on the front door. I got out of my bunk, went to the door, and opened it. The district ranger was standing there and he was angry. I thought he was going to yell at me, but instead he said there was a report of drunken college guys bothering people in the campground. He asked who else was around and I told him it was just me.

At that time, there probably were no two people on the planet who were as opposite of each other as him and me. Looking at me with a doubtful expression and likely thinking I was a useless, long-haired, anti-war hippie, he said, "Okay, it will have to be just you and me." I got in his truck and we drove off to the reported campsite. It was like John Wayne driving a truck with one of the hippie characters from *Easy Rider* sitting next to him. It was a fascinating situation because we both felt that the campground was our territory and that we had to team up to defend it from outsider troublemakers.

On the way, he turned to me and asked somewhat skeptically, "Do you know how to fight?" By then I knew his personality well and figured he was likely looking forward to breaking some heads and wanted me to join in on that. Since I had dealt with a lot of college guys during my time as a dance promoter, as well as during my night security work in women's dorms, I was pretty confident that I knew how to talk drunken men out of causing trouble without coming to blows. But this was not the time to argue with the district ranger about the most effective methods of crowd control, so I answered him by just saying, "Yeah." I did not mention that I had never hit anyone in my life.

As he drove, I planned what I would do to make sure no one got hurt. When we approached the scene of the reported trouble, I would jump out of the truck before we came to a full stop, run over to the problem guys, and ask them to help me out by quieting down. Then I would say if they did not, I would not be able to stop my ex-marine boss from smacking them around. I would be the Good Cop warning them what would happen if they had to deal with the Bad Cop coming up behind me.

When we got to the campsite, however, everything was quiet and calm. Maybe the drunken college guys had seen us driving up and had run off. The district ranger seemed disappointed because, I think, he was looking forward to a fight. He turned around, drove back to the crew quarters, and dropped me off without saying a word.

IN LATE AUGUST, toward the end of our season, there was a huge forest fire on the Wenatchee National Forest in Washington state. Forest Service crews from all over the country were being sent there to help. We got word that two guys from each of our forest's six districts would be flown out to work on that fire. All of us desperately wanted to go, because working on such a big fire would be a hugely valuable experience to add to our résumés.

We all knew that one local guy was sure to be selected, as he was the town's golden boy and liked by the district ranger. That meant only one other guy could be chosen out of fifty other employees. As I was on the bad side of the big boss, I figured I had no chance and stopped thinking about the fire. Then I got a call from my supervisor. He floored me by saying the district ranger had picked me to be the second man. (In those days, all the firefighters were men. Now crews have a mixture of men and women.)

Being chosen to go out west on that fire set me on a career path that eventually ended up with me working with wolves in Yellowstone decades later. I never knew why the district ranger picked me for that slot, but I guessed he grudgingly respected that I had stood up to him on the visitor center issue and was willing to stand with him when he thought we would have to fight a mob.

The twelve of us who were chosen from our districts drove to the nearest airport and were directed to a charter flight that was warming up on the tarmac. The other guy from my district and I got on the plane first. I did not know much about airplanes back then. I figured I would just take a seat in the front row so that I would be out of the way of the other guys when they went to seats farther back. After we took off, the flight attendant who worked that section of the plane came to us and said, "Congratulations on being in the first-class section." We got special treatment, fancy meals, and some alcoholic drinks, while the firefighters behind got far less attention.

When we landed in Wenatchee, we were driven to a Forest Service campground that had been closed to the public. We would camp there for the duration of the fire. The rest of the guys in the campground were from other National Forest or Washington state firefighting crews. There were also a lot of National Guard troops.

The next morning, our New Hampshire crew was loaded into a truck that normally transported cattle and dropped off where we would be fighting the fire. We had to stand for the long trip. In the coming days, we built fire lines and put out fires that jumped those lines. Using a term that came out of the Vietnam War, we proudly called ourselves grunts. Like soldiers in a war, we had no idea what was happening anywhere other than at our assigned spot. One day we were working on a steep slope with the fire above us when a huge log rolled downhill directly at us. We scrambled away just in time.

We spent a week on that fire and went back to the campground every evening. They served us hot dinners and breakfasts, so we ate well. Toward the end of that deployment, I had a little time off. I went to the Forest Service Headquarters, looked at the slides that had been taken of the fire, and arranged to have copies made and sent to me. I decided that when I got back to college, I would put together a slideshow on my experiences using shots I had taken, along with the ones from the HQ file. Luckily, firefighters were getting the big fire under control just before the semester started, and I was able to get back to start my senior year on time.

DURING MY SENIOR year, I took a few elective classes to expand my horizons. I signed up for a class on park administration, which gave me some exposure to how National Parks were managed and the history of conservation in the United States.

I also took a class on environmental interpretation, which is what I had just done in my summer job in New Hampshire. My class project involved laying out a nature trail and writing a guidebook on the designated stops on the route. It got me thinking about ways to present nature to the public.

During spring-break week, our class went on a field trip and visited Cape Cod National Seashore. It was the first National Park area I had ever been in. A ranger met with us and talked about his job. What he said really resonated with me and got me thinking about finding alternatives to the forestry career I was being trained for.

That year, the forestry major admitted its first female student. She was the daughter of one of the forestry professors and smarter than most of us. When I started at UMass, there were no women studying in the departments of forestry, fisheries, or wildlife. These days, I often give talks to college wildlife classes in Yellowstone, and in recent years those classes have usually been majority female. I once talked to a male supervisor and he told me if the two best candidates for a wildlife job were a man and a woman, he would hire the woman because he felt women were better at the detail work that wildlife research is based on.

In the last semester of my senior year, I took a five-credit course called Forest Management to finalize my training as a forester. Most of the grade was based on designing a hundred-year management plan for making clear-cuts on a hypothetical National Forest. Clear-cutting means sawing down every single tree in a given area for lumber and other uses, then planting seedlings of the most valuable commercial species so that forest could later also be cut down. I can now look back and see that the forestry professors regarded trees as a crop to be planted and later harvested, rather than as living things that had an intrinsic value.

I got an A in that class, but it made me realize I did not want to kill trees for a career or be in the business of exploiting nature for human use. The park administration class had exposed me to the preservationist management philosophy of National Parks, and the ranger at the National Seashore had really impressed me. I began to think I would be much happier working in a National Park rather than in a National Forest.

That last semester, I looked into joining the Peace Corps and was offered a two-year assignment in Morocco, where I would help local people plant trees. It would have given me a draft deferment, which was a major enticement. But by that time, I was not looking to continue in forestry work. I also was offered a master's program studying recreational use of National Forests and state parks. I also turned that down.

After finishing college in the spring of 1971, I worked for a nonprofit organization for a while and had to raise the funding for my position. I knew nothing about fundraising and found it the hardest thing I had ever done, but I got it done. I did not know it at that time, but gaining that experience in fundraising would turn out to be an extremely valuable skill later in life. I also had to do a lot of public speaking for that job. That experience, along with the Forest Service naturalist job I had in the summer of 1970, got me to the point where I felt comfortable and confident giving talks.

In the early 1970s, the Vietnam War was winding down because of public opposition. The Selective Service agency announced that in 1971 they would not be drafting anyone that had a lottery number higher than 125. Since I was 141, that meant I was safe. But I did not consider that a thing to brag about or bring up in conversations. In total, more than 58,220 US service members, nearly all of them from my generation, died in Vietnam. Many others were seriously injured or suffered throughout their lives after being exposed to Agent Orange.

I have great respect for the men and women who served honorably in World War II and in Vietnam, both the ones who were drafted and the others who volunteered.

When that nonprofit job ended, I stayed with a college friend and his wife in a rural part of Vermont. They had just bought an old farmhouse and were beginning to renovate it. I earned my keep by chopping firewood, milking their goat, and doing whatever other chores needed to be done. In the fall, I moved out and rented a room in nearby Barre, Vermont, where I got a job as a darkroom technician at the local paper, the *Times Argus*.

While I worked there, I branched out into taking photographs for the paper and writing articles and book reviews. One of my articles was on the reintroduction of a weasel-like animal called a fisher to the Vermont woods. Fishers had been a native animal in the state but had been killed off. Twenty years later, I started working in Yellowstone and advocated for a wolf reintroduction program there.

My newspaper job was only half-time, and it did not pay well. For a short time, I got food stamps to make ends meet. I decided to seek out jobs that were more in line with what I wanted to do as a career. I got an offer to work for the Vermont Department of Forests and Parks in the southern part of the state and moved to a rented room in the town of Springfield. Much of my work involved marking trees that local people could use for firewood. I would snowshoe through the forest, seek out dead standing trees, and mark them with red paint. That job and the summers I spent working and hiking in the New Hampshire woods were much like the many times I explored the woods and fields of my rural part of Massachusetts when I was a young boy. I was very happy to have that job but felt I had not yet found the position I was best suited for.

3

Starting Out With the National Park Service

THAT WINTER IN Vermont, I bought a book called *Desert Solitaire* by Edward Abbey. It was about his time as a park ranger in Arches National Park in Utah. Reading it changed my life, for it confirmed what I had already begun to suspect: working in National Forests might not be the best choice for me.

In the 1999 film *The Matrix*, Neo, the main character, has to make a life-altering choice between taking a red pill or a blue pill. In my case, I ended up taking the National Park pill.

Luckily, my forestry degree made me eligible to apply for jobs in the National Park Service. I sent out ten applications and got an offer to work as a firefighter in Sequoia and Kings Canyon National Parks for the summer. I was selected partly because I had worked on fires in New Hampshire but mostly because of the big fire I had worked on in Wenatchee. I owed my first National Park Service job to the district ranger who had unexpectedly picked me for that assignment.

The job offer was contingent on my ability to run a mile and a half in under twelve minutes. To meet that requirement, I started to run after work in Vermont, and by the time I left the state, I knew I could easily pass that test.

In May 1975, I drove out to California and stopped off to buy my National Park Service uniform before arriving at my new job. I was put on a helitack crew with four other guys at the Grant Grove section of the park. Once the fire season began, two or more of us would periodically be flown by helicopter into the backcountry to put out lightning-caused fires. We would camp out for however long it took to extinguish the blaze.

When we were not camping out, we lived in a bunkhouse with steel closets for storing our clothes and gear. I had a great time getting to know the other guys on the crew. They taught me the trick of getting a cool drink on a hot day when we were on a fire. You put whatever warm water you have in a canteen, then wrap a wet rag around it. As the moisture in the rag evaporates, it draws heat from the water and cools it. A man on our crew named Raoul, who was always in a good mood, introduced me to the joys of Mexican food. It is still my go-to favorite.

We could bring our own food when sent out on fires, but we often ate Vietnam-era C rations (officially called "Meal, Combat, Individual"), which were contained in small cans inside cardboard boxes. Our favorite dessert was pound cake. Each box had a small metal GI can opener that we used to get access to the food in the cans. That opener also served as a kind of universal tool. You could use it as a screwdriver and to cut things. Decades later I still have one of them from that job on my key ring.

I learned a lot that summer, not only about fighting fires, but also about working on a team. We came from very different backgrounds and educational levels, but none of that mattered when we were on a fire. We had to rely on each other and watch out for fellow crew members.

When we were not fighting fires in the backcountry, we did prescribed burns in sequoia stands. That began with cutting out thick brush growing near the base of the sequoia trees. Then we would build a fire line around the area, just as I had done on the Wenatchee and New Hampshire fires. When the weather conditions were right, meaning no wind and high humidity, we started fires inside the fire lines, which we then monitored closely. That season we never had any of our prescribed burns get out of control.

It was a humbling experience to work under stands of immense sequoias. It was also rewarding because we felt we were doing valuable work that would protect those massive, ancient trees. Some sequoia trees live for well over three thousand years and grow to three hundred feet. I much preferred planning prescribed burns that benefited sequoia trees to planning and carrying out clear-cuts, the job I had been trained for.

We had a big Park Service campground in our district, and I went to all the evening slideshows put on by rangers on the naturalist staff. After getting a feel for how they did those talks, I volunteered to do an evening program on fires and controlled burns in National Parks. I also put together a program on fighting large fires. For that presentation, I used the slides I had from the Wenatchee fire.

Because our jobs were scheduled to end in the fall, when cooler temperatures and wetter weather greatly lessened the chance of wildfires, I spent a lot of time that summer researching winter naturalist jobs in the California desert. The two main possibilities were Death Valley National Monument and Joshua Tree National Monument. In the National Park system, the difference between National Parks and National Monuments is that parks are created by Congress while monuments can be set aside by presidents. Both Joshua Tree and Death Valley National Monuments later became National Parks under the California Desert Protection Act, which was passed in 1994 during the Clinton administration.

In July I made arrangements to have job interviews at Joshua Tree and Death Valley. We had a California state park ranger working on an exchange program in Sequoia and Kings Canyon, and he gave me contact information for Anza-Borrego Desert State Park in eastern San Diego County, so I added that park to my interview list.

I had to make the long round trip for my interviews on my two days off. Just as I was about to leave, I had a chance to earn a lot of money by working overtime on a fire, but I turned it down. The fire crew guys thought I was crazy, but I stayed with my plan. I left right after work and drove through the night. After hundreds of miles, I arrived in Death Valley in the early morning. That park was my top choice because of its legendary reputation.

After my interview with the chief ranger, I sensed I did not have enough experience to be given an offer. I then drove to Joshua Tree, a few hundred miles farther south, and had my interview there. My car had no air conditioner, so I had to endure the peak of the summer heat. As with Death Valley, I got the sense that my limited experience was going to be an issue.

I then continued to the small desert town of Borrego Springs, where I was interviewed by Bud Getty, the manager of the 596,000-acre Anza-Borrego Desert State Park. Bud was friendly and seemed impressed that I had called him up and then driven all that way to talk about a job. It was a big help that I had a recommendation from the state park ranger stationed in Sequoia, for Bud knew him. I felt I had a pretty good chance of getting an offer. A few weeks later, Bud called to say I was hired.

I STARTED MY new position at Anza-Borrego in October 1975. Anza-Borrego was named in part after the Spanish explorer Juan Bautista de Anza, who came through the area in the 1700s. *Borrego* is the Spanish word for "sheep" and refers to the desert bighorn that live in the park's mountains. Anza-Borrego is the largest state park in California and the second largest in the United States.

The two winters I worked there were good times for me. My boss, Glenn Mincks, allowed me to do a lot of naturalist programs, including evening slideshows and nature walks. It was there that I began to improve as a public speaker and started to understand that a good talk needs to be more than a list of facts; it needs to tell a story and it should have a good ending.

My first talk to center on a story was about a colorful old-timer called Pegleg Smith. Pegleg, a trapper, a guide, and sometime horse thief, lived in the mid-1800s. When he arrived in what later became Anza-Borrego, he tried to make a living as a prospector, but he got in trouble with the local Native people and had to flee.

Pegleg began telling stories about how he had found gold but had to abandon his discovery because of the conflict he had with the Native tribe. After telling his tale, he would offer to sell a map showing the location of what became known as the Lost Pegleg Mine. Knowledgeable people in that part of the California desert regarded all that as a moneymaking scam.

Decades later a prospector came to Anza-Borrego to look for the lost mine. He said that after many failed attempts, he stumbled upon a site where gold nuggets were strewn across the desert. But a massive sandstorm came through the area, forcing him to seek shelter. When the storm was over, drifting sand had obscured all the landmarks and the gold was lost once again.

I ended the talk by implying that the second version of the lost gold was probably as suspect as Pegleg's version. But it was a good story that let me tell visitors a lot about the history of the area.

The park had issued me a jeep and a motorcycle so I could patrol the desert dirt roads. Twelve sections of the park are designated wilderness areas, where only foot travel is allowed. When I was on foot patrol, I got to see the desert bighorn sheep that lived in the park.

One of the other park rangers was George Leech, and I often went on desert patrols with him. He had been a professional boxer and once sparred with Joe Louis. I also went on patrols with ranger Kate Foley. She took me into the Carrizo

Impact Area, a section of the park closed to the public. It is a forty-five-square-mile area that was used as an aerial bombing range by the US Navy during World War II and the Korean War, and later in the 1950s. Some of the thousand-pound bombs never exploded, and a bomb buried under a shallow layer of desert sand could explode if a vehicle drove over the site.

Kate knew the area well and followed routes she had safely taken on earlier patrols. It was spooky to see so much unexploded ordnance lying around. When I saw Mel Gibson's 1981 postapocalyptic movie *The Road Warrior*, the devastated scenery in the film reminded me of the country Kate took me through. Decades later I spent some time with Gibson when he came to Yellowstone to see wolves.

I mostly did patrols by myself. On the main road, that included picking up litter. One time I grabbed a discarded can of soda and a lizard jumped out of it right at me. It apparently had been living inside the can and was upset I was stealing it from him.

I lived in a small trailer in Tamarisk Grove Campground, where I helped register people, collected camping fees, and answered questions about what to do in the park. I also cleaned two restrooms and several outhouses every morning. Having done the job myself, I thank every man and woman I happen to see cleaning restrooms now.

One day I was scrubbing the urinals in the campground's men's room. A middle-aged man came in and used the facilities. As he washed his hands, he turned to me and asked me how I liked my job. I told him it was a great job because I got to drive around the desert by jeep and motorcycle, hike all the trails, and do talks for visitors. As he watched me scrubbing away, he told me something I will never forget: "I am the top heart surgeon in Cincinnati and do very well for myself, but if I could, I would trade my job for yours in an instant."

The climate of the Southern California desert is mild in the winter, so I started a habit of running after work. There was a dry wash full of mesquite trees, coyotes, and lizards near my trailer, and I ran a few miles out and back on it most days. On my days off, I hiked all the trails in the park and did a lot of off-trail routes as well.

San Diego was about an hour-and-a-half drive from the campground and I often went to the famous zoo there. I still had my Minolta camera from college, and I bought some telephoto lenses to up my photography game.

Soon after starting in Anza-Borrego, I bought a Datsun pickup that came with a camper shell and foam pad. In the years that followed, I would sleep in the back of the truck many nights when traveling. That made my life so much easier. Before that, I had to get out my sleeping bag and spend the night on the ground near my parked car. I tried not to think about the scene in *Easy Rider* where Jack Nicholson's character is beaten to death by locals when he did that.

I had become fascinated by Death Valley and vowed that one day I would work there as a ranger. One of my first road trips in the truck was a three-hour drive to visit that National Monument. I bought tapes of my favorite records to play in the truck's cassette tape player. I had never had a vehicle with a tape player before. Listening to tapes made long road trips so much more enjoyable, as I was no longer beholden to local AM radio stations, which usually did not play the type of music I liked.

DURING MY FIRST winter at Anza-Borrego, I applied to a lot of summer naturalist jobs in National Parks. My top choice was Mount McKinley National Park in Alaska because of the wildlife, especially the grizzlies, wolves, moose, caribou, and Dall sheep. But since I had not yet worked as a naturalist in the Park Service, I was worried that I would not get any offers. There were no phones at the Anza-Borrego campground and mail only got to us periodically. The phone number I put on my Park Service applications was the state park headquarters line in the town of Borrego Springs. If they got a call for me, it would take a few days for a message to be delivered.

One day I got a note from headquarters. It said I needed to call Bill Truesdell, chief naturalist at Mount McKinley National Park. To call Alaska, I had to drive ten miles to a phone booth at a gas station and put in a pile of coins. It turned out Bill was a desert guy and knew Anza-Borrego well. He asked me if I minded working at remote sites. That was easy for me to answer. I told him that not only did I not mind, but working in remote areas was my preference. Bill told me there was a Park Service visitor center sixty-five miles out into Mount McKinley Park and they needed a naturalist to work and live there. I immediately said that would be perfect.

As I drove back to the campground, I thought about how strangely some things had led to other things in my life. I had not wanted to do the visitor programs on the White Mountain National Forest, but they made me do them. Then, despite what had started out as a difficult relationship, the district ranger had picked me to go on that big fire in Washington state. That assignment got me my first National Park Service job in Sequoia and Kings Canyon, where I was a firefighter who volunteered to do evening slideshows for the public. That experience, along with the summer I did programs for the Forest Service and my winter job at Anza-Borrego, gave me enough background to get the offer in Alaska at my dream National Park.

I had about a month to prepare for my drive from the Southern California desert to central Alaska. After doing some research, I booked a passage for me and my truck on the Alaska state ferry. The ferry would take me from Prince Rupert, British Columbia, to Haines, Alaska. From there I would drive north to the Yukon Territory, then west to Alaska, and after many more miles I would end up at Mount McKinley National Park. The ferry ticket back then was about $200 and I had to pay in advance. That was a lot of money for me, but it was worth it because I was about to set off on a big adventure.

Life Lessons From Wolves

Teamwork

My time as a firefighter taught me the importance of teamwork. In dangerous situations, you have to look out for other members of your crew. This is a lesson wolves have also taken to heart, and when I later worked in Yellowstone, I observed many instances of teamwork out on hunts and witnessed times when the whole pack would rally around an aging or injured family member. One such wolf was Yellowstone wolf 253.

In October 2001, there was a serious battle between the Druid and Nez Perce packs in Lamar Valley. After the fight was over, I saw that yearling male 253 had been bitten on his left hind leg. The injury was bad enough that he could not put any weight on that leg. I later saw that 253 had a hard time making any movement, including walking around or bedding down. He was essentially an invalid.

When the other wolves left on a hunt, 253 stayed behind. I later saw alpha male 21 return. He went straight to 253 and gave him some food. I was impressed by that, but 21 was the father of 253, so his caretaking of a young son was something to be expected. A few days later, I saw a six-month-old pup leave a carcass site carrying a huge elk leg. I expected it would soon bed down with the leg and feed on it. But the pup continued carrying that leg a long way farther. The little wolf went to the disabled 253, its big brother, and gave the leg to him. With the help of his family, 253 partly recovered from his injury but for the rest of his life limped on that leg.

I have often thought the teamwork of wolf packs is similar to how the Yellowstone wolf researchers, wolf watchers, and wildlife tour guides work together to spot wolves and share sightings and information with others in the park. It's a team I am proud to be a part of.

I tell wolf 253's story in *Thinking Like a Wolf: Lessons From the Yellowstone Packs.*

4

The Denali Years

MY JOB IN the desert ended in late April 1976 and I immediately drove north to Prince Rupert, where I caught the ferry headed for Alaska. You could reserve a small cabin, but most people—including me—just rolled out sleeping bags and spent the night on the deck. I stepped off the boat briefly when it called in at Ketchikan, my first time setting foot on Alaskan ground. When the ferry reached the end of the line at Haines, I headed north once again.

Partway to Alaska, the truck broke down. I got a tow to a gas station at Beaver Creek, Yukon, where I had to wait a few days to get a new alternator. The employee was happy to install the part, but he was continually interrupted by customers who needed gas. That was before self-service gas pumps, so I told him I would pump gas if he would continue to work on my truck. It took several hours, but he got my truck going that day. I paid him and continued on.

When I finally arrived at Mount McKinley National Park, I drove to Park Headquarters to check in with Bill Truesdell. He told me I would be living in an employee cabin at headquarters for a week of training, then would go out to the Eielson Visitor Center, where I would live and work for the summer tourist season.

The Eielson Visitor Center has a commanding view of the 20,310-foot Mount McKinley, the highest peak in North America. The mountain and surrounding area became a National Park in 1917, originally named for President William McKinley. The name of the mountain and park was officially changed to Denali in 1980.

In the Koyukon Athabascan language, *Denali* means "the High One." I will use that name from now on, including references to times before 1980, out of respect for Alaskan Native people. The congressional bill that changed the name also expanded the park from two million acres to six million (9,400 square miles). That is three times the size of Yellowstone National Park.

When I later got to Eielson, I immediately went down to the basement of the visitor center to see where I was going to live. There was a small bathroom and a medium-size room with a kitchen area, a table, and two beds. I preferred the bed on the side of the room that faced Denali, so that when I woke up in the early morning, I could move the window curtain aside and immediately see whether the huge granite mountain was visible or fogged in.

When I checked that bed, I noticed that someone had already claimed it. A two-pound Arctic ground squirrel was rolled up in a ball, hibernating on the mattress. I picked it up, walked outside, unraveled the sleeping animal, and left it in a sunny spot to warm up. I unloaded the rest of my belongings from the truck and by the time I was finished the squirrel was gone.

In the Park Service, there are several categories of employees. That summer in Denali, there were about twenty-five park naturalists, most of them new like me. Our job was to do programs for park visitors. Twenty naturalists were based near the park entrance and another four lived fourteen miles to the east of the visitor center at a Park Service housing area along the Toklat River. I was the only naturalist living at Eielson.

There were also law enforcement rangers, scientific researchers, maintenance workers, and administration staff. I was sharing a room with the maintenance worker for the building. After I met my coworkers, we all pitched in to clean up the visitor center, then we waited for the tourists to arrive.

The road that runs eighty-five miles from the park entrance to the Wonder Lake Campground, twenty miles past Eielson, is mostly unpaved and narrow, so the park allows only limited access to personal vehicles. The Park Service rents a fleet of yellow school buses for the summer to ferry visitors from the park entrance to Eielson and beyond.

When I started working at Denali, employees who worked and lived out in the park were allowed to use their own cars during their time off. In later years, the rules became more restrictive, but fortunately, by that time I was getting enough photographs published in books and wildlife magazines to qualify me for a professional photography permit, which allowed me to drive around the park in my own car on my days off.

The first buses would arrive around nine in the morning, and the visitor center would soon fill with people. Huge picture windows gave them a spectacular view of the Alaska Range, including Denali and the impressive Muldrow Glacier, which flowed down the eastern side of the peak. As the tree line in Denali is around 2,790 feet and the Eielson area is at 3,700 feet, there are no trees to obscure the view of animals browsing near the visitor center.

Caribou and grizzlies could be seen most days. On one memorable morning, I had moose, caribou, Dall sheep, and a wolf in view through those windows. That covered most of the large mammals to be seen in the park. And on one of my days off in late summer 1989, I saw two wolverines just west of Eielson, traveling together. That turned out to be the only wolverine sighting in my life.

People were welcome to use our big telescope inside the visitor center to get a closer look at the wildlife and the mountain. One day a woman at the scope yelled out that she had found a grizzly. Everyone rushed over to look for the bear, but no one could spot it. I asked the woman where it was, but she had a hard time explaining its location. Then she got even more excited and said the bear was now standing up. The other people were getting frustrated over missing the bear, so I asked her to let me look through the scope. I saw the animal right away. It was a ten-inch-tall Arctic ground squirrel. Then I had to tell everyone that there had been a bit of a misunderstanding. At least they all got to see the squirrel.

My duties included staffing the visitor center desk as well as leading walks through the tundra meadow outside the building. The main attractions in the meadow were wildflowers in spring and early summer. Once or twice a week, I drove twenty miles west to Wonder Lake Campground and did evening campfire talks there. The subject I chose for my initial campground program was the first ascent of Denali. And I was able to give the talk in the perfect setting: as I faced my first audience of about twenty-five people, Denali was directly behind me.

In early 1910, a group of miners from the area north of the mountain decided on a lark to climb Denali. None of them had done anything like that before, but they knew the country and figured they could travel up the Muldrow Glacier to the summit. They came back a few weeks later with a story of making it to the summit and leaving a fourteen-foot pole there. Their epic adventure became known as the Sourdough Expedition. Back then *sourdough* was a term for men who had lived in Alaska for a long time and could handle themselves in the backcountry.

Two years later, another expedition approached Denali from the south. They came close to reaching the summit but had to turn back before they reached the highest point. When they came back down, the climbers were asked if they had seen the pole on the summit. The answer was no.

The following year, 1913, a climbing party finally reached the summit. There was no pole or any evidence anyone had been there before. It turned out they were on what is known as the South Summit of Denali, which is 20,310 feet above sea level. While there, the party looked over at the North

Summit, which has an elevation of 19,470, and saw the pole the miners had carried up the mountain. That proved their story of climbing Denali was true. Their goal had been to reach what looked like the summit from the north and they really did get there.

The first person we know of to stand on the true summit of Denali was Walter Harper, an Athabascan, whose people have lived in the interior of Alaska for thousands of years.

OVER MY YEARS as a summer naturalist in Denali, I worked up fifteen different campfire talks. The one that always got the best reaction was called "Why Are Ground Squirrels Such Jerks?" Arctic ground squirrels live throughout Alaska. In the museum at the University of Alaska in Fairbanks, I saw a Native winter parka made from about two hundred ground squirrel pelts. That is the traditional component of parkas in the Far North. For that reason, Native Alaskans call them "parky squirrels."

Male Arctic ground squirrels can weigh up to three pounds. Females are smaller and usually live in colonies with related females. That enables them to team up and drive off marauding groups of male ground squirrels, who often try to kill and eat the females' newborns.

The squirrels eat a wide range of vegetation, including grasses, roots, fruit, mushrooms, and seeds. They also consume insects, young snowshoe hares, lemmings, and other squirrels. Predators that hunt ground squirrels include grizzlies, wolves, golden eagles, and red foxes. Ground squirrels can make up 90 percent of the diet of golden eagles and 50 percent for foxes. If they are not eaten by predators, Arctic ground squirrels can live for up to ten years, a long life for a species that size.

Arctic ground squirrels have a sophisticated alarm system. If one sees an aerial predator flying above the colony, such as a golden eagle, it will call out with a single high-pitched whistle. But if a ground predator such as a wolf is spotted, the call will start with a three-note chatter and switch to five notes if the wolf comes closer. When a predatory bird lands in the colony, the alarm switches from the aerial whistle to the ground chatter.

Alaskan ground squirrels hibernate for up to eight months, starting as early as August. In summer a normal squirrel body temperature is around 99 Fahrenheit (37 Celsius), but during hibernation it can drop as low as 27 Fahrenheit (–3 Celsius) without any tissue damage from freezing. By the end of winter, a squirrel may have lost around a third of its weight.

A chemical in the squirrels' blood appears to trigger hibernation. In an experiment conducted by researchers Albert Dawe and Wilma Spurrier, some blood was drawn from a hibernating squirrel in the winter. It was stored, then injected into squirrels in the summer. They dropped into a hibernation state soon after injection. In my campground talk on ground squirrels, I half jokingly suggested that we could put astronauts into hibernation on long space missions by injecting them with squirrel blood.

The title of my talk "Why Are Ground Squirrels Such Jerks?" referred to the squirrels' habit of darting across the road in front of the park buses, which was really unnerving for the drivers. It seemed like they were challenging the buses, but actually all they were trying to do was get to a burrow on the other side of the road. Many squirrels ended up run over and other squirrels would eat them. Visitors, not realizing what was going on, would see a squirrel dragging a dead or injured squirrel off the road and say something like, "How cute. That squirrel is trying to save its friend!"

IN ADDITION TO giving campfire talks, I led multi-hour hikes. It was up to the rangers to choose where to hike and what to teach visitors while hiking. On some of my hikes, I taught people how to safely wade Alaskan rivers, rivers that originated from glaciers. On others, I went to areas where we could watch Dall sheep, pure white relatives of the bighorn sheep I used to see in Anza-Borrego.

My most popular hike was to a small valley that had a large population of hoary marmots and pikas. The fifteen-to-twenty-pound marmots are related to ground squirrels and like to den in areas with rocky outcrops, places where they cannot be dug out by grizzlies. Marmots mate for life and usually keep their young for two years. They work hard all summer to put on fat layers, then hibernate in family groups during the winter months. Just before hibernation, marmots are so fat they look like Jabba the Hutt from the Star Wars movies.

Pikas are related to rabbits and look like chubby gray chipmunks without tails. They are about four inches long and weigh just a few ounces. They also like to live where there are rock piles, but they have a different life strategy from their marmot neighbors. They collect vegetation during the summer, hide the material under rocks, then feed on those caches throughout the winter. Those food caches are defended territories, but pikas use food-gathering areas such as meadows in common. Their territorial calls are high-pitched squeaks. I never saw any conflict between the tiny pikas and their much larger marmot neighbors, probably because the two species use the same habitat in such different ways.

Denali has 158 bird species that live in the park, mostly migratory ones. The champion migrator is the Arctic tern. Arctic terns spend the spring and summer in the park, then fly to Antarctica for the summer season there, a round trip of about twenty-five thousand miles.

Species that live year-round in Denali include three species of ptarmigan. The willow ptarmigan is the state bird. They are white in winter and a mottled brown in summer. In really cold weather, they burrow into snow. *Ptarmigan* is a Gaelic word from Scotland, home of my ancestors, that translates as "croaker," a reference to the birds' harsh-sounding calls. Their genus name is *Lagopus*, which means "rabbit foot." That is because the feet of ptarmigan are covered with feathers.

Another bird that lives year-round in Denali and the rest of Alaska is the raven. I later worked in desert National Parks such as Death Valley in Southern California and ravens are permanent residents there as well, even in the scorchingly hot summers. Ravens are tough birds and in captivity they have lived to be up to sixty-nine years old.

People attempting to climb Denali often had trouble with ravens stealing food. Ravens can fly nearly to the top of the twenty-thousand-foot mountain. To protect food caches, climbers had to bury edible items in snow. At first they marked the sites with red flagging, but ravens quickly figured out the meaning of those flags and dug through the snow to get to the hidden food.

In traditional stories told by Alaskan Native people, a major character is Raven, a trickster who can assume any shape. For a talk I did on ravens, I found out that anthropologists believe Raven Trickster stories originated in Siberia and were brought to North America when people migrated across the Bering Land Bridge.

We also had periods of roving interpretation in our schedule. I would take ram horns, caribou antlers, and animal pelts to lots where the buses stopped, set those items up on a folding table, invite people over to let them handle the objects, then talk to them about the park's wildlife.

I learned that first summer that I had to get up early in the morning to study the park wildlife because that was when the animals were the most active. I bought myself a Bushnell spotting scope so I could see animals in more detail when they were far off, and I got into the habit of writing up my wildlife observations at the end of every day. Those Denali field notes and my later field notes during my Yellowstone years were the basis for many books I went on to write about wildlife.

ANOTHER OF MY responsibilities in Denali was managing people's interactions with wildlife so that neither the people nor the wildlife came to any harm. People arriving at our visitor center liked to feed the Arctic ground squirrels. The extra high-calorie food created a much higher density of squirrels than would have been normal for the area.

My first spring at Eielson, that overpopulation attracted a blond-colored young female grizzly. She quickly learned our area was the best squirrel hunting area in her territory. When she arrived, our staff had to get every visitor back onto the building's front porch for safety. But there were always some people who defied us and stayed in the yard taking photographs.

I was learning more about how to manage crowds and came up with a method that always worked. Whenever someone ignored repeated requests to come back, I would walk up to the offender and stand right in front of them. That got their attention, because they could no longer take photos. I then repeated my order to go to the building. By that time, they began to realize they were the only person risking their life by being near the bear and would agree to back off. Often the crowd on the porch would clap as the offender walked back toward the building.

When the blond bear was near the visitor center, I had to constantly monitor her location. One day she started to circle around to the west side of our building. That put her out of my sight. I ran down to my quarters in the basement so I could look for her through the west-facing window by my bed.

When I got there, she was an inch or two away from the window, looking in at me. I suddenly remembered that several squirrels had gotten into my room that morning. I thought I had chased them all out, but now I worried that if the bear saw one through the window, she would crash through it and end up in the small room with me. After a minute or so, she turned around and walked off. But she left a reminder of her visit: a big grizzly nose print on the window glass.

Despite our best efforts, people continued to feed the squirrels, and that bear just could not stay away. We reported the problem to higher-level Park Service people. Without consulting with us, a ranger from Park Headquarters came out and shot the grizzly. The staff at the visitor center were devastated because it was not the bear's fault and she did not deserve to die.

I vowed I would never let that happen again. Soon I came up with a plan. I got five Havahart live squirrel traps, baited them with food, and positioned them around our visitor center. The traps worked great. In no time at all, I would have five captured squirrels. I would load the traps into my government car, drive down the road about five miles, and let the squirrels go. After catching five more, I would repeat the process.

I soon thought of a more efficient method. After cleaning out an old garbage can, I would drop captured squirrels into the can, put the lid on it, catch more, and after getting about ten of them in the can, I would drive off to the release site. On one of those trips there was a problem. I stopped on the park road, took out the garbage can, put it on the road, took the lid off, and got ready to tilt the can over so the squirrels could get out. I took a moment to look around and saw a grizzly charging at me. It must have heard the squirrels calling from inside the can. I ran back and got into my car.

The grizzly stopped near the can and looked around for the squirrels. It did not understand they were all in the can, just a few feet away. As the bear tried to figure out the problem, one of the squirrels jumped out of the can and almost landed on the grizzly. It ran under a nearby vehicle where the bear could not reach it.

The grizzly went back to the garbage can and smacked it with its front paw. When the can landed on its side and all the squirrels escaped, the bear caught and ate one of them. It was only then that I noticed the whole incident had been witnessed by a busload of tourists. I cringed as I realized they had seen a uniformed park ranger feed a grizzly a garbage-can load of squirrels. I boarded the bus to explain but I doubted they believed my story.

We eventually managed to stop most of the squirrel feeding, and that, along with my squirrel relocation program, solved our grizzly problem at our visitor center.

DURING MY FIFTEEN seasons in Denali, I was mostly at the Eielson Visitor Center, but sometimes I was based at Park Headquarters near the entrance to the park. When I was there, I did slideshows in an auditorium and campfire talks in a large campground. I also did dogsledding demonstrations.

In the early years after Denali had been designated a National Park, there had been a lot of problems with poachers who would sneak into remote sections of the park in the winter on dogsleds, illegally shoot caribou and moose, then sell the meat. Rangers acquired their own dog teams so they could patrol the backcountry. In modern times, Denali rangers continue to do dogsled patrols to deter poachers, to check on park visitors, and to conduct research.

Because I was not in the park in winter months, I did not do those patrols, but I did do a lot of dogsledding demonstrations on a dirt loop at the kennels. I would tell audiences of several hundred people about the dogsledding tradition in the park, then hitch up a team of dogs to a sled with wheels on the runners, yell "Mush," and drive the sled around the loop. The dogs loved to pull sleds, so they were enthusiastic about getting to participate, running at top speed while I tried to hang on.

On one of my demonstrations, everything went normally, but when I got back to the crowd, people excitedly told me that a cow moose had been near the far side of the loop and had chased us. She had a calf and probably mistook the dogs for wolves that might go after her offspring. Luckily, the dogs outran her and saved me from an attack. I had not seen her because I was concentrating so hard on looking forward.

In mid-June one year, we had a storm that dumped twelve inches of snow on the ground in the kennel area. That day we took the wheels off the demonstration sled and the dog team raced off with me on my first experience on snow. It was a much faster run than a usual trip.

When off duty we could come down to the kennels and take dogs for a walk. I did that a lot with a huge male named Silver. Actually, it was more like Silver took me for a walk, for he was very strong. He liked pizza, so I tried to make friends with him by giving him pizza slices. Silver was a wheel dog, which means he and another big male were positioned right in front of the sled so they could use their size and strength to help a stationary sled accelerate. Usually, a smaller dog, male or female, would be out in front as the team leader and that dog had to be good at following voice commands from the musher, meaning the human driver.

People are always surprised when they hear I never had a dog. My life of seasonal jobs, including twice-yearly migrations to different National Parks, where pets were not allowed in government housing, made it impossible to have one. But if I could have had a dog, I would have taken Silver when he reached his retirement age.

One summer we heard that a controversial cabinet-level bureaucrat was going to visit Denali. He was well known for making policy decisions that adversely affected National Parks and wildlife. Several of the seasonal rangers announced that they would hold a protest event during that visit. The park superintendent responded by forbidding any demonstrations. He had the power to fire seasonal employees, so things got tense. The organizers of the protest reluctantly agreed to cancel the event. We all thought that was the end of the issue.

The high-level bureaucrat arrived with Secret Service protection and was taken to the kennel to see the dogsledding demonstration. As the ranger in charge finished explaining how dogsledding operated in the park, another ranger was bringing a big male dog from his kennel to the sled. The controversial official happened to be standing near the sled to be used for the demonstration. The big dog suddenly veered away from the sled and dragged the ranger to the bureaucrat. Before the Secret Service agent could react, the dog went right up to the dignitary, lifted his leg, and peed all over the man's pants.

Since the incident was an accident, no one could be blamed or fired. Later, we found out how the clever setup had been planned. The ranger responsible had taken a walking stick and rubbed it on the post that a male dog was chained to. He likely had peed on the post hundreds of times. That dog was a rival of the one that peed on the official. No one had noticed earlier that the ranger had strolled toward the dignitary and "accidentally" brushed that stick against the side of his pants while passing by. When the ranger brought the dog toward the sled, the dog got the scent of the rival male's urine on the pants of the bureaucrat and reacted by peeing over it.

5

Grizzlies in Denali

DURING THE TIME I worked there, Denali had a population of two hundred to three hundred grizzlies. Each bear had a home range. The size of the range depended on the amount and quality of food in that area. In a study in the Yukon Territory, which had bear habitat similar to Denali's, male grizzlies had home ranges that averaged 178 square miles and females had ones that were about 53 square miles. There was usually a fair amount of overlap in bear territories. Grizzlies can coexist with neighboring bears as long as they keep apart from each other.

Based on the weights of grizzlies captured and weighed in the park, most adults are probably in the two-hundred-to-three-hundred-pound range. But some have reached an estimated seven hundred pounds. In zoos grizzlies have lived up to forty-seven years, but in Denali the oldest known bear died in its thirty-second year.

Denali grizzlies can be black, brown, or blond. Scientists had never seen a blond grizzly until one was shot in the Denali area in the early 1900s, before the establishment of the park. It was taken near the Toklat River, so since then blond bears have been known as Toklat grizzlies.

Park grizzlies usually den in late October or early November and normally dig out new dens every year. Most dens are located in high-elevation areas where snowfall tends to be deep. The more snow, the better the dens are insulated from the cold. Bears usually line the spot where they sleep with dead grass. The den chamber temperature rarely drops below freezing throughout the winter, regardless of the outside weather.

One October I investigated an empty grizzly den on a slope near the Toklat River. The entrance was twenty-eight inches wide and the tunnel went back seven and a half feet. The tunnel had been dug at a slight upward incline, which would allow any melting snow or ice that got into the den to drain outside.

The grizzlies in Denali greatly increase their food intake in fall to prepare for their winter sleep. Once they have stored enough fat, they gradually lose interest in eating. I have heard that grizzlies living in captivity ignore offered food for about three weeks before denning as their bodies switch to winter mode.

Bears usually roll up in balls for the winter, a position that conserves their body heat. Breathing and heartbeats are lowered, but body temperature drops only a few degrees. Researcher Erich Follmann found that a denning grizzly has a temperature of 94.1 Fahrenheit (34.5 Celsius), which is 5.8 degrees below normal. That means that grizzlies are not true hibernators like marmots and ground squirrels, whose body temperatures drop to near freezing levels. The more proper term for the winter state of grizzlies is *torpor*, but as that word is not commonly used or understood, many people continue to use the term *hibernation* for bears.

While sleeping through the winter, grizzlies lower their metabolism to about 35 percent below normal. That enables them to survive long periods without food. A 1988 study by P. D. Watts and Chuck Jonkel found that a 440-pound grizzly needs only 44 to 88 pounds of stored fat to survive a 150-day hibernation. Because fat has a high moisture content, the bear does not need to drink during the winter.

When grizzlies come out of their dens in the spring, it may take a few weeks for their normal appetite to come back, so they are somewhat lethargic. I heard of one captive grizzly that did not eat for three weeks after leaving its den.

The grizzly mating season starts soon after the bears leave their dens. Females can have cubs when they are four years old, but Harry Reynolds and John Hechtel, who researched grizzly bears in the Alaska Range area, which includes Denali, found that the average age of females having their first litter is eight years. The biggest factors influencing sexual maturity are the nutritional quality of available food and the bear's body weight.

I saw many examples of grizzly courtship over the years in Denali. One took place near the Toklat River when a brown male moved toward a blond female. She allowed him to approach, then playfully nipped him on a front leg. The pair stood up and wrestled and nipped at each other. After that they sat down and pressed their open jaws together in a playful manner.

On another occasion, I watched a pair of grizzlies that looked like they were getting ready to mate. At times they slept side by side. Then they would get up and feed on tundra plants. Later, they wrestled with each other. That led to a mounting attempt by the male, but the female pulled away. The male continued to try to breed her, but she got into a pattern where she would run away from him, then go back. It looked like she was not quite ready for a mating, and the male seemed to accept that, as he never tried to force himself on her.

Another mating pair I observed were tied together when I spotted them. The male, who was much bigger than the female, had mounted her from behind. He stood on his hind legs and his front legs dangled over her back. At times he rested his head on her back. They stayed that way for about fifteen minutes, then they moved slightly out of sight, still in their mating tie.

After a female has been bred in the spring, her fertilized eggs stay in an undeveloped state until the fall. When she dens, the eggs implant in the wall of her uterus and begin to grow. The cubs will be born in the den in January or February, assuming the mother bear is healthy and has enough stored fat. If that is not the case, the fertilized eggs are reabsorbed by the female.

Most females have litters of one to three cubs. Newborn grizzly cubs weigh just a pound or so, far smaller than a newborn human. The cubs start to nurse on their mother right away and continue to do so throughout their time in the den. The mother usually goes back into a deep sleep after nursing her cubs, while the cubs sleep normally between nursing bouts. The cubs stay warm by resting on their mother.

As most Denali grizzly mothers keep their cubs until they are about two and a half years old, the family will spend two more winters in the den after their first winter. This also means females seldom breed more often than every three years.

AFTER WATCHING THE park grizzlies for some time, it became obvious to me that once they have shaken off the lethargy of their long winter sleep, they are obsessed with finding food. One Alaska study found that adult grizzlies spend about 91 percent of their waking time eating or looking for food. Most of that is plant material, but grizzlies supplement it with high-protein meat from caribou, moose, and Dall sheep. Usually, they feed on carcasses, but sometimes they make their own kills.

During my time in Denali, I got a report that a grizzly mother and her three yearling cubs had found a big bull caribou that had been wounded by a wolf pack. The wolves had walked off and bedded, probably intending to rest before finishing off the bull.

I arrived in time to see the grizzly mother and her cubs heading toward the injured bull. When the mother charged, the bull ran into the river, then turned and faced the bear. The bull tried to use his big antlers to fend off the grizzly, but she reared up and grabbed him around the head and neck with her front paws. As they struggled, the bear gradually pulled the caribou down into the river.

The cubs, who had remained on the riverbank, looked worried and were making crying sounds, probably because they thought the bull was attacking their mother. When the bull finally died, the cubs joined their mother and fed on him. After the four bears had eaten their fill, they took naps on top of the carcass.

The following day, a big male grizzly approached and ran at the mother bear, likely intending to chase her away so he could take over the site. The three cubs ran off, but the mother stood her ground. That was enough to cause the big male to turn around and leave.

As long as the bears were on the carcass, the wolves could not access it. This was a dynamic I often observed in Yellowstone in later years. The grizzly family stayed for four days before they moved on. By then there was not much for the wolves to scavenge. The cubs had even climbed up on the huge antlers to get every scrap of velvet.

Grizzlies also often use their superior size and strength to claim an animal that wolves have worked hard to bring down. In 1989, however, I witnessed an unusual interaction between an adult grizzly and wolves. Even today, I've never seen anything quite like it.

Twelve members of Denali's East Fork pack were traveling together east of their den. They spotted a mother grizzly with three yearlings and ran at them. One yearling stuck close to the mother, but the other two panicked and ran off. The wolves chased them, and we lost all the animals in a gully. But soon wolves came out of that area with red meat in their mouths, a strong indication they had killed one of the yearlings.

I later saw the mother bear with just one yearling. The mother had a wound on her back, probably inflicted by one of the wolves. She sniffed the ground and the air and also repeatedly looked around. I took that to mean she was searching for her two missing yearlings. She also stood up to full height to get a better view of the area. At one point, she got near the park road and charged at nearby cars and shuttle buses. I think that was due to her high stress level. If a person had accidentally gotten near her, she likely would have killed them.

After that sighting, I thought about all the times the wolves had done the hard, dangerous work of killing a caribou only to have a grizzly steal it from them. The attack on this bear family might be considered retaliation for those incidents.

Grizzlies often take over wolf kills, but they are also capable of taking down caribou, moose, and Dall sheep, mostly animals that are young or injured. Because of their size, grizzlies give the impression that they might be slow, but they can run almost as fast as a racehorse. Healthy caribou, however, are even faster. I often saw caribou passing by grizzlies without much concern because of their confidence in their speed.

Young bears have to learn the hard way that caribou are faster than they are. I was watching a mother grizzly with twin yearlings near a small group of caribou. One of the yearlings ran at them. The caribou sped off and effortlessly outran the young bear. The mother grizzly and the other, wiser yearling ignored the caribou and continued to feed on plants when the young bear gave chase. Things are different when caribou calves are very young, for they have not yet developed the ability to run at top speed. But it only takes them a few days to run as fast as the adults.

Moose, which are much bigger than caribou, use a different tactic to avoid bear attacks. Adult moose usually stand their ground. If a bear comes closer, the moose will likely charge forward and try to stomp it with its rock-hard front hooves. But if a bear finds a cow moose just after she has given birth, she might not have recovered enough to fight it off. Bull moose often get injured during fights with other bulls in the fall mating season, which weakens them and makes them vulnerable to bears.

Moose calves are easier prey for grizzlies. The most dangerous situation for a calf is when it gets separated from its mother. One spring I saw a moose calf running alone across the tundra. A grizzly spotted the calf and pursued it. At first it looked as though the calf was outrunning the bear. But when it ran into a willow thicket, the bushes slowed it down.

The bear must have seen that, as it ran faster, plowed through the thick brush, and was right behind the calf when it ran back out into the open. The young moose soon collapsed from exhaustion and the grizzly was immediately on it. I looked around for the mother moose for some time and failed to spot her. If the mother had been with her calf and had recovered from giving birth, she would have had a good chance of protecting her calf from the bear.

In May 1985, I saw a major fight between a mother moose and a male grizzly. The cow had newborn twin calves with her when the bear came on the scene and approached them. The cow moose charged at the grizzly at top speed. On reaching him, she kicked forward with her front hooves. The bear crumpled to the ground from the blows. The mother moose then stomped the prone grizzly with her hooves.

He somehow squeezed out from under her and ran off, but the cow was not finished. She chased the bear and once again stomped on him. I thought she was going to kill him, but the grizzly slipped out from under her and ran off. The cow let him go and went back to her twin calves, who were hiding behind some trees.

I thought that was the end of it, but apparently the grizzly could not resist making another attempt to get the calves. He approached the mother and calves and she charged forward. The bear ran off, but the cow was faster. When she got right behind the bear she kicked forward and hit him on the rear end. As he dropped to the ground, she stomped on him again. The bear finally got away and did not make a third attempt on the calves.

But things do not always turn out in the mother moose's favor, especially if more than one bear is involved. In my early years in Denali, I knew a mother grizzly who had triplet yearlings. The family charged at a cow moose with twin calves. The moose seemed to be confused by the charge of so many bears. As she hesitated about which of the grizzlies to deal with, the mother bear rushed in and killed both calves.

Several years later, the same mother bear had another set of triplets. By the time they were two and a half years old, the cubs were almost as big as their mother. The bear family spotted a mother moose with twin calves and charged. The cow singled out the mother grizzly and chased her off, but as that was going on, two of the cubs got both calves. After the bear family left, moose researcher Dale Miquelle and I went out to one of the calf carcasses and Dale examined it. We saw that the killing bite had been to the head. The jaw had been broken by the force of the bite. The young calf weighed thirty pounds.

Grizzlies are a far greater threat to moose calves than wolves are. In one Alaska study, forty-eight moose were radio-collared soon after birth. Thirty were dead by July. Grizzlies had killed twenty-four and wolves had only gotten one. Biologist Warren Ballard, after doing a study of moose calf mortality in Alaska, wrote of the findings: "The wolf, which we first suspected to be the most important predator on the moose (the 'butler' in our whodunit) turned out to be only slightly guilty—an accomplice, as it were."

After feeding on a carcass, grizzlies usually cover up the remaining meat to save it for later meals. I once found a bear on a freshly killed moose calf. It straddled the carcass and used its front paws to scrape dry grass and soil over the remains. Within a few minutes, it had a foot of material covering the calf. That would hide the smell and likely keep wolves and other bears from finding the meat.

Another time, I found a caribou carcass with a pile of vegetation and dirt covering it that was three feet high and eight feet long. I watched from a safe distance and soon saw the grizzly return. It dug up a portion of the carcass and fed. Then it lay down on top of the caribou, took a nap, and later resumed feeding. That pattern continued for a long time: eating, sleeping, then feeding again.

Covering a carcass is a learned skill. One spring I watched a mother bear and cub feeding on a moose calf. As its mother napped, her cub tried to toss a big clump of tundra dirt onto the carcass. But it missed its target, and the dirt landed on the sleeping mother bear and woke her up.

ALTHOUGH GRIZZLIES CAN take down large prey, their hunting success is much higher with Arctic ground squirrels than with caribou, moose, or Dall sheep, mostly because they can dig the squirrels out of their burrows. When I was working up my campfire talk on Arctic ground squirrels, I read a lot of research papers on them. A graduate student named James Gebhard estimated a mother grizzly had caught and eaten 397 ground squirrels during one spring-to-fall period. Just before denning, that bear was eating an average of 12.5 pounds of squirrel meat per day. On especially good days of squirrel hunting, she was getting up to twenty-six thousand calories, about the same as if she ate twenty-six triple cheeseburgers.

One time when I was watching a mother bear and her two big yearlings feeding on tundra plants, the mother bear stopped grazing to chase and catch a squirrel. Her cubs ran over right away. One stole the squirrel from its mother and quickly gulped it down. The sow must have learned from that, for when she got a second squirrel, she ran away from her cubs, stopped, and started to eat it. Despite her precautions, one of her cubs ran in, pulled half the squirrel away, and swallowed it.

The following year, I had another great view of a grizzly getting a squirrel. A bear had been digging out a ground squirrel burrow for a good ten minutes, using its claws to pull out big chunks of dirt. It often paused, peered into the hole, then resumed digging. At times the bear would pounce on the ground with its front paws, then look around to see if the squirrel had run out of another tunnel. That plan worked. When the squirrel darted out a few feet away, the bear grabbed and ate it.

I looked around and saw that the grizzly had dug two earlier holes in its attempts to reach the squirrel. Each hole was about two and a half feet deep. Later, the bear moved off, saw a squirrel running toward its burrow, and caught it before it got there.

Grizzlies also use their claws to dig out beaver. I once saw a grizzly trying to reach a beaver hiding in a burrow on the shore of a pond. The hole it dug was big enough to allow the bear to get almost entirely inside it. I watched as the bear backed out of the hole, moved to a nearby section of the bank, and started digging there. Soon the bear pulled out a big adult beaver. The beaver frantically flopped around, trying to break free, but the grizzly bit it on the back of the neck and killed it. After that, the bear ran off with the beaver and ate it out of my sight.

Salmon do not run as far north as Denali, so park grizzlies lack a food source that is so important to coastal Alaskan bears and helps them grow so large. Most of what park bears eat in spring and early summer is low-calorie vegetation, but they can add a lot of weight once berries start to ripen in late July. When that happens, bears flock to berry patches and devote most of their time to eating high-calorie fruit, including blueberries, soapberries, and crowberries.

I came across a grizzly study by Arthur Pearson. He watched a grizzly feeding throughout the day on a soapberry patch in the Yukon Territory. After the bear left, Pearson studied a pile of its droppings and estimated there were twenty thousand soapberry seeds in the pile. He had already found that bears there tended to produce ten bowel movements per day. That meant the bear had likely eaten two hundred thousand berries that day, which could add two pounds of fat to a grizzly. Imitating the bears, I began a custom of picking blueberries and putting them on my morning cereal. I still put them on my cereal every morning many decades later, but now I buy them at the supermarket.

I WAS OUT in grizzly country nearly every day during my fifteen seasons in Denali and only once had a problem with a bear. I had gotten a mountain bike and would leave the visitor center in the early morning and bike east on the road to look for wildlife. I had to go up a long uphill section of road, then had a long downhill coast for nearly a half mile. As I reached the crest of that hill, I looked in my mirror and saw a grizzly chasing me.

Bears have poor eyesight, and the grizzly probably mistook me for a prey animal such as a caribou or moose. As grizzlies can run at speeds of up to thirty-five miles per hour, I had to make a quick decision: should I stop and take out my bear spray, a cayenne pepper–based mixture that usually causes grizzlies to turn around and run off, or should I try to outrun the bear?

That long downhill stretch would allow me to get up to perhaps forty miles per hour. That meant I would be faster than the bear. But if it continued to pursue me, the grizzly would catch me when the road started up another hill. I could not take that chance, so I stopped, positioned the bike perpendicularly between me and the oncoming bear, and got ready to use the spray on it.

As soon as I got off the bike and stood up, the bear stopped, looked at me, and, apparently realizing I was a human, turned around and walked away. Alaskans jokingly refer to people who bike in grizzly country as "Meals on Wheels." That was almost me that day.

Many bear attacks involve people camping out with food smells that attract grizzlies. Denali is mostly treeless, so hikers cannot use a rope to put food out of reach of a bear. For that reason, the park tested several types of bearproof food containers. I was involved with some of the field testing.

In one case, two other rangers and I were out in the backcountry when we spotted two sibling bears on the tundra. I was carrying the container and the other rangers had shotguns in case we needed to scare off the bears. We put fish scent on the container, then I was told to walk toward the bears and put it down out in front of their direction of travel. After doing that, we all backed off to see what would happen. One bear went to the container, sniffed it, fooled around with it for a while, then lost interest and left. We repeated the test with another bear and had about the same results. The two tests showed us what we needed to know: the containers did seem to be bearproof.

The design that worked best was a round tube made of heavy-duty plastic. The tube was about ten inches in diameter and had a locked lid. The Park Service made a lot of these containers and loaned them out for free to people camping in the backcountry. During my time in Denali, those food containers, and prompt aversive conditioning when a grizzly caused a problem, reduced food-related incidents by 90 percent. Aversive conditioning can include hitting a problem bear with projectiles such as rubber bullets, or scaring it with loud noises.

Not all clashes with grizzlies were food-related. One morning when I was on duty at the Eielson Visitor Center, there was a grizzly on the road east of the building. I went to my car in case I had to deal with the bear if it came closer. I then saw the grizzly charging a man who had walked toward it for photos. I drove over and scared the bear away. Then I got the man into my car and took him back to the visitor center.

Soon after that, I saw the bear chasing a woman and her young daughter. The bear veered off when the pair ran toward the building. When the local law enforcement ranger arrived on the scene, I told him what had happened, and he said he would give me a shotgun to deal with any future bear incidents. I did not tell him, but I had no intention of ever shooting a bear. I figured I could manage any future incidents without killing anything. I would do that by managing the people.

One day a grizzly stopped by an empty tour bus in front of the visitor center just as a passenger came out of the building and started to head to the bus. I told him he had to go back to the building because of the bear, but he responded by saying "You're not my driver" and tried to go past me. I had to physically stop him, then escort him back inside the building. That grizzly continued to prowl around our visitor center over the next few days. The rangers captured the bear, then flew it out to a remote western section of the park and dropped it off there.

In another case, a man approached a mother grizzly and her cubs about ten miles east of Eielson. In defense of her cubs, the mother mauled the man. The rangers decided not to do anything to the grizzly, as she was just protecting her young. I kept track of that family the rest of the season and the following year and they never caused any more problems.

A different bear situation developed a few weeks later. An older female cub that had been driven off by her mother had approached people on several occasions. That day, some other rangers and I went to where the bear was hanging out, and one of us walked toward her to test her reaction. The bear charged him but veered away at the last moment. We darted the bear and tranquilized it. She was big for her age, and it took eight of us to drag her to the road. It was spooky to be so close to a grizzly, especially since her eyes were open the whole time and she was watching us. We had to give her new injections periodically to keep her sedated. She was put on a helicopter and flown out to a distant section of the park, far from any people.

During my fifteen years working in Denali, there were ten incidents where bears mauled people. In seven of these ten cases, the grizzlies likely attacked because they felt threatened.

Two incidents took place when people were hiking through thick brush and they surprised grizzlies at close range. In four cases, young people ran into grizzlies while out walking in the dark in an area known to be frequented by bears. Then there was a sudden encounter with a mother bear and cub on a riverbank. The bear likely attacked because she was surprised and wanted to protect her cub. In all seven cases, the situation probably could have been avoided if the hikers had made a lot of noise to alert the bears of their presence.

In the other three maulings, people made poor decisions that put them close to grizzlies. In two cases, young men deliberately approached grizzlies for close-up photos. The third mauling involved a man without a tent sleeping on a bear trail near a moose carcass. The area was closed because of the danger of bears coming to the carcass. When a grizzly came to the site and found the man in his way, he smacked him and left.

I have lived and worked in three National Parks that have grizzlies—Denali, Glacier, and Yellowstone—for forty-nine years now (1976 to 2025). I had only one close call with a bear during my time in Denali. That was when the grizzly ran after me when I was on my bike. In Yellowstone there was also one incident. I was walking through a thick stand of sage when I suddenly heard the sound of running animals. A moment later, I saw a mother grizzly and her two cubs running away from me.

The critical thing is to pay attention while you are walking off road in grizzly country. Most of the hiking in Denali and Yellowstone is in open, treeless country, so you have good sight lines to look for bears. When hiking through a forest or thick brush, I regularly yell out to alert a bear that might be in the brush that a human is coming. Usually, the wording in the yell is something like, "Hey bear, I'm coming through."

It is highly preferable to hike in a group, but because of my wolf research, I often am alone when I hike off road. I always carry within easy reach a canister of bear spray that contains cayenne pepper, which is very noxious to grizzlies. So far, I have never needed to use it. If a grizzly charges and you do not have bear spray, the best response is to drop on your stomach and play dead. That hopefully will convince the bear that you are no threat.

Life Lessons From Wolves

Empathy

To be able to put yourself in someone else's shoes requires empathy. This is a value I connected with at an early age and have tried to embrace throughout my own life. I was later to see it expressed in one of the most famous Yellowstone wolves, wolf 21.

Yellowstone wolf 21, one of the pups raised by wolf 8, grew up to be the biggest and strongest male wolf I have ever known. When 21 was young, he witnessed how wolf 8 defeated a much bigger alpha male, then showed mercy by letting him live. 21 followed that example for the rest of his life. He never lost a fight with another wolf, but he never killed a defeated opponent. In every case, he used the minimum amount of force and showed mercy to his rivals.

21 was totally devoted to his longtime mate, wolf 42, and to his large family. He often pretended to lose chasing games and wrestling matches with his young pups. That reminded me of my own father, who let me win wrestling matches with him on our living room floor.

My favorite 21 story took place when he was a young adult. That spring his mother had a pup with health problems that often kept it apart from the other pups. One day I saw 21 come back to his family with food from a kill. After feeding his mother and the healthy pups, 21 looked around and seemed to be searching for something. He saw the isolated sick pup, went to him, and stayed with the pup for some time: a big brother looking out for his little brother.

I think about the story of 21 giving special attention to the sick pup when I am asked to take Make-A-Wish kids and boys and girls from Texas Children's Hospital out to see wolves in Yellowstone and try to give them the same extra attention that 21 gave to that pup.

I tell wolf 21's story in *The Reign of Wolf 21: The Saga of Yellowstone's Legendary Druid Pack.*

In 1970, when I was in college and working summers for the US Forest Service in New Hampshire, I was picked to help fight a wildfire on the Wenatchee National Forest in Washington state. I am in the back row, on the far right. That experience led to my first National Park Service job in 1975 as a firefighter in Sequoia and Kings Canyon National Parks. **Rick McIntyre photo collection**

In 1976, after working for a winter season in Anza-Borrego Desert State Park in California, I landed my dream job as a park ranger in Denali National Park in Alaska. It was here that I first got to watch and study wild wolves and honed my skills as a storyteller, translating my field notes into compelling campfire talks for park visitors. **Robert Kenkel/Rick McIntyre**

I worked summers in Denali from 1976 to 1990. The Eielson Visitor Center, where I lived for most of my time in Denali, offered stunning views of the 20,310-foot mountain. **Rick McIntyre**

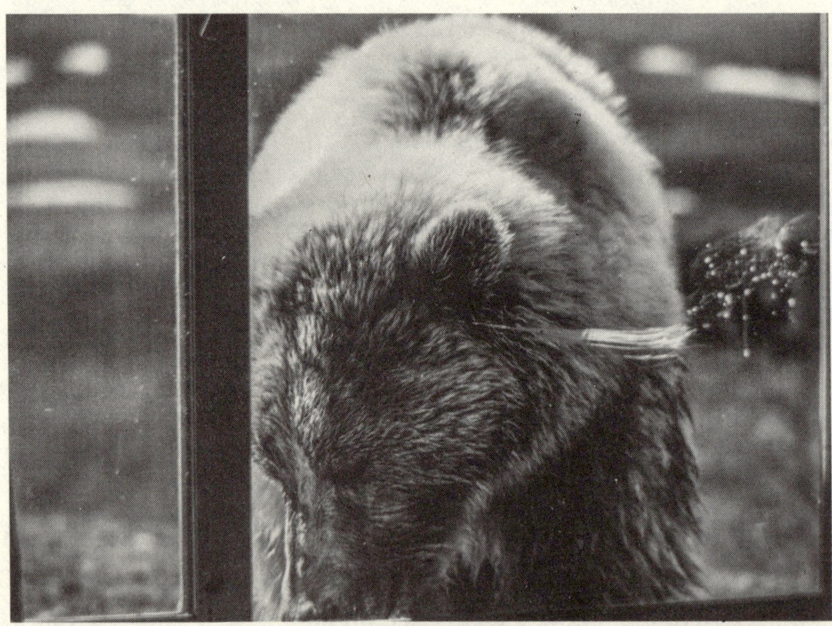

Grizzly bears were an issue near the Eielson Visitor Center. I caught this one getting a good look into my living quarters, possibly hoping to find a ground squirrel or two to snack on. **Rick McIntyre**

I got to know individual grizzly bears in Denali, including this cub—Stony. Because of the thoughtless behavior of park visitors, Stony became habituated to human food in adulthood. I tell his story in one of the first books I wrote, *Grizzly Cub: Five Years in the Life of a Bear*. **Rick McIntyre**

In Denali, I witnessed and photographed many dramatic fights between gigantic bull moose during the mating season. Their massive antlers can inflict significant—and sometimes fatal—damage. **Rick McIntyre**

Denali was where I began my transition from wildlife photographer to wildlife researcher. In the 1980s, following in the footsteps of famed wolf researcher Adolph Murie, I found a spot where I could watch the den of the East Fork pack from a distance, without interfering with the pack's family life. **Rick McIntyre**

The East Fork alpha male (top) and his mate (bottom). The East Fork male was the first, and the most impressive, alpha male wolf I have ever known. It was while watching this pack that I developed protocols I would later use when observing wolves in Yellowstone. **Rick McIntyre**

While I was working summers in Denali, I had winter jobs in various desert parks in California, including Death Valley. Here I am in 1982 with C-3PO during the filming of *Return of the Jedi*, the third film in the original Star Wars trilogy. **NPS**

I began my job as wolf interpreter in Yellowstone National Park in the spring of 1994, eight months before wolves were reintroduced to the park. My role was to prepare the public for the arrival of the wolves. I used this wolf pelt in my talks when I described how early rangers killed off the original wolf population. **Rick McIntyre**

6

Stony's First Year

STONY WAS THE most memorable grizzly bear I ever got to know in Denali. It all began when I was driving along the park road in the spring of 1984 and saw a newborn cub about the size of a teddy bear. I stopped and the cub stared at me, then turned around and ran after its mother. She veered toward the park road and crossed it, with her cub following her. They passed within a few yards of my car. I had never been so close to a grizzly family.

The mother and her son stayed near the road, and I spent the next ten hours watching them. She spent much of that time feeding on tundra plants while the cub explored the surrounding area and found things to do. He picked up a rock and carried it around for a while. After that, he tried to climb a willow bush but fell off it to the ground. Determined to conquer that bush, he got higher up on his second attempt but began to fall once again.

The cub grabbed a branch with his teeth and tried to reach out to other branches with his front paws. As he dangled from the branch, it broke, and he fell to the ground. Ending up on his back with the broken branch on top of him, he turned the branch into a toy. The cub juggled it with both front paws, then with his hind paws. After that, he stood up on his back legs and carried the branch around in his mouth.

Tiring of that game, the cub next went to a nearby snowbank, positioned himself at the top, sat down, and slid down on his rear end. He ran back to the top of the snowbank and did many more slides, always on his bottom.

The cub and his mother lived near Stony Hill, a few miles west of Eielson, so I began referring to him as Stony and his mother as Big Stony.

He was getting bored with the snow-sliding game, so Stony went to his mother and tried to get her to play by nipping her on the side of her face. She continued to feed on tundra plants and ignored him. Then the cub got in front of her, blocking her path. The mother bear bumped into him and knocked him over. He tumbled down the nearby slope but ran right back up to her.

Refusing to be ignored, Stony squeezed in under her hind legs, moved forward under her belly and front legs and ended up under her face. That was a position that blocked her from the tundra plants she was feeding on. He got on his back, waved his paws in the air, and tried to playfully bite her. She ignored him and kept on walking. The cub chased her and nipped her hind legs, but she paid no attention to him.

Undeterred, the cub ran forward, got in front of his mother, smacked her in the face, then ran off, hoping that would start a game of chase. He stopped to look back at his mother. Once again, she ignored him and continued to graze.

His failed attempts to get some attention from her went on for a few more hours. Then the mother bear, who was likely now full, stopped and lowered her face to his level. This is what Stony was waiting for. He smacked her on the head with his front paws and repeatedly nipped her face. In a gentle manner, she nipped back at him. He rolled on his back and the mother and son wrestled, nipped, and smacked each other.

Soon the play slowed down. At that point, the mother rolled on her back. The cub knew what that meant. He climbed up on her and nursed. After that, tired from all the traveling and playing, Stony napped. But soon he opened one eye and saw that his mother had moved off and was continuing to feed on grass. He ran to her and resumed his nap beside her. When he next woke up, he saw that she was once again far from him. He ran to her and started a new nap under her belly. That pattern continued four more times. By then it was 11 p.m., but still light enough to see. I headed back to Eielson so I could get some sleep. That day was the best one I had ever spent with wildlife.

GRIZZLY CUBS ARE famous for their playfulness. They chase and wrestle for long sessions throughout the day as their mother grazes. The cubs stand up on their hind legs and wrestle with their front paws, they smack each other with their paws, and they nip their playmates on the face and body.

One spring I saw two first-year cubs play King of the Mountain on a snowbank. One cub ran up on the snow and its sibling followed. Both cubs stood up and boxed with their front paws. One would then lose its balance and slide down the snow, but would instantly run back up and resume wrestling. Later, they played the same game on a hilltop. When both of them fell over, they continued to wrestle as they rolled down the slope together.

Another game involved climbing up willow bushes. I once saw two cubs climb up a fifteen-foot-high willow. When both cubs got high up on the bush, they started to wrestle. One of them lost its balance and was about to fall to the ground. It grabbed a branch with its front paws and managed to hold on. The second cub moved over and bit at the other one's paws. The hanging cub lost its grip on the branch and fell to the ground. It climbed right back up in the willow and pushed its sibling off the disputed branch. After all that rough play, the cubs went to their mother and nursed.

On another day, I found a mother grizzly with three yearlings. Two of the yearlings wrestled with each other while the third one played in a snow patch. That bear found a piece of snow crust and carried it around in its jaws. Then the yearling dropped it and pushed it back and forth with its nose and then a paw. Later, it got another piece of snow crust, rolled on its back, put the crusted snow on its belly and played with it there.

Then there was the time when I watched a mother bear with three new cubs that were small enough to walk under her belly. She lay down on her back. The cubs climbed up on her chest and nursed. After that, the cubs played together. Much of that was wrestling and biting. They also smacked one another with their front paws.

Later, I watched the cubs chasing one another up and down a steep slope for forty-five minutes. Then they ran back to their mother and ran in circles around her. As they played around and under her, she dug out roots and ate them. After the joint play session, one cub tried to climb a big willow bush but repeatedly fell to the ground.

Then the mother bedded and gently played with one cub. That included licking and gently nipping the cub. In response, the cub nipped the fur on her face. After that, it was time to nurse again. While the mother stood, the cubs got under her, stood up to reach her nipples, and nursed. The best moment came later when a cub stood up behind the mother, turned around, and scratched its back on the mother's bottom.

Stony was missing out on play sessions like these with siblings. I think that was why he was so insistent on getting attention from his mother, the only playmate available to him.

BIG STONY AND Stony continued to live near the park road, just a few miles from Eielson. I eventually concluded that the mother bear was staying near the road to avoid big male grizzlies who might try to kill her cub. Most other park grizzlies stayed away from the road, but Big Stony did not seem concerned about cars and buses stopping to watch her and her son.

As I watched that bear family, I saw how persistent Stony was in wanting to nurse. A study of grizzly bear milk by James Gebhard found that a quart has about 2,300 calories. First-year grizzly cubs nurse about every two hours, but older ones feed less often. Mother grizzlies have six nipples, so there is plenty of milk to go around.

I once watched twin cubs nursing. Each one finished on a nipple, then moved on to another one. Soon after that, both ended up at the same spot. That set off a fight on top of their mother's chest. The two cubs fell off the mother. When they scrambled back up on her, they went to separate nipples and continued to nurse. Mother grizzlies often go to sleep after nursing and the cubs often do the same thing, using their mother as a pillow or mattress.

Stony would often sneak under his mother's belly while she was grazing on tundra plants and try to nurse. The mother bear usually reacted to that by stepping forward. Sometimes he would fall over and be left behind. Other times he would hang on to one of her nipples and be dragged along the tundra. If he failed repeatedly to be nursed, Stony would cry out with a call that sounded like "*Waugh*." When he finally got to nurse, he made a different sound that resembled the buzzing of bees.

One day I watched as Stony pestered his mother for a nursing for some time. She finally sat upright, then leaned back to a position where her belly and chest were fully exposed. I could see her six teats because of missing fur around them. Stony climbed up on her and nursed vigorously as his mother held his head and rear end in her front paws. When the milk in that nipple ran out, he went to the next nipple, then to another. He was still nursing when she had finally had enough and got up and walked off. Stony continued to hang on to a nipple and was dragged across the tundra as his mother moved on.

When he grew a little older, Stony often climbed up willow bushes that were up to fifteen feet tall. He learned to use both his front paws and his jaws to pull himself up the branches. The mother bear seemed to be concerned when she saw her cub climbing so high and frequently kept an eye on him while he was up there. One of those times, the cub fell, tumbled through the air, and landed right next to her. I expected that would end his climbing expeditions, but he ran right back to the bush and climbed up well past where he had fallen. A bit later, rather than backing down, he turned upside down and climbed headfirst back to the ground.

Soon Stony graduated to a new game: chasing caribou. They can weigh two hundred to four hundred pounds, so it was a comical sight to see a little bear, who probably was around ten pounds, pretending to be a mighty hunter. He never caught one, which was good, for he would not have known what to do next.

THE BIGGEST THREAT to grizzly cubs is big male bears. If they kill a mother bear's cubs, that can bring her quickly into estrus and the male grizzly might then breed her. I found out more about this when there was a major grizzly incident in May 1984. I missed seeing the initial altercation because I was helping people doing research on caribou calf survival in another section of the park. But I got a detailed account from my friend Fred Dean, a professor at the University of Alaska, who was studying grizzlies.

The incident took place on the Toklat River. It involved a mother grizzly and her two yearling cubs. A big male grizzly ran toward them, perhaps with the intention of breeding the female bear. The mother and her cubs ran off. The male bear caught one yearling and smacked it on the back with his front paw. The mother ran back to protect her cub and she and the male had an all-out fight for about fifteen minutes. That included bouts of standing up and fighting and fierce wrestling on the ground. Fred told me the male was about 25 percent bigger than the mother bear. She was losing but refused to give up and save herself. In the end, the big male killed her.

Fred then looked at the cub and saw it was seriously injured. It was crawling along the ground, using its front legs to pull itself away from the male bear. After going about two hundred yards from the attack site, the young bear collapsed. The other yearling, who was uninjured, had run off and gone out of sight.

I joined Fred the following morning and saw that the big male had buried the body of the mother bear and was sleeping on top of his cache. I watched the male for five hours and he stayed bedded at the site the whole time. He must have fed on the mother bear during the night and was waiting as that meat was digested. Occasionally, he would wake up, look around, wave off mosquitoes, and scratch himself. He also yawned a lot.

The helicopter we were using for the caribou study was nearby, so the pilot flew over the big male. The sound of the copter frightened the male from the mother bear's remains, but as soon as the helicopter left, he came right back. When I checked the site five days later, the male bear was gone and the carcass was in plain sight. The injured cub had crawled to the road, perhaps thinking the male bear would stay away from people and vehicles, but it was clear it would not survive. To end its suffering, a ranger shot it.

Eighteen days after the male bear killed the mother grizzly, another ranger and I watched the site for some time. There was no sign of bears or wolves in the area, so we hiked out to investigate. When we got there, we saw that only the internal organs had been eaten. There were a lot of bear droppings there, likely from the male that killed her, but no wolf tracks. After moving off and going up on a hill, we looked back and spotted a grizzly going to the carcass and standing by it. We backed off farther to see what would happen next.

This was not the big male, but the mother grizzly's surviving yearling cub. The young bear did not seem to understand its mother was dead. It was a tough emotional moment for us when we saw it lie down and rest its head on the mother's body. Later, it walked off and fed on plants. The orphaned grizzly cub was still near its mother's remains a week later. I continued to monitor it and saw the cub still visiting the site and resting on the remains over a month after her death. Eventually, it disappeared. We never knew its fate.

STONY SEEMED TO instinctively know big male bears were a threat. One day I saw a large male grizzly approach the cub. Big Stony saw what was happening and she also moved toward her cub. Stony knew what to do in dangerous situations: he ran to his mother and got behind her. I next saw him stand up on his hind legs and look out past his mother at the big male who was coming at them.

Despite being much smaller than the male bear, Big Stony charged. The male must have been smart, for rather than deal with an enraged mother bear, he ran away. I looked back at the cub and heard him making crying sounds like a frightened human child. The mother bear rushed back and calmed him down with a nursing session.

As I have mentioned, grizzlies have long front claws that are perfect tools for digging ground squirrels out of their den tunnels. On seeing a ground squirrel, Big Stony would immediately chase it. But most of the time, the squirrel would get to a burrow entrance and dive down into it. I once saw Big Stony spend thirty minutes digging out a burrow. I never saw her share a caught squirrel with her son. She needed protein to help produce her milk for him, and that was apparently more of a priority than giving him part of the squirrel meat.

Later that summer, Stony, who had been gaining weight, approached his mother when she dug out a squirrel. He lunged at the prize, and mother and son tussled over it. They rolled around on the ground for about thirty seconds. Then, apparently in defeat, Stony ran off. But when he stopped to look back at his mother, I saw he had that squirrel in his mouth.

It was approaching fall on the tundra and Stony was getting more and more independent. He had learned how to dig out squirrels and often concentrated on that. I began seeing him well away from his mother. She frequently got far ahead of him and would have to go back and find her cub.

Around that time, a wolf approached the mother bear and cub. The mother bear spotted the wolf, then stood up on her hind legs to monitor it. She was a big bear, much bigger than the wolf, and it left, apparently unwilling to risk dealing with an angry mother grizzly.

That was my last view of the cub and his mother that season in Denali. Back then I worked in Death Valley in the winter months, so I had to leave. While there, I often pictured mother and cub curled up together in a den.

7

Stony Grows Up

IN THE SPRING of 1985, I got back to Denali and immediately started searching for Stony and his mother. I failed to find them for six weeks. Finally, on July 5, a few miles east of Eielson, I spotted a mother bear with a one-year-old cub. But this yearling was blond and Stony had black fur in his first year. I saw the yearling go up to its mother and smack her in the face with a front paw. Then the two bears wrestled for ten minutes. Despite the color difference, this had to be the mother and son I was looking for. In the coming years, Stony's fur often changed colors. I later learned that it is fairly common for young bears in Denali to have different-colored fur (black, brown, or blond) from year to year.

After that, I saw Stony and Big Stony just about every morning in the same territory they had the previous year. Their relationship was similar to what I had seen during

Stony's first year. The mother bear spent most of her time feeding on tundra plants but took breaks to nurse and play with her son.

One morning Stony got a little too insistent on a play session when his mother was concentrating on eating. He got between her and the plants she was feeding on. She lunged at his rear end with an open mouth and he dodged just enough to avoid getting a painful bite on his bottom. He ran off and she chased him. They soon went around a hill and accidentally ended up on the park road, where three busloads of tourists were taking photos of the scenery. The mother bear realized that was not a good place for them to be, and she led her cub away.

That should have set a good example for her son, but Stony seemed curious about those big metal objects. One day the driver of a truck stopped to watch the bears, and the cub bit a rubber portion of a bumper. In other cases, he sniffed car tires and once looked into a bus at the passengers. That behavior worried me and the other rangers, because it was dangerous for a grizzly to be unafraid of cars and people.

I later saw an incident that showed the cub seemed to have learned from his mother that cars and other vehicles were all right to be near. A big male grizzly approached the pair when they were near the park road. As he moved toward them, the mother bear ran off, with Stony following her. She headed to the road, saw a tourist bus nearby, and took him there. Mother and cub sat down close to the bus and watched the big male off to the south. When the male bear spotted that bus, he turned around and left.

One hot summer day, the two bears found a pond and swam around in it to cool off. Always looking for play sessions,

Stony swam over to his mother and deliberately splashed water in her face. She swam after her son, caught him, and tossed him around in the water. He got away and swam to shore but turned around right away and did a belly flop into the water next to his mother. The pair continued to play in the water for a long time.

When I had to leave at the end of that season, I figured Stony's mother would want to mate the following spring, which meant she would have to drive off her son before she met up with a big male who might harm him.

I often thought how tough it must be for cubs to be driven off by their mothers. They usually try to come back to her over the course of several days, but each time they are chased off aggressively. That continues until the cubs finally leave for good. What can help at that point is for siblings to stay together for a while. Wolf researcher Adolph Murie reported seeing twin cubs in Denali continuing to pair up for three years after leaving their mother. I knew it would be a particularly traumatic experience for Stony because he had no siblings to hang out with.

WHEN I RETURNED to Denali in the spring of 1986, I found Stony and his mother right away in their usual territory. Stony was now blond, nearly two and a half years old, and getting big. I realized they were in a crisis moment, because a huge male bear was chasing them. As she had often done in past dangerous situations, the mother ran toward the park road. It was a bad decision, because a cliff on the other side of the road blocked any further retreat. The mother bear frantically looked around for an escape route as Stony pressed up against her side in fear of the oncoming big bear.

Seeing a steep gully that offered a possible escape route, she ran up it and the cub followed. She led Stony up to a ledge well above the road, then both of them turned around and looked down at their pursuer. He had stopped and was looking up at them. Perhaps wary of the steep climb, he turned around and left.

I saw that mother and son were both panting rapidly in an effort to displace the body heat their running had created. When things calmed down, the mother bear got into a nursing position and her son immediately came over and suckled on her. They stayed up on the cliff for the rest of day.

By that time, Stony was almost the size of his mother and had a prominent diagonal scar on his forehead, likely a wound from a male grizzly. But he still nursed on his mother—after one nursing session, the tired cub took a long nap as he lay down on his mother's soft belly—and he still loved to play. He found an orange traffic cone and batted it back and forth with his front paws. When he came across a snowbank on a hill, he would go to the top of it and slide to the bottom.

In late July, I found a lone grizzly feeding near the park road. He looked up and I saw the diagonal scar on his forehead. Stony was finally on his own in a dangerous world. As the weeks went by, he continued to be alone. By then his coat had become a mixture of black, brown, and golden fur. There was a ring of whitish fur around his neck. He had grown much bigger and now looked to be about two hundred pounds. But his behavior was much the same. He still played with rubber traffic cones and chewed on wooden road signs.

There was a contract crew working in the park that summer. They were preparing to build a new bridge over the

Toklat River. The crew lived in a camp near that river and it was a place frequented by Stony. The Park Service had given the workers strict instructions to put all their garbage into bearproof containers.

I passed through that area a lot and often saw Stony walking through the construction zone and the housing area for the workers. The young bear showed a lot of interest in the human-related objects there and would sniff and touch them with his front paws. When he came near the workers, they would get in the nearest truck.

Then one day we got a report of a terrible event. One of the construction workers had thrown a sandwich to Stony. The bear went over to the sandwich, sniffed it, then ate it. He was never the same after that, for now he had learned he could get tasty food from people. The following day, he returned to that area and found a garbage can that was not bearproof. He knocked it over and found some food from the workers' lunches. Things had gone from bad to worse.

A patrol ranger was notified and drove to the scene. The bear was still sorting through the garbage and unconcerned about the arrival of the vehicle. The ranger turned on his loud siren and that scared Stony into leaving. After that, the ranger went to the man in charge of the construction crew and gave him a ticket for violating the food-storage laws in the park. He added that there would be a detailed inspection of the area the following morning.

I drove over to the area the next morning to monitor the situation and was distressed to see Stony trying to break in to a metal bearproof Park Service trash can. He failed to get in, but I assumed he had smelled food inside the can and would continue to look for ways to get at it.

A big crowd of park visitors were watching and photographing the bear at the garbage can and many were laughing at his antics. It was not funny to me, for I was now really worried about what would happen to Stony if we could not turn this new behavior around.

A week or two later, I met up with the law enforcement ranger in that area and we saw Stony approaching the workers' camp. When we positioned our vehicles to block him, he moved off and fed on nearby plants. The ranger had to leave, so I stayed on the scene for the next few hours.

During that time, it was just me and Stony. About every twenty minutes or so, he would try to circle around me to get to the garbage can, but I would move my car and block him. In some of those interactions, he would look me right in the eyes. I felt tremendous sympathy for Stony. He was just trying to find something to eat, and because of thoughtless human behavior, he was focusing on getting food from garbage cans.

It was now well past our tourist season and time for me to leave Denali and drive to my winter job in Death Valley. On my way there, I worried about Stony and hoped that his winter denning might break his human-food addiction.

WHEN I GOT back to Denali in May 1987, Stony was nearly three and a half years old and had become a big bear. In my first sighting, he was digging out Arctic ground squirrel burrows. That was a good sign, as squirrels are a natural food for bears. Stony was blond again but still had that scar on his forehead.

He walked toward the park road, headed right to my truck, and bit the front bumper. I honked my horn and he ran off. Over the next few weeks, things went fairly well for Stony and there were no major problems.

That spring I saw Stony's mother in her usual territory. She had two new cubs with her. Both had light fur rings around their necks that looked like collars. I later found out that both cubs were females, so they were Stony's younger sisters.

On a later day, I saw that two men had walked off the road and were approaching Stony for close-up photos, a very dangerous situation. I called the men back to the road and explained Park Service rules about not approaching grizzlies. I had to go to work at Eielson soon after that. A few hours later, I heard a disturbing report on the park radio: a grizzly had bitten a man on the leg. He described the bear as blond and it had a scar on its forehead. That meant it was Stony.

I was needed at the visitor center, so I could not go to the scene of the incident. I soon heard more about what had happened. The man said he was walking off road, saw the bear, stayed in place, and started to take photos of him. The grizzly came right toward him, stopped a few feet away, and sniffed his tripod, then sniffed the man's arm. The hiker flinched and Stony backed off a few feet.

The Park Service recommends lying down and playing dead if a grizzly is close to you, so the man did that. Stony came back, sniffed him some more, then bit him on the leg and licked the blood that flowed from the wound. The man moved a bit at that point. The motion apparently scared Stony, for he moved away. This is one of the two mauling incidents I described earlier, when young men got too close to bears while trying to take photographs.

The rangers later interviewed witnesses to the incident. Their story differed from the young man's. They said the man spotted Stony and walked toward him as he took photos. The witnesses estimated the man got to within fifty feet of the bear. Approaching that close would likely cause a grizzly to feel threatened and attack. Based on that information, it was the man who was at fault, not the bear.

When my shift was over, I went to the scene of the incident. Stony was still there, feeding on plants. I talked with the other rangers about Stony. Some of them felt he should be killed. Others suggested capturing him and moving him to a distant section of the park where it would be unlikely for him to encounter humans. In the end, the park superintendent instructed the bear management rangers to capture and radio-collar Stony, then monitor his behavior. After being collared, he was known as Denali grizzly number 115.

Part of the plan to monitor Stony was to have armed rangers approach him and watch his response. In those tests, he either moved away from the rangers or ignored them. All that was a good sign.

We made it through the rest of that tourist season without any more problems from Stony. Because the park road in Denali is not plowed in the winter, the animals have the place to themselves. Stony spent that winter in a den.

WHEN I RETURNED to the park in 1988, Stony was close to four and a half years old. On seeing him for the first time that spring, I noticed that his fur was now brown. He was near a mother grizzly who was with two tiny new cubs. She saw Stony in the distance and ran off with her cubs, apparently fearful that a stranger might harm them.

Stony followed them but got distracted and soon was feeding on tundra plants. Later, he moved toward the mother and cubs. Those cubs had already been taught well by their mother and ran behind her for protection.

A few moments later, the mother grizzly charged at Stony and he ran away, wisely choosing to avoid a confrontation with an angry mother bear. But he soon came back, something I did not understand. In the next few minutes, he was chased off three more times after moving toward the mother and cubs. After that, he left for good. I suspected that Stony intended to play with those cubs, but if so, the mother could not take a chance of them being accidentally harmed.

As the summer progressed, Stony was well behaved. He did not approach any people and stayed away from garbage cans. One day the local wolf pack killed a caribou near Stony. He later got the blood scent and traveled to the kill site. Now a big bear, he easily chased the pack off their kill and claimed it as his own.

As the weeks went by, Stony continued to stay out of trouble. He wandered off to the west, well away from the park road and people. By that time, the battery in his radio collar was getting low on power, so rangers tranquilized him and put a new collar on him. They estimated his weight at 280 pounds, big for a Denali grizzly.

He came back to the western end of the park road and feasted on blueberries. That put him near the Wonder Lake Ranger Station, where several Park Service employees live.

The wife of one of the employees had two young children playing outside the cabins there. She looked out a window to check on them and saw Stony.

After getting the kids inside, she watched Stony through a window. Stony spotted the little inflatable pool the kids played in, climbed into it, and played in the water, just like the kids would do. He soon left the area, and the mother and kids went out to look around. The bear had apparently bitten the plastic pool, which was now deflated and empty.

After that, Stony moved north and out of the park. He wandered into an area where a tourist facility had a dump. Discarded food was there and Stony ate it. That was the worst possible news. It had looked like the rangers had successfully changed his behavior of seeking out food from human sources, but now all that had been upended.

Two bear management rangers were sent out there and they found Stony sniffing around the kitchen area of the facility. Stony then found another garbage dump and ate food scraps there. The rangers hit him with rubber bullets but he repeatedly returned to the dump. The next day, he found bags of dog food in the back of a pickup and ate them. Later in the day, he broke into an unoccupied trailer but found no food there. After that, he went back to the dump. Stony was still there the following morning and showed no sign of leaving.

I was off that day, so I drove over there and offered to help the bear rangers out. They were getting Stony's radio signal but he was not in sight. I got permission to go into the trailer he had damaged. Stony had broken through the front door, then left by breaking through a window in the kitchen.

I went back to the bear rangers and they told me their plan. They hoped to dart Stony and fly him off to a distant section of the park where there were no people or cabins. That meant they were giving him another chance. But we knew from past events that once a grizzly gets addicted to high-calorie human food, they rarely break that habit. That makes them too dangerous to tolerate and they have to be put down. If the rangers did not dispatch him, the local people would have the legal right to kill him.

The rangers captured Stony, and a helicopter flew him to a far-off location. I am an optimistic person, but I doubted the bear would stay out there. He likely would come right back, and if he did that, the rangers would have to put him down.

The next day, a plane circled that area and got Stony's signal, but it was in mortality mode, meaning he had not moved for some time. The crew in the plane saw Stony in the exact same place where he had been left. He was obviously dead. No helicopters were available in the coming days, so it was a week before a crew landed at his site. They determined that the drug dosage to tranquilize him was normal for a bear of his weight. The ranger on the scene felt Stony might have thrown up while unconscious and choked to death.

Stony's death deeply troubled me. I had never known a grizzly as well as I had known him. I kept on going back over the incidents that eventually led to his death. It started with the worker throwing a sandwich at him. From then on, Stony was drawn to food from human-related sources. The sequence continued when he bit the hiker who approached him for photos. Then it got far worse when he found the garbage dump outside the park. I later wrote a book about Stony called *Grizzly Cub: Five Years in the Life of a Bear.* Its purpose was to show what can happen to a bear when people feed it and try to get close for photographs.

There was a bright spot that gave me some hope. Stony's mother and her two daughters, who were yearlings that year, were doing well. They often were near the Eielson Visitor Center. In July I spotted the family on the park road. A ground squirrel ran by them and all three bears chased it in a side-by-side formation. As the squirrel ran uphill, then downhill, the three grizzlies sped after it. Then one of the yearlings got the squirrel.

The mother bear and other yearling moved off without trying to steal the squirrel. The first yearling put the squirrel down on the ground and prepared to eat it, but the squirrel turned out to be still alive and ran off. It tried to hide in a jumble of rocks, but the young bear snatched it up. The other yearling ran over in hopes of getting part of the squirrel, but the first yearling would not share, even when her sister whined at her.

The family was still together the following summer, 1989. The sisters were now two and a half years old. When I got back to the park in May 1990, I spotted the two sisters on their own near the Toklat River. By mid-June, they usually were near Eielson, so I saw them a lot. One day I watched them get in a friendly wrestling match. But in the following days, they were apart.

In late June, I found one twin feeding on a carcass. A wolf approached and the young bear aggressively chased it away. When the wolf later came back, the bear lay down on top of the carcass as a way of keeping the meat all to herself. I later heard that three or four wolves showed up and the young bear drove them off.

The two sisters were back together in August. They fed on berries, then spent time in a friendly wrestling match. On a later day, both bears were separately trying to dig out squirrels. One of the sisters chased a squirrel and it ran toward the other sister. That bear chased it back toward the first sister and the two bears smashed into each other. That set off a fight, with both of them standing up on their hind legs. I could hear them growling. But the two sisters soon went back to looking for squirrels to eat.

In September, the two bears were separated once again. They continued to eat berries and hunt ground squirrels. They would sometimes come together, then would drift apart. I saw them on my last day in the park, on September 15. They had been together, then one went up a ridge toward some Dall sheep, while the other stayed below, eating berries.

As far as I know, unlike their older brother, the two sisters never got into any trouble and never became curious about people.

Life Lessons From Wolves

Finding Your Place

Each of us has a specific set of skills and our own definition of success. Not everyone is destined to be a leader, to be wealthy, or to fit into a role defined by society. Some of us find something we are comfortable with and try to live our lives true to our own values and choices, being the best we can at what we have chosen to do. This is what I have done in my life: I have chosen a path less traveled, one that has allowed me to watch and study wild wolves for over forty-six years. I would not want things to be any other way.

Yellowstone wolf 1109 was very much a wolf who chose her own path in life. She was a low-ranking wolf in the Junction Butte pack, but she never seemed to care much about her place in the hierarchy. She often left to live as a lone wolf for a while, before returning to her lowly spot in the pack. When she was with her family, she chose denning sites away from the main pack so she could minimize contact with the more aggressive female wolves. After all but three of the pack's pups died in 2018, 1109 was the wolf that stepped in to care for the survivors, even though they were likely born to another female. Thanks to 1109's devotion and care, all those pups survived their first year. Although she was a low-ranking female, in the end, she was the wolf that saved the pack.

From the beginning of my career, I have lived a life that is very different from the life others might choose, but it is a life that suits me well. I chose what I felt matched my skill set and have always tried to learn and improve. I got my start watching wildlife in Denali; now I devote my days to watching wolves in Yellowstone. In addition to that, I do what I can to look after the people in my "pack": the people who watch wolves with me.

I tell 1109's story in *Thinking Like a Wolf.*

8

Moose in Denali

MOOSE ARE THE biggest animals in Denali, with bulls getting up to sixteen hundred pounds in the fall. Cow moose can weigh thirteen hundred pounds. The bulls and cows attain that weight by eating as much as sixty pounds of vegetation per day in the spring, summer, and early fall.

Moose eat a variety of plants that grow in ponds, but willows tend to be their main food, with willow leaves making up to 85 percent of their intake during the growing season. I read a study that found that willows browsed by moose regrow leaves and twigs at a rate 350 percent higher than unbrowsed plants. Later in the fall, after the leaves have dropped off the willows, moose consume the branches on the bushes, a much less nutritious food. Because of that change in diet, moose lose weight throughout the winter months, then start to regain body mass in the spring.

Denali's moose spend most of their time in areas that have a mixture of forests and willow bushes and rarely appear in the high-elevation meadows around the Eielson Visitor Center. I would have to drive to find them in the lower sections of the park.

In the spring of 1980, I saw a mother moose, who had just given birth to twin calves, deal with her male calf from the previous year. Like grizzly cubs, moose calves hang out with their mothers for as long as they can and usually only leave when their mothers drive them off. This yearling, who looked to be at least four hundred pounds, had already been driven off several times. I saw him come back and once again approach the bedded cow. She got up, stared at him, then chased him off. The cow went back to her newborn calves, who were around thirty pounds. They got up and nursed on her for some time. As that happened, her son fed on willows at a nearby site. He was still trying to get back with his mother the next day.

Mother moose can produce up to six quarts of milk per day, which translates to a daily weight gain of one to two pounds for very young calves and three to five pounds for older ones. By the fall, four-month-old moose calves can weigh several hundred pounds.

I often hiked to Horseshoe Lake at the eastern end of the park to watch the moose families that were frequently seen there. In late May 1982, I watched twin newborn calves go to their mother. She was bedded but stood up as they approached. The mother touched the nose of one calf and sniffed it, then did the same to the other twin. After that, both got under her and nursed for several minutes. When done, they went back to her face and she licked one, then the other.

I had a very different experience with a mother moose as I walked back to the trailhead through a thick forest. As I went around a turn in the trail, I saw a moose near two calves. She charged at me and I ran off through a thick stand of trees. Satisfied with that, the mother soon turned back and rejoined her calves. I was grateful she did not get close enough to kick out at me with her front hooves.

For most of the year, a cow moose and her calf or calves hang out together apart from others of their kind, but as the fall mating season approaches, cows and their calves form groups, which soon attract bull moose. Typically, the biggest bull moose in the area guards a band of cows and calves, hoping to breed all the adult females. But almost always, other bulls come along and challenge the original male to fights.

As the cows do not come into breeding condition until later in the fall, there can be a succession of bulls controlling the band of females. In theory, the biggest and strongest bull will get to mate with those cows, but if he gets injured during the rutting season, a smaller bull might challenge him and win.

According to Denali moose researcher Dale Miquelle, there are three main levels of fights between bull moose. On the first level are sparring matches that are often short and nonviolent. Then there are fights to determine who is dominant. Finally, there are the fights for breeding rights to the female moose, which are the most violent because the stakes are so high.

One fall, I saw the dramatic aftermath of a fight between bulls when I came across a Park Service truck stored in a small parking lot. There were signs that two bull moose had been fighting in the lot. The hood of the truck was damaged and the windshield had a big hole in it. I studied the hood and saw moose hoofprints on it. Two bulls must have been fighting, and one apparently pushed his opponent backward onto the hood. When the losing bull tried to step back, his hoof went right through the windshield. If a person had been sitting at the wheel, that hoof could have killed them.

The fights I saw mostly consisted of two bulls using all their strength to push each other backward. The two bulls would first go toward each other in a swaggering gait. When they got close to each other, both would stop and seem to pose to show how big and strong they were. Then both would charge forward and slam their antlers into their opponent's antlers. When one bull was clearly winning the pushing contest, the other male would usually turn and run off.

Moose have the largest antlers of any animal in the world. They are grown from scratch every year and shed after the rutting season is over. I once saw a big bull moose walking through a forest. His antlers were so massive, he had to turn his head sideways to fit between trees. At one point, he rubbed his antlers on a tree with a diameter of about eight inches. The bull was so strong, he nearly pushed it over. I did some research and found that in Alaska the biggest set of bull moose antlers measured seventy-seven and a half inches from right to left, about six and a half feet. A good-sized sample of moose antlers were weighed in Denali and the heaviest pair tipped the scale at sixty-four pounds.

While the antlers are growing, they are covered with what is known as velvet, a living tissue that supplies blood to the developing antlers. When the antlers reach their full size, the velvet is no longer needed, and the moose rub it off. In late August 1983, I had a good view of a bull moose rubbing the velvet from his fully developed antlers. He went to willow bushes and spruce trees and thrashed their branches with his antlers. At one point, a spruce twig hung down from an antler like an earring. He grabbed it with his mouth and pulled it off.

All that thrashing seemed to attract a cow moose, for she came toward him. When he stepped in her direction, she moved off a bit, but she soon returned. The moose sniffed noses, then they walked off in separate directions. I took that to mean neither one was quite ready to mate. Maybe that would happen on their next meeting. I later learned from moose researcher Vic Van Ballenberghe that cow moose come into heat for only a few hours. He thought they most often breed just once. If they do not breed or get pregnant, they can come into a second estrus a few weeks later and try once more.

THANKS TO DALE, I was learning to tell one bull moose from another and getting to see a lot of fascinating behavior. One September morning, I parked near Dale's car and followed his tracks two miles to where he was watching moose. A bull with the intimidating name of Slasher had a harem of seven cows. Two of the cows were not getting along. They came at each other, laid their ears back, reared up on their hind legs like stallions, and sparred with their front hooves. The stronger cow pushed her rival backward, and soon that one ran off. Later, a cow ran in my direction and I thought she was about to attack me. But she was really charging a rival cow nearby.

One fall, Dale was mainly following three bulls he called DW, Cut Ear, and Scarface. DW's name referred to a dry wash where he often was seen. Early one morning, I found Dale watching DW as the moose pawed out a wallow. When finished, DW peed in the shallow hole he had dug and vigorously slapped the puddle of urine with a front hoof as he lowered his antlers nearly to the ground. That caused the urine to splash onto his antlers, which was the point of the behavior.

From where Dale and I were standing some distance away, that smell of urine was very strong. Dale told me that bull moose urine in the rutting season has a scent that attracts females. The biggest bulls with the most potent urine scent usually end up with the largest harems of cows. Dale also said that if several cow moose are nearby, they will fight each other to get to a fresh bull moose wallow, which suggests they find that strong urine scent irresistible during mating season.

That fall day, Dale and I watched as DW swaggered over to rival bull Cut Ear in an aggressive posture. Cut Ear apparently was intimidated, for he made submissive-sounding whines and moved off. DW trailed him for a while, then bedded down.

A few days later, we saw DW following two cows. Soon he stopped and glared at another bull moose half a mile away. Looking like he was showing off, DW thrashed some bushes with his big antlers, then strode toward the rival bull. That guy moved away from DW. I now saw that two cows were following DW. They must have been rivals for DW's attentions, as one cow chased the other away.

We saw a young bull moose bed in a wallow DW had made. I wondered if he was deliberately trying to get the urine scent on him from the older and bigger bull to impress the cows. DW came over and chased him off. Then DW grunted and several nearby cows grunted back at him. All that seemed to be communication between DW and his harem. He ended up bedding down near them.

I soon saw that three other cows were nearby, along with a yearling male moose. DW chased the young male away from the cows, then went back to the females. Later, the yearling bull returned, but this time it was a cow that chased him off. Apparently, she preferred to be courted by the older and bigger male. That allowed DW to rest a bit.

All that happened during the morning hours. I knew the moose would be inactive during the warmer midday hours, so I took a break to look for other animals, then came back at 4:30 p.m. I saw that DW now had a harem of five cows. Two of them fought and one kicked the other in the side.

DW concentrated on herding his cows together. If one strayed off, he would circle around and drive her back into the group. After that, he scraped out a wallow, urinated into it for some time, then splashed the muddy urine on himself. That worked like a charm and the scent immediately drew the five cows to DW.

When DW lay down in the puddle of muddy urine, two of the cows bedded beside him. Soon DW got up and a newly arrived cow pushed him away with her nose so she could lie down in the muddy pool of his urine. Later, other cows competed to bed in DW's wallow.

The following morning, DW, who now had a harem of three cows, ran off another bull who was about the same size as him. That was September 14. The following day, a big new bull was in DW's territory. It was Scarface, a real tough fighter. The three cows that had been with DW were now with him, which suggested that Scarface had beaten DW in a fight during the night.

Two days later, we saw Scarface get into a violent fight with a collared bull known as 59. They ran at each other, crashed head-on, then fought violently as each bull used all his weight to push the other guy back. As I watched the battle, I thought it was one of the most awesome sights in nature.

Finally, 59 turned around and ran off. Scarface pursued his opponent and tried to gore him in the rear end with his antlers, but 59 got away. It was a smart move to run off. I later read a research paper describing how a big bull moose killed his opponent by goring him in the stomach with his antler points.

Sometimes, when bull moose fight, their antlers get locked together and the two males cannot get untangled. That usually leads to the death of both animals. One Alaska moose researcher over the course of his career found three pairs of bull moose skeletons where the antlers were entangled. He concluded that all six bulls had died of starvation.

In Denali the remains of two bull moose with locked antlers were found. One bull had a broken neck and must have died from that injury. The break must have happened after the two had locked antlers. That meant the other bull had starved to death still tied to his dead opponent. That would be a gruesome way to die.

Another biologist found two live bull moose locked together. Based on their appearance, he estimated they had not eaten or taken in any water for six days. The man had his tranquilizer rifle with him, so he darted both bulls. When they went unconscious, he sawed off an antler from one bull, then stepped away. After the drugs wore off, the two bulls disentangled themselves and walked off in opposite directions.

I later thought how intense the mating season is for bull moose. They stop feeding for two to three weeks. Dale estimated that the fighting can cause them to lose as much as 18 percent of their body weight, perhaps two or three hundred pounds. Vic found that although male and female moose numbers are about equal at birth, by the time bulls mature and fight over harems the ratio changes to thirty to thirty-five bulls for every hundred cows.

Toward the end of the mating season that fall, I saw a bull moose who had a harem of twenty-one cows. A nearby bull had only one. Sometimes life is unfair.

THE 1984 SEASON in Denali started off with a big event. A cow moose with newborn twin calves was trying to cross the park road. She and one calf made it to the other side, but people got between them and the second calf. To make things worse, some people went up to the calf and petted it as they took photos.

The rangers cleared the people out to give the mother time to return to her calf. I went to the area in late evening to see if there was anything I could do to help. There was no sign of the mother. When Dale arrived, he decided to intervene. He picked up the calf and carried it toward the area where its mother was last seen. This was a dangerous move, because on seeing Dale with her calf she might think he was going to harm it.

I went over and offered to help Dale. He put the calf down, and we searched the area together. Eventually, we spotted what looked like the mother, but we could not be sure, because all cow moose look pretty much the same. As I monitored the situation, Dale went back to the calf and carried it toward that cow. By that time, she had moved into some thick brush and was out of sight. It was a very risky thing to do, but Dale carried the calf into the brush, and I lost sight of him.

A few moments later, Dale ran out of the bushes without the calf in his arms. But the calf, who had gotten used to being with Dale, was running after him. Behind the calf, I saw its gigantic mother charging out of the willows and running at full speed toward the calf and Dale.

Dale made it to the road near me. The calf reached that spot a few moments later. Then the mother moose ran in. Dale was on the other side of her calf and moving away from it. The cow moose got to the calf, looked at it for a moment, then licked its face. After that, she turned around and led the calf off into the bushes. From Dale's angle, he could see her nurse her calf there. Her second calf was there as well. It was a happy ending for all of us, thanks to Dale.

Dale Miquelle later worked for the Wildlife Conservation Society and was stationed in the Russian Far East, where he studied tigers and helped protect their populations. He now is based in Bozeman, Montana, and often comes down to Yellowstone, where we reminisce about our days with moose in Denali.

Later that fall, I helped Vic Van Ballenberghe radio-collar a bull moose. Vic fired a tranquilizer dart at a four-year-old, 950-pound bull and hit the animal on the rear end. The bull was startled by the sound of the gunfire and ran off.

When the drugs took effect, Vic and I went to the bull and Vic put the radio collar around his big neck and took some measurements. The bull was lying on his side and seemed to be breathing irregularly. Vic and I rolled him upright so he could breathe more easily. We moved off to some nearby trees and monitored the bull to make sure he recovered properly. After a while, the bull tried to get up but could not quite manage it. Every time the bull rolled back onto his side, we walked back and pushed him upright again. After many more tries, he finally stood up and walked off without any apparent ill effects from the drugs.

In September, I found the bull moose DW. He already had a large harem of cows. Several young bulls came on the scene and DW chased them all away. After that, he rested for a while. When he got up, DW confronted a bull nearby who had a harem of fifteen cows. We called this other big male Split Ear. He was so big and intimidating that no other bulls had challenged him for a week.

DW and Split Ear started to walk parallel to each other in the swaggering gait John Wayne used in his movies when he confronted the bad guy. The two bulls slowly came closer, and when they got a few yards apart, each charged forward. They locked antlers and both pushed forward with all their strength. Split Ear was bigger and forced DW to back up. But DW made a powerful lunge and that pushed Split Ear back.

This was now a serious, all-out fight. Partway through the battle, one of DW's antler points broke off. Then both bulls switched to lighter pushing, which allowed them to rest a bit. That cycle continued for some time: strenuous pushing, then less intense sparring. Gradually, the fighting got more serious. As they pushed each other back and forth, they broke tree trunks with a diameter of four inches. That was enough force to break a man's leg.

At times, one bull would reposition, then charge, hit his opponent on the side, and push him back for some distance. The two bull moose looked like Japanese sumo wrestlers shoving each other with all their might. The fighting was now much faster than anything earlier, and I was getting worried for my own safety. The bulls were moving rapidly and cared nothing for what was around them.

I had a tree between them and me, but it was thin enough for them to easily knock over. I considered running away to a bigger tree but could not take the chance of being noticed. At that point, the two bulls were only ten feet away from my skinny tree. I could hear their heavy breathing. It was just like the sound Darth Vader made when he breathed through his mask.

The fight continued and, much to my relief, the bulls moved off to a meadow a little farther away. I could see that hair had been torn out of the sides of both bulls and was strewn all over the ground. For such huge animals, the bulls were lightning fast. Each one tried to cause serious injury by aiming its antler points at the side or rear end of his opponent.

There were brief pauses in the fight, then they renewed all-out attacks. On what seemed to be a third round, DW looked away for a moment, perhaps at a cow. Split Ear lunged forward and drove the other bull backward a long way. I saw that Split Ear had an advantage by being slightly uphill from DW. That enabled him to win a lot of pushing contests.

Now both bulls came at each other with lowered heads, engaged their antlers, and pushed with all their strength. The battle had gone on for a long time by then and both bulls looked exhausted. Then everything changed. DW had enough. He ran off and Split Ear chased him away from the cows.

Owing to the intensity of the fight, I had no idea of how long it had lasted. Then I remembered that I had looked at my watch when the fight started, and it was now one hour later. That was a long fight. A human heavyweight championship boxing match has fifteen three-minute rounds with a one-minute break between rounds.

After the fight, neither Split Ear nor DW had any energy left to go back to the cows. They had to rest for some time. The following morning, I went back there to see the aftereffects of the fight. DW was left with just one cow, while Split Ear had thirteen, a massive reward for his victory.

I found DW on October 1, and he now was with four cows. Things were calm, so I left to check on other moose. I rushed back as soon as I heard that Split Ear had come back and was fighting DW once again.

At first the rematch was slow-paced, then the two bulls went all out, using their full strength on each other. I saw that Split Ear was winning. He pushed DW farther and farther back. Somehow DW managed to stop his opponent's momentum and pushed Split Ear back. They disengaged, then each bull repositioned and tried charging into his opponent's side.

Everything was now happening too fast to see details of the fight. Finally, the exhausted DW turned away from Split Ear and was chased off. The winning bull went back to his nearby harem of cows.

Vic went out the next day and saw Split Ear and DW near each other. DW walked away from his rival, but Vic felt that both bulls were respectful of each other. That may have been because Split Ear had a big harem of cows, while DW had a smaller group. Perhaps now both bulls were paying more attention to their females than to each other.

There is a footnote to that story. The moose researchers saw that during the second match between Split Ear and DW, a young bull sneaked in and bred one of the cows without either of the much bigger bulls noticing him. If I come back as a bull moose, that will be my strategy.

9

Denali's East Fork Pack

IT WAS FAIRLY easy to see grizzlies in Denali because they often traveled and fed on the treeless tundra within sight of the park road. Wolves were harder to spot. During my first summer in the park, I got word that two wolves were trying to get a moose calf down the road from Eielson. As soon as I got off work, I rushed over and arrived in time to see the wolves close to a big mother moose and her newborn calf. The cow was aggressively defending her calf, and the wolves soon gave up and traveled out of sight. After that initial sighting, I was hooked on watching wolves. I had no more wolf sightings that summer, but in later years I saw and watched them much more often.

One of the first books I read after arriving in Denali was Adolph Murie's *The Wolves of Mount McKinley*. He was assigned to research the park wolves in 1939. Originally, the study was to be on wolves' impact on prey animal populations. Back then many Park Service employees feared that wolves would decimate Denali's wildlife species, such as moose, caribou, and especially Dall sheep. Murie discovered that he could watch the den site of the East Fork pack from a distance. He quickly realized it was a golden opportunity to research wolf social life, as well as their hunting behavior. Murie's work was considered the first scientific study of wild wolves.

In my early days in Alaska, I also read *Journey to Caribou Land* by Martin Cole. He came to the Denali area in 1930 and got a job working on the road that would bisect the central section of the park. One day, when Cole and his boss, a man named Wallace, were surveying possible routes, they saw a huge herd of caribou. When he later wrote about that experience, Cole added a section regarding the Park Service's attitude toward wolves: "Because the wolves were preying heavily on the caribou they were not protected. The Park Service was anxious to eliminate them. In this respect, Wallace...was furnished a Springfield army rifle." The context of that story made it clear the men were to shoot as many wolves in the park as possible, especially members of the East Fork pack, the pack Murie began studying nine years later.

Not everyone agreed about killing the park wolves. I came across an opposing point of view from Park Service assistant director Arthur Demaray. In *Changing Tracks*, author Timothy Rawson quotes a 1938 letter Demaray wrote to a man demanding the killing of wolves in Denali to protect the Dall sheep: "If sheep, wolves, and caribou have lived together for many thousands of years without one exterminating the other then, all other things being equal, there seems to be no reason why they cannot now." Demaray accurately predicted that in years to come people would seek out places where they could "see and hear a timber wolf in its natural state."

After arriving in Denali in March 1939, Murie hiked seventeen hundred miles in Dall sheep habitat to determine whether wolves were killing too many of them. He collected hundreds of sheep skulls and found that wolves were primarily killing the oldest, youngest, and least fit individuals, rather than prime age breeding adults. We get similar findings in Yellowstone with our wolf population.

After that, Murie concentrated on watching the park wolves, especially the East Fork pack. He achieved a legendary accomplishment when he spent thirty-seven continuous hours watching that wolf family. He published his milestone book *The Wolves of Mount McKinley* in 1944. In that book, he wrote eloquently about the day-to-day lives of the East Fork wolves, including stories about how they hunted for caribou and Dall sheep, observations of their social life, and accounts of how they raised their pups. He concluded that the park wolves were living in a rough balance with their prey: caribou, moose, and Dall sheep.

Murie's work was highly respected by the Denali rangers, and they suspended their wolf extermination program. But outside political players used their influence to reinstate the killings in 1945. They continued until 1954, when the antiwolf program finally ended forever.

The East Fork pack somehow survived that era, and their descendants were still living in the pack's traditional territory when I started in the park in 1976. During my time, they ranged as far west as the Eielson Visitor Center area, and for many years I regularly spotted their pack members as I traveled along the park road.

THE WOLF I got to know the best during my Denali years was the East Fork pack's alpha male, a big, dark gray who limped on his left front leg because of an injured paw that had never fully healed. At times, he also limped on his right front leg. His injuries slowed him down and the other wolves in the pack would periodically stop and wait for him to catch up. His mate, the alpha female, had a lighter gray coat. At the time, it was accepted wisdom that a wolf pack consisted of a family group led by a breeding pair, referred to as the alpha male and the alpha female, and the alpha female would be the only female to have pups.

One day in 1981, I watched the two alphas hunt. The female, who was out in front, suddenly stopped and sniffed the air. She spotted three cow caribou and a young calf and ran at them. As the caribou raced off, the female wolf closed in on the calf. Just as she was about to reach it, it collapsed from exhaustion. It was dead by the time the male caught up with his mate. After that chase, the alpha male licked his left front paw for a long time.

Another time, I saw the alpha pair traveling with three other pack members. They stopped to rest but soon jumped up and ran off at top speed. I looked ahead of them and saw they were chasing a grizzly. When the lead wolf was about ten feet behind the bear, it slowed down to match the bear's speed. The grizzly and the wolf disappeared behind a hill, but the wolf soon returned to its companions, and all five members of the pack had what looked like a celebration as they romped around and played together. The bear chase seemed to be a game to them. When the pack moved on, the alpha male was slower than his companions, but he caught up when the pack stopped.

A few weeks later, I spotted the limping wolf traveling alone. He ignored nearby caribou as he headed west. I noticed he was traveling on snow patches as much as possible, probably because the soft snow was easier on his bad paw. Often he would stop at caribou tracks and sniff and paw at them. I guessed that he was seeking out an animal whose scent indicated a weakness.

Later, he bedded down for a fifty-minute rest. When he got up, he stared to the south, dropped into a stalking posture, then charged toward a small group of caribou. He got to within a few feet of the slowest one, but it sped up and easily outran him.

After resting, the wolf went farther west and I lost him. I later spotted him bedded down. Two cow caribou and a calf were running away from him, then I saw he had taken down a caribou calf. As he fed on it, he took breaks to lick his damaged paw, which was probably sore from his travels. I watched him for nearly eight hours that day, then finally headed back to Eielson at 8 p.m.

A ranger told me that at 10 p.m. the wolf got up and headed back to the family's den with a leg from the calf in his mouth. The den was about fifteen miles east of where he got the calf. That meant he traveled at least thirty miles round trip that day and did it on only three good legs. A wildlife researcher got a good look at the male's damaged paw when he crossed the park road and told me that the pads on the bottom of the paw were swollen to twice normal size.

FROM READING MURIE'S book, I knew the East Fork pack denned on the East Fork of the Toklat River. In late May 1984, I hiked up on a ridge north of the road and used my spotting scope to scan that river drainage. After some time, I finally spotted two adult wolves coming out of the den. Like Murie, I could now observe the pack at their den from a distance.

I deliberately stayed miles away from the den area out of respect for the wolves. I did not want to do anything to bother them or cause them to abandon their den. I was much too far away for photographs, and I found I liked concentrating on the wolves without dealing with camera equipment.

The day I found my observation site was a big deal for me because I had never seen wolves at an active den site before. What made it even more significant was that this was the same den site that Murie had watched in 1940 and 1941. As far as we knew, the wolves at the site were descendants of the ones that used the den during Murie's time.

A few days later, I went back to my observation spot and saw the alpha female and several other adult wolves at the den. One of them slipped into the entrance and the alpha female bedded down with her head partway in the den opening, periodically wagging her tail. Meanwhile, another pack member was chasing a caribou east of the den but failed to get it. Later, the wolf saw two short-eared owls land on the tundra. The wolf ran over and searched around, probably looking for a nest with eggs or chicks in it, but left without finding anything. That evening one wolf stayed at the den as other wolves went on a hunt to the east.

Some days later, I saw three black pups walk out of the den entrance. On June 19, I watched the three pups nurse on their mother. The mother wolf was standing and the little pups had to balance on their hind legs to reach her nipples. The following day, one young adult was babysitting the pups. They pestered it and one climbed up on the wolf's back. The adult got up, walked off about a half mile from the den, and hid under a bush to take a nap. This was behavior I would later witness many times in Yellowstone. Wolves definitely have their patience tested when they are tasked with looking after little ones. My wolf sightings dropped off after the adults moved the pups closer to the pack's hunting grounds.

I RETURNED TO the park in 1985, eager to resume my wolf observations. I was to observe the East Fork pack for a total of seven years, from 1984 to 1990. As I did so, I honed my observational skills, and every night, I would write up my wildlife sightings for the day in a series of notebooks. This protocol would serve me well in the future in Yellowstone.

In late May 1985, I saw four adult wolves, including the limping adult male, leaving the East Fork den and going east. Two adult wolves stayed behind. Later, I saw the four wolves heading back to the den from the west. Two of the four wolves looked young and were likely yearlings, meaning they had been the pups I had seen at the den the previous year. They usually traveled side by side and often playfully nipped at each other. One of the yearlings chased a caribou, but the alpha male did not join in. I figured he had judged the animal to be too fast for his group to catch. Despite his limp, the male often led the party as they traveled.

In mid-June, I saw four wolves at the den, including the alpha female. She opened her mouth and either howled or made some other vocalization. Five pups ran out of the den in response and clustered around her. A few days later, an adult carried a pup from the den about a hundred yards, then bedded down with it. I figured the adult wanted to play with the pup.

Meanwhile, another East Fork adult was chasing a caribou at top speed across the nearby river. The caribou crossed the river at a faster speed than the wolf, then stopped to watch the wolf running toward it. When the wolf got closer, the caribou ran off, but in the confusion of the chase it ended up veering toward the den area. A wolf at the den saw it and charged. Swerving past that wolf, the caribou continued to run, and I lost it and the two wolves behind a hill. Later, I found those wolves feeding on what likely was the caribou they had pursued.

The following week, I saw the mother wolf returning to the den. A young adult at the den ran to her, licked her face, then rolled on the ground under her in a submissive manner. Another young adult ran over and behaved the same way. It looked like they were both yearlings. Then the new pups ran out of the den and nursed. I was beginning to get a sense of how hierarchies work in wolf families and how the young gradually get integrated into the pack.

I began to make connections between the behavior of wolves and the behavior of their domesticated descendants. For example, on one occasion, I saw two young adult wolves bedded down with three pups three hundred yards from the den. When an older adult came into that area, the pups and one of the younger adults licked its mouth repeatedly to solicit a feeding, which involves the older one regurgitating a pile of fresh meat. Apparently, the newly arriving wolf had not eaten much recently, for it walked away without feeding the younger pack members. After watching that incident, I realized that when pet dogs excitedly lick the face of a returning human friend as a greeting, it is likely a remnant of how their wolf ancestors begged for a feeding from adult pack members.

I learned that wolves are willing to take risks when hunting, even when the odds are not in their favor, and that, like some people, they sometimes overestimate their skills. Dall sheep, for instance, are adapted to steep, rocky terrain, whereas wolves are hunters that usually inhabit less extreme terrain, adapted to outrunning their prey. A fellow ranger saw a band of Dall sheep crossing the Toklat River to reach a high ridge. An East Fork wolf saw them, ran at the sheep, and pulled down a lamb. So far, so good, but the wolf then tried to get a second sheep, a young ewe, which got away. While that chase was going on, the lamb, which apparently had not been seriously injured by the wolf's bite, got up and escaped up a nearby steep cliff.

I also began to appreciate wolves' ingenuity when it came to problem-solving. In early July, the pack had a bull caribou carcass by the river. A yearling wolf carried off a small section of meat. Then the alpha male arrived and, despite his bad leg, attempted to carry off the bull's head with the antlers and rib cage still attached. It was a heavy load for any wolf, but this male had only three good legs. He struggled to carry his prize up a steep riverbank. After several failed attempts, he seemed to give up. Then he surprised me. The wolf got on the uphill side of the heavy load, grabbed the head with his jaws and walked backward up the bank as he dragged his prize to the top.

I realized how quickly pups become independent when I saw six pack members, including the mother wolf and the limping male, traveling upstream on the East Fork that month with three of the pack's six pups. The three pups that had been left behind walked away from the den on their own as they played together, and ended up about a half mile from the mother wolf. She seemed to have no concern about her pups going off on their adventure without any adult supervision or protection.

When the pups are mature enough, a wolf pack moves them to a site closer to the pack's hunting grounds. The East Fork pack's rendezvous site, as these sites are called, was more difficult to observe, for it was two miles farther away than the den area.

Having moved the pups, the family was in full hunting mode. I watched one evening at 6:15 as the adult wolves got up, greeted each other, and had a big group howl. Then they romped playfully around together. All that was apparently a rally to prime the whole family, including the pups, for a hunt, and they then took off to the east in single file to search for prey.

The alpha female led the group, and at one point she rolled on what was probably some sort of interesting scent. Behind her, five other wolves played on a snow patch and rolled on the snow. That particular hunting foray did not result in any kills, and at 8 p.m. the alpha pair turned around and led the group back to the rendezvous site. Despite their long hike, those pups had a strenuous play session among themselves that evening.

IN THE SPRING of 1987, I noticed that there appeared to be two mothers with pups: the alpha female and a younger female. I watched as the alpha male arrived at the den and walked off to bed down with the younger female. I began to think about how packs are structured and which wolves mate with which other wolves. It seemed that the alpha pair were not always the ones producing pups to further the family line.

Earlier that spring, the limping male had been captured and radio-collared. He was missing the outside toe on his left front paw, evidence that he had been caught in a trap but had broken free. There was also damage to his right ear, which was sliced in half. That probably happened during a fight with another wolf. Despite his injuries and his advanced age, he had plenty of body fat and was in excellent condition.

My favorite memory of the limping male that year took place one morning when he played with the pups for a long time. He licked them, playfully pounced on them, pulled their tails, smacked them with a front paw, and chased them around. They responded by standing up on their hind legs and putting both paws on his face, then hitting him with their paws. When he bedded, they climbed around on his back. At one point, he suddenly jumped up, probably because a pup bit him a little too hard. How different this was from male grizzlies, moose, caribou, and Dall sheep, who have nothing to do with their offspring.

On July 9 and 10 that summer, there was an epic battle between the East Fork alpha male and a young bull moose in the Teklanika River. Combining the various eyewitness accounts of the fight, I determined the battle lasted thirty-six hours, during which the old wolf attacked his much larger opponent fourteen separate times.

Each time, the moose fought back vigorously, kicking the wolf and stomping on him with his front hooves. At one point, the moose must have come down on the wolf's injured paw, for it bled profusely. The alpha male licked that paw between attacks and at one point licked it for a full hour.

Toward the end of the epic duel, the weakened moose waded out to a deeper part of the river. The wolf followed but had to swim the final few yards to his opponent. Then the fight resumed. At one point, the moose reared up, came down on the back of the wolf, held him underwater, and nearly drowned him. The wolf managed to squirm away and swam back to the shore to rest.

When he later went back into the river, the bull moose had lost so much blood he was too weak to put up much of a fight. One last bite to the throat finished the drawn-out duel. Soon after that, the other East Fork wolves arrived and fed alongside their alpha male.

We could not tell how badly the alpha male was injured in that battle. Our later sightings of him indicated he was moving extremely slowly and was likely in a lot of pain. Around four weeks after the fight, we stopped seeing him. I hoped he was just in a section of his territory that was out of sight to us, but more time went by without sightings. Knowing him, I felt only death would keep him from being with his family and serving them as their alpha male.

The death of the East Fork alpha male hit me hard. He was the first wolf I had ever come to know well. When I later studied wolves in Yellowstone, I got to know many accomplished alpha males, but as great as they were, none was tougher than the East Fork alpha male.

IN 1990 I used a mountain bike to explore the park on days when I was not on my professional photographer's permit. One evening in late May, I biked a few miles east of Eielson and saw a wolf. It was a different experience than seeing a wolf from my car, because there was nothing between us when he crossed the road a few yards from me. The wolf seemed to ignore me as he trotted off.

In late June, I had several sightings of adult East Fork wolves in the Toklat River area. On the last day of the month, I spotted four wolf pups close to the park road near the Toklat River Bridge. They were making crying and whimpering sounds, then they howled. Earlier, two adults and five pups had been seen there. The four pups must have gotten separated when the other wolves crossed the road. I figured the best thing I could do to help was to move on and get out of their way.

A few miles farther down the road, an East Fork wolf was feeding on a caribou carcass. It was getting warm by that time, and the adult wolf took a break from feeding to lie down in a small stream to cool off. If that adult howled, the pups would likely hear it. That would enable them to reunite with a pack member.

On July 6, I found another caribou carcass near the Toklat River Bridge. Three East Fork wolves were feeding on it. Then the new alpha male wolf arrived and the other wolves acted in a subordinate manner to him. He was the wolf who had succeeded the limping male after his death. There was a good chance he was a son of that male.

Later, wolves carried off parts of the carcass. I saw one wolf dig a hole, put meat in it, then use its nose to push dirt back over the hole. I thought using the nose might help the wolf memorize the scent of that cache site. Other wolves carried legs off from the carcass. A wolf later gnawed on one of the bull's antlers, which was covered in velvet, an edible material that is rich in nutrients. Later in the day, a big adult wolf had enough jaw strength to crack a thick leg bone. It then ate the marrow. That day, I watched wolves come and go from the carcass, from 7 a.m. to 10 p.m., a total of fifteen hours.

Later in the month, I saw three pups alone in that area. They howled in a low, mournful tone, likely in hope of having adults come back and feed them. We saw one of the mother wolves nearby and she howled back at the pups. That seemed to calm the pups down, and they were soon playing together. They got into wrestling matches and pounced on each other. The pups were still there the next day, without any adults. That suggested the area was a rendezvous site where the pups could be stashed when the adults went out on hunts.

In August I saw a wolf from another pack chasing a ground squirrel. The squirrel got to its burrow and the wolf started to dig it out using its front paws. At times, to speed up the excavation, the wolf bit into the tunnel and tossed chunks of dirt away over its shoulder. All that worked, for it soon grabbed the squirrel from the hole. It took three or four minutes for the wolf to eat it. Later, the wolf crept forward in a crouched posture, looking like a dog trained to get in a pointer position when it saw a target. It spotted a squirrel and chased it. The squirrel ran in a zigzag pattern as it desperately tried to get away. The two went into some bushes and I could not tell the outcome of the hunt.

Soon after that, a friend saw a wolf chase a Dall sheep ewe down a steep slope. The wolf gave up, but then another pack member farther down the ridge ran uphill and got the ewe. The two wolves fed on the sheep and buried pieces of meat for later consumption. I arrived as one of the wolves left the site and trotted east down the road. I followed well behind the wolf in my car so I could slow down any traffic that might come along. It was going about six miles per hour. At one point, the wolf found a run-over ground squirrel and ate it.

In mid-September, the East Fork wolves killed a Dall ram. It happened when the ram was trying to cross the Toklat River and was far from any escape terrain such as cliffs. The alpha male wolf was bedded on the other side of the river from the carcass where several lower-ranking members of his pack were feeding.

The big male got up and started to move toward the carcass site. A younger wolf at the site saw him coming and went into a nervous attempt to carry off one of the ram's legs. But when the bigger male approached, the young wolf dropped the leg and moved away from it. The alpha picked up the leg and carried it off. After he ate the leg, I saw him wipe blood off his face on a willow bush.

Then he went back to the carcass, and despite its size and weight, he dragged it into the river channel, apparently intending to feed on it on the far bank. His plan did not work because the fast current caused him to lose his grip. The carcass floated four hundred yards downriver. The wolf found where it ended up, tore off a leg, and carried it off, probably to give to the pups back at the den.

I frequently hear anti-wolf people say wolves often do not eat what they kill and use that as a justification to promote killing wolves. As I continued to watch the East Fork wolves feed on the last bits of that carcass, I saw one pack member eating the stomach lining, something I would hesitate to try even if I was starving.

As it turned out, that was my last season and my last wolf sighting in Denali.

AT THAT TIME, I thought of myself as a park naturalist and wildlife photographer. It never occurred to me that I might one day become a wolf researcher.

The first wolf researcher I ever met was Gordon Haber. He came up and introduced himself to me after my first talk at Wonder Lake Campground in 1976. I knew his name because everyone in the park talked about him. Gordon had originally been a Park Service naturalist at Eielson, like me, but he had moved on and was now doing a PhD on wolf behavior. He often got into arguments and long-running feuds, especially with other wolf researchers.

I would be around Gordon for all fifteen seasons I worked in the park, and he often gave me tips on where to see wolves, tips he usually did not share. I think much of that good relationship was because I had chosen to talk about the miners' climb of Denali's North Peak, a story people who call Alaska home love to hear. Of all the subjects I could have picked, that was the one that apparently impressed Gordon and led to a friendship that lasted for the rest of his life.

In 1964, during his undergraduate years at Michigan Tech, Gordon got a summer job at Isle Royale National Park. At that time, it was the only park in the lower forty-eight states that had a wolf population. Gordon was in fire control, which happened to be my first National Park Service job as well. One day a coworker accidentally came into contact with a live fallen power line. At great risk to his life, Gordon somehow separated the man from the line and saved the man's life. The secretary of the interior later honored Gordon with a federal government valor award for his heroic action. Even though I knew Gordon for many decades, he never mentioned that incident or the award.

Gordon began his PhD study of the park wolves in 1966. After finishing his thesis, he continued to do research on the Denali packs for many decades. Much of his work was centered on the East Fork wolves. He was especially interested in the social behavior of packs. Adolph Murie was still in the park in Gordon's early years, so Gordon consulted with him on the history of that pack. It would be fair to say Gordon's wolf research was a continuation of the research Murie began many decades earlier.

When I started in Denali in 1976, Gordon had already been watching the park wolves for ten years. At times Gordon had funding for research flights, so he frequently studied wolves from the air rather than from the ground as I did. He also had wolf study areas outside the park.

While Gordon repeatedly clashed with other wolf researchers, I stayed out of his feuds and concentrated on asking him what he was learning about the park wolves. I remember one dispute, however, that accidentally involved me.

Back then I was doing a lot of wildlife photography and getting my photos published in major magazines and scores of books. I got a call from the editor of a prestigious nature magazine. He had commissioned a wolf biologist to write an article on how wolves hunt and he needed photos of wolf packs chasing and attacking prey animals. I did not have much on that, so I told the editor to call Gordon. He had the best aerial shots of wolf hunts in Denali. I gave him Gordon's contact information and finished the call thinking I had done a good thing.

The editor called back a few days later and I could tell right away that something had gone wrong. He asked me a blunt question: "What is the deal with Gordon Haber?" I responded by saying, "What did he do?" When the editor had reached Gordon and asked him to send photos of wolves hunting, Gordon's response was to ask who the writer of the article was. On being told the man's name, Gordon went into a tirade, in which he essentially said the man knew nothing about how wolves hunt.

The editor tried to steer the conversation back to wolf photos, but Gordon would not drop his criticism of the other biologist. When Gordon finally calmed down, he told the editor he would send in some shots only if he had editorial control over what was in the story. That was something the magazine editor could not grant and he ended the call. I knew that Gordon was low on money at the time and really needed what would have been a lucrative payment for his photos, but he lost out on that because of his stubborn demand for control of the story.

That was one side of Gordon's personality, but there was another side to him: he was a heroic protector of wolves. Seven years after I spent my last season in Denali, Gordon was doing some wolf research in an area east of the park. He found a wolf that had been caught in a wire snare. The trapper had not checked his traps in some time, so that wolf was in pain and had not had any food or water for many days.

Caribou carcasses were positioned near the snare, an illegal form of wolf baiting. Gordon called the Alaska Department of Fish and Game to report the violation, and they told him they would come and free the wolf. When no one showed up, Gordon decided to release the suffering animal himself. To do that, he had to get within about ten inches of the wolf's jaws. The wolf calmly watched Gordon get its paw out of the snare, then ran off.

Gordon could have kept quiet about freeing the wolf, but he was not a guy to keep quiet. He told the story of that suffering animal far and wide. The trapper sued Gordon and a trial was held in the man's hometown. The jury, made up of local people, sided with the trapper and ordered Gordon to pay him $190,000. I later heard that back around that time, a trapper in Alaska might get $200 for a wolf pelt.

Because of the outrage over what had been done to that wolf, a conservation group paid Gordon's fine. I often thought about what I would have done if it had been me who had found that suffering, snared wolf. Like Gordon, I would have freed it, but I would have told no one.

After that incident, there were rumors that anti-wolf Alaskans were telling bush pilots they would be boycotted if they flew for Gordon. Gordon called me periodically during that difficult time. By then, I had written a few books, and Gordon wanted me to write a book about how the state of Alaska was mismanaging its wolf population. I declined, but it did spark an idea that later turned into a book I did write. In *War Against the Wolf*, I laid out the many ways in which people have persecuted wolves throughout the history of this country.

In 2009 Gordon hired a bush pilot who was somewhat new to the area to fly him over the wolf packs in Denali. The plane ran into turbulence while flying low and crashed into a ridge in the east end of the park. The pilot survived but Gordon was killed. Friends of his and editor Marybeth Holleman gathered Gordon's writings about wolves and published them in the 2013 book *Among Wolves*, a compilation of Gordon's experiences with wolves in Denali.

In my Denali years, I also got to know Dave Mech, who is considered the top wolf biologist in the world. Unlike Gordon, Dave was not argumentative and loved to talk about wolves to everyone. I was often with him on the side of the road when park visitors would stop to tell us about a wolf sighting. Dave would listen intently to their story, ask questions, and then thank them profusely for sharing that information with him. He is the epitome of the type of scientist who still gets excited about his field. In later years, Dave and I would coauthor several scientific papers on the Yellowstone wolves.

During my years in Denali, I progressed a lot in my ability to tell stories in my Park Service programs, stories about grizzlies, wolves, and moose that were emotional and captivating. I moved away from primarily listing facts about a species to being a storyteller whose talks had a beginning, middle, and climax.

Life Lessons From Wolves

Redemption

Watching the East Fork pack changed my life. Before I discovered the pack's den, I had been most interested in grizzly bears and ravens. As I watched the East Fork pack raise its pups, I began to see that in many ways wolves are not so different from humans, and individual wolves show many traits I recognize in people. One of the things I have reminded myself throughout my life is that even if people make unfortunate choices, it is never too late to change. And as I was to learn when I later began observing wolves in Yellowstone, wolves can change as well.

I have never known any wolf like Yellowstone wolf 302. He was a big male who seemed destined to become an alpha. But he showed himself to be selfish and unreliable, the exact opposite of his father, wolf 2, and his two uncles, wolves 8 and 21. Specifically, he ran away when rival males challenged him. For years 302 would get females pregnant and abandon them, then go back to live with his parents. In human terms, he was a slacker.

I was fascinated by 302 and spent many years watching him in hopes of seeing him turn his life around. And that is exactly what happened. When he was an old wolf, 302 formed his own pack with some nephews and several females. For the first time, he raised pups he had sired and did a good job being a father. On the last day of his life, 302 became one of Yellowstone's greatest heroes when he saved his pups by fighting an entire pack alone.

I talk to park visitors a lot about 302 because his story shows that those of us who have made mistakes in life can change our behavior and be better individuals.

I tell wolf 302's story in *The Redemption of Wolf 302: From Renegade to Yellowstone Alpha Male.*

10

Winter National Park Jobs

WHEN I STARTED my seasonal employment for the National Park Service in Denali in the spring of 1976, my goal was to get a permanent Park Service job with retirement and health benefits. But competition was fierce, especially in the most desired parks, and you usually had to work for years in a series of less coveted sites, often historic places in or near cities, before an opportunity came up.

Thanks to my forestry degree, my good grades in college, and my work experience, I was getting offers for jobs with the US Forest Service. Toward the end of my second summer in Denali, I was offered a permanent Forest Service job with retirement and health benefits on the Tonto National Forest in Arizona. I accepted the offer, hoping to work there for a while before transferring to a career job with the Park Service. I started that fall.

The position turned out to be mostly an office job, something that did not suit me or my skill set. To make the situation worse, there was a chain smoker in the room. I left the job after seven months and went back to my summer position in Denali in 1978. For the next twenty-one years, I was a migrant seasonal worker for the National Park Service, meaning I had a summer job in one park and a winter job in another park. I had traded paperwork for adventure and never doubted that was the best choice for me.

The one benefit of my Tonto job was that it gave me reinstatement status, which meant I would be considered for jobs in the National Park Service before applicants who had not worked for the federal government in a career job. I eventually got seasonal job offers from all the parks I wanted to work in, including Yellowstone. That fall, however, even though I applied to a lot of desert National Parks, nothing came through.

Eventually, I tracked down an obscure Park Service operation: the Los Angeles Field Office. They offered me a job and I drove to the big city. I was too poor to rent an apartment. Back then you could stay in the Hollywood YMCA for fifteen dollars a night, but only for three nights in a row. I would sleep in my truck for the fourth night, then start another three-night stretch in the Y. Technically, I was homeless.

When I left the Y in the morning in my uniform to walk to my car, I expected people to ask why a ranger was in the city, but no one paid any attention to me. Maybe they thought I was an actor on the way to a movie set. I drove the Hollywood Freeway to the federal building downtown, went to the Park Service office, and sat down at my desk. My job was to answer phone calls, which were mainly from people wanting information about visiting parks such as Yosemite and Sequoia. I worked in an office, but I did not have to do any paperwork or write any reports. After three weeks, I got an offer for a winter naturalist job at Padre Island National Seashore on the Texas coast. That three-week stint in Los Angeles was the last office job I ever had.

THE PADRE ISLAND job came with housing in Corpus Christi. The small apartment was on a canal that connected boaters with the ocean. My job involved staffing a small visitor center and doing nature walks and other programs. One program my supervisor signed me up for was unique to that park: a craft demonstration on fish printing. I would go to a fish market and get a flounder, the flatter the better. Visitors would meet me in a building near the beach and I would teach them how to make fish prints. The process is simple. You coat the top side of the flounder with ink, then press the fish against the rice paper. When you lift the fish, there is a perfect imprint on the rice paper, suitable for framing. Everyone got to take home their fish print and put it on their wall. After the show, I took the flounder home and ate it.

Also, as part of my job, I prepared a slideshow on the planned reintroduction of Kemp's ridley sea turtles to the island, a species that had been wiped out locally. They are the smallest and most endangered sea turtles. Adults are about two feet long and weigh seventy to one hundred pounds. When I was a young boy in Massachusetts, I had a passion for learning about the turtles that lived in our freshwater ponds, so it was exciting to study the life history of sea turtles.

To get an update on what happened with the turtle program in the years after I left, I called Dr. Donna Shaver. She started working at Padre Island National Seashore in 1980, a year after I left, and was still there forty-five years later. Donna was put in charge of the recovery program in 1986 and has dedicated her life to saving the species.

Kemp's ridley sea turtle is classified as a critically endangered species in the United States. Historically, they nested on beaches in Texas and Mexico. There was a record of forty thousand females nesting at Rancho Nuevo on the east coast of Mexico in 1947. By 1985 fewer than three hundred females nested there, the last nesting site in use by the species. The tremendous reduction in the population was due to a number of factors: collection of eggs in Mexico as a supposed aphrodisiac, killing of adults for human consumption and leather, accidental capture in fishing nets, and environmental degradation of the Gulf of Mexico waters.

A major part of the recovery plan was to establish a secondary nesting site at Padre Island National Seashore, where park rangers could protect the turtles and eggs. From 1978 to 1988, around two thousand eggs were collected in Mexico each spring as the mother turtles laid them. Before the eggs touched the sand in the nests the mother turtles had dug, they were caught and placed in containers with sand from Padre Island. Then the containers full of eggs were flown to Texas.

The eggs stayed in the containers until they hatched. The newborn turtles were then allowed to crawl across the beach at Padre Island, get into the ocean water, and swim out about ten yards before they were recaptured in nets. Taking the young turtles from the ocean saved them from high predation rates. In the wild, only one out of an estimated three hundred hatchlings reaches adulthood.

The next stage involved transporting the young turtles to a facility in Galveston, Texas, where they lived for about a year. By that time, they would be large enough to avoid most predators. That part of the recovery program was called "head starting." Each turtle was fitted with a tag for later identification. Most of the turtles were then brought back to South Texas and released into the Gulf of Mexico, about five miles offshore from Padre Island and nearby Mustang Island, and allowed to swim away.

The recovery plan was based on the premise that as the young females crawled across the Padre Island sand, they would imprint on the scent of that exact beach and years later return there to nest. Over the years of the project, about twelve thousand young turtles were released at the National Seashore. The first adult females began returning to Padre Island to nest in 1996, and females have continued to come back annually to the present time. The population of Kemp's ridley sea turtles is slowly recovering. Now each year about fifty-five hundred females nest on the beach in Mexico and another fifty-five at Padre Island, which has eighty-three miles of beaches.

I did not know it at the time, but now I realize that experience explaining a proposed wildlife reintroduction program to park visitors in the late 1970s gave me a good background for explaining Yellowstone's wolf reintroduction plan in the mid-1990s.

My winter job at Padre Island ended in the spring of 1979 and I drove back to Denali for another season.

BECAUSE THERE ARE far fewer parks that have their prime tourist season in the winter than in the summer, it was hard to get hired at a winter park. I had always wanted to work in Death Valley, partly because I liked watching movies set in the desert and partly because of the mystique of the park's name. I decided to apply again. My experience in Anza-Borrego Desert State Park had given me a good background in desert wildlife and plants. That job, combined with my years in Denali and my previous employment with the federal government, got me an offer to go to Death Valley.

When I started at Death Valley in the fall of 1979, I joined six other seasonal naturalists. All but one of us were new to the area. The first week, Chief Naturalist Virgil Olson took us on field trips throughout the two-million-acre National Monument. In the evenings, I read books on Death Valley.

As I did my research, I discovered that Edward Abbey was working in Death Valley when he wrote *Desert Solitaire*, the book that inspired me to have a career with the Park Service. He got a job as a school bus driver and every morning took the children of the Death Valley rangers and other employees to a school in a nearby small town. While school was in session, he sat on the bus and worked on *Desert Solitaire*, then he drove the kids home when classes were over.

All seven seasonal naturalists were scheduled to start doing programs for visitors about two weeks after we arrived. The most important program would be an evening slideshow talk in the main Death Valley Visitor Center at Furnace Creek. The auditorium there seated 450 people and usually was full during our busy season. During holiday periods, the crowds in the park were so big that we did two shows each evening. By that time in my career, I preferred to talk to the largest possible audiences because I found I got a better response from big crowds.

For my first talk, I picked Death Valley's ghost towns because that would be a fairly easy talk to research. I knew the park had a great collection of slides that showed what those towns looked like in the heyday of mining. I also knew that National Park visitors liked talks on history.

I later branched out into slideshows on the borax mining days and the history of Death Valley since it was set aside as a park. The story of borax mining in Death Valley was especially interesting to park visitors because the president at the time, Ronald Reagan, had hosted the television series *Death Valley Days*. The show ran on the radio from 1930 to 1945, then the television version was on the air from 1952 to 1970. Ronald Reagan hosted the show from 1964 to 1966 and acted in twenty-one episodes. Then he left to successfully run for governor of California.

Reagan had also done commercials for 20 Mule Team Borax products. A huge deposit of borax, a type of salt, was discovered in Death Valley in 1881. It needed to be transported 164 miles to a railroad in Mojave, California. Owing to the weight of the borax, the mining company used teams of twenty mules to pull the load. Those teams became famous, and the company named its laundry and cleaning products after them.

In another evening program, I spoke about desert bighorn sheep and the issue of nonnative wild burros. On the following day, I led a convoy of cars to sites where people could see for themselves the harm the burros caused to desert plants and water sources. Then we went back to Park Headquarters and met with the Death Valley superintendent so the visitors could express their support for burro removal.

After being in the park for a few years, I tried a different type of program that the Park Service calls "living history." I played the role of William Manly, who was in a party of people traveling to the California Gold Rush in 1849. The party's map was inaccurate, and the group accidentally entered Death Valley. By that time, their food had run out and they were starving. Manly and his friend John Rogers volunteered to go for help. The two men walked about 250 miles west and ended up near Los Angeles. They returned to Death Valley with food and horses, then led the party to safety.

Other programs I did in Death Valley included nature walks through many of the spectacular natural formations in the park, such as the salt flats, sand dunes, and narrow canyons. One of the other new naturalists was Larry Norris, and he knew desert ecology better than I did. Larry and I shared one of our days off, so we nearly always went out on hikes on those mornings to learn more about the park.

Many of our hikes were out on salt flats that lie below sea level. One site, Badwater, is 282 feet below sea level and is the lowest point in the United States. On one hike to another area, we went into an old horizontal mine without flashlights and almost fell into a deep vertical shaft.

The average rainfall in Death Valley is about two inches per year. That water flows downhill to the below-sea-level salt flats, where most of it evaporates and leaves behind the salt and other minerals it picked up on the way. Temperatures in Death Valley are moderate during the day in the winter, often in the 60s and 70s, but very hot in the summer. There was a recorded temperature of 134 Fahrenheit (57 Celsius) in Furnace Creek on July 10, 1913. It stood as a world record for decades but is now a disputed figure, owing to how temperatures were taken at the time. It got to 130 Fahrenheit (54 Celsius) in Death Valley in both 2020 and 2022.

Because of the spectacular desert landscape, at least eighty-eight Hollywood movies have been filmed in Death Valley. They were mostly low-budget westerns going back to the 1920s, but there were also big-budget films such as Kirk Douglas's 1960 *Spartacus* and Marlon Brando's 1961 *One-Eyed Jacks*.

Parts of the original *Star Wars* movie were filmed in the park in the mid-1970s. Some of the rangers from that time were still working there when I arrived in 1979. They told me the crew for that film did not impress them. After arriving in the park, one of the people on the movie crew realized they had not brought enough actors to play the three-foot-high Jawa characters, who lived on a desert planet. He went to a ranger and asked if Death Valley had an elementary school. The man went there and hired the kids to wear the Jawa costumes.

I was the supervising ranger on some of the movies shot in the park in the 1980s, including the third Star Wars film, *Return of the Jedi*. The scene they filmed in Death Valley appears near the beginning of the movie, when R2-D2 and C-3PO are traveling toward Jabba the Hutt's castle on a desert planet. The only actor in the scene was Anthony Daniels, who played C-3PO. R2-D2 was a radio-controlled unit. The crew needed many takes to get the scene right because R2-D2 kept falling over.

The movie crews always treated me very well. I often was asked how their sons and daughters could become park rangers.

WHEN I STARTED in Death Valley in the fall of 1979, all the new rangers were warned about the Manson family. Death Valley rangers had been involved in capturing Charles Manson and his followers just outside the park in October 1969, a few months after the group murdered nine people in the Los Angeles area.

The story had been set in motion the previous month, when a $35,000 Park Service maintenance vehicle was vandalized and set on fire in the northern part of Death Valley. District Ranger Don Carney followed the tire tracks of the suspects' vehicles a long distance south through the desert and up into the mountains on the west side of Death Valley. Dick Powell, the district ranger for that region, joined Carney in the high country and helped him search the area.

The subsequent investigation turned up reports of a group of what at the time were called hippies living at the Barker Ranch, a remote ramshackle building near the southwestern border of Death Valley. It looked like members of that party had vandalized the Park Service vehicle.

A combined force of park rangers, California Highway Patrol officers, and Inyo County Sheriff officers raided the property in mid-October. They arrested everyone in sight but could not find the leader of the group. CHP patrol officer Jim Pursell went into a small bathroom and noticed a long strand of black hair sticking out of a cabinet under the sink. He opened the door and found Charles Manson hiding there.

In total twenty-four people were arrested on suspicion of arson, vandalism, and grand theft auto.

Manson and five of his followers were later convicted of the murders in Los Angeles and sentenced to long prison terms. If it had not been for Carney's dogged determination to follow those tracks to the hideout, many more innocent people likely would have been killed.

Manson vowed to have his followers kill the Death Valley rangers for revenge. Park Service rangers tend to be self-confident people, so our response was to laugh off the threat. Manson died in prison in November 2017 at the age of eighty-three. By that time, he had been incarcerated for close to fifty years.

I did a lot of photography in Death Valley, mostly of the spectacular desert scenery. I especially liked to photograph the sand dunes at sunrise and sunset. One year a law enforcement ranger asked for my help in photographing the scene of a death by suicide. We drove out to a remote section of the park, then walked out about a half mile to the site. It was not a pretty scene. A very overweight man had taken off all his clothes, slit both wrists, and bled to death. That had been a few days earlier, so the body was bloated. As the park ranger had told us the man had been wanted in the Las Vegas area for some very serious crimes, we felt little sympathy for him.

My winter jobs in Death Valley usually ended in mid-April with the onset of the summer heat. I would pack up my belongings in my truck and start driving north to Denali for my summer job, a trip that varied from four thousand to five thousand miles, depending on my route. That meant I was going from the park with the lowest elevation in the country to the park with the highest mountain.

We celebrated the fiftieth anniversary of the establishment of Death Valley as a National Monument in 1983. Many high-level Park Service employees joined us for the event, including a man in his nineties called Horace Albright. He began working for the National Park Service as the assistant director when it was established in 1916. Albright was the superintendent of Yellowstone National Park in the 1920s and was director of the National Park Service in 1933, when Death Valley became a unit. I got to meet Albright and thanked him for what he had done for the National Parks.

Years later, in 2016, I was to have another connection with Horace Albright. *National Geographic* published a book called *The National Parks: An Illustrated History* by Kim Heacox. I had worked with Kim for many years in Denali. The book selected ten people to represent the one hundred years of the National Park Service. Albright was one of the ten, and much to my surprise they also picked me.

AFTER MY 1986 summer in Denali, I got a call from Bill Truesdell, the man who had hired me for my first summer in Alaska back in 1976. He was now chief naturalist at Joshua Tree National Monument and he offered me a winter seasonal naturalist job. That park is located 227 miles south of Death Valley, not far from Anza-Borrego Desert State Park. It was time for a new challenge, so I took the job and ended up working at Joshua Tree for six winters.

I started there in the fall of 1986 and was assigned to the Cottonwood Ranger Station area in the southern section of the park. During my first few seasons, I lived in an old Park Service trailer that had a resident pack rat. In later years, I moved to a newly built modern home across the street. There was a Park Service campground in our area, where I did evening talks. We also had a small visitor center nearby, which I staffed off and on throughout the week. One day Johnny Cash walked into the visitor center by himself and we had a brief conversation. I had great admiration for him, but Johnny acted like a regular guy who was modest about his career.

Interstate Highway 10 was about five miles south of my area. On some of my days off, I would go to the nearby towns of Palm Desert and Palm Springs for food and supplies or to see movies. I often went to the Living Desert Zoo in Palm Desert to photograph desert animals, including desert bighorn sheep. I did talks there and at the Palm Springs Desert Museum (since renamed the Palm Springs Art Museum).

Back then I was doing a lot of research on ravens, which were common birds in the desert parks I worked in, as well as in Denali. Initially, my research was for a Park Service program in Joshua Tree, but I later thought I might write a book about ravens.

My friends at the Living Desert asked me to rehabilitate a raven named Shadow. He had been a wild bird that had caused a lot of trouble. Shadow, like all ravens, was exceptionally smart. He noticed that people in a Palm Springs neighborhood would go out to their mailboxes every day, pull objects out of them, and take the objects back into their homes. Shadow figured those things must be food, so he developed a habit of going to one mailbox after another.

Opening the lid, he would take out each item and toss them away if they were just letters.

I built a large cage behind my trailer, placed a perch in it, along with a water container, then put Shadow in it. I collected run-over animals on the desert roads and put them in the cage for food. The scent of those dead animals attracted local coyotes. When one would show up, Shadow would croak out in loud warning calls. I would go out and chase off the coyotes.

After a few weeks, I felt Shadow had gotten used to our area well enough to be released. I opened the cage gate and walked off. When I came back, he was gone. I thought that was the end of his story, but I was wrong. He quickly figured out that our nearby visitor center was the ideal place to hang out and beg for food. He would fly in, strut back and forth in front of the building, and go right up to newly arriving people. Shadow was very insistent on being fed. If someone did not hand him food, he would grab their clothes and tug on them.

After a week or so, I noticed Shadow was not around as much as he had been. We got our mail dropped off at a truck stop on Interstate 10 known as Chiriaco Summit. When getting my mail, I found him there accosting people for food. He was causing so many problems that the staff told me to capture and remove him. That was going to be difficult because he was so intelligent. It turned out someone solved the problem for me. I heard that a truck driver was seen feeding Shadow. He grabbed the bird and drove off with him. We later were told the man had a large aviary on his property, where he put Shadow.

WHEN I FIRST arrived in Joshua Tree, I looked for a good story to tell at my campfire talks and found it in the case of Bill Keys. He came to the region in 1910 to work on a gold mine called the Desert Queen. Later, Keys acquired some land. He intended to earn a living ranching and mining, and called his operation the Desert Queen Ranch. Keys married Francis Lawton in 1918.

Keys and a man named Worth Bagley had a long-running argument over a mining claim that came to a head in 1943, when Bagley took a shot at Keys. That led to a gunfight, and Keys killed Bagley. Keys was found guilty of murder and sent to San Quentin for ten years. Keys's wife Francis wrote to Erle Stanley Gardner, the lawyer who wrote the Perry Mason books, and Gardner found proof that Bagley had planned and started the gunfight by shooting at Keys. That meant Keys was acting in self-defense.

The case was brought to the parole board in 1950. The board paroled Keys, and in 1956 the governor of California gave him a full pardon. When he got back to his land in Joshua Tree, Keys erected a stone monument at the scene of the shooting and chiseled the following words on it: "Here is where Worth Bagley bit the dust at the hand of W. F. Keys, May 11 1943." I would tell that story at our campground evening program and the next day take people to the Keys Ranch to show them where the events took place.

I was always looking for new stories and found one in March 1989, when the oil tanker *Exxon Valdez* ran aground in Prince William Sound, south of Anchorage, Alaska. Eleven million gallons of oil polluted the ocean and shorelines in that area. After getting back to Denali in early May,

I drove 460 miles overnight to the coast to document the disaster. I talked my way onto a plane that took me to one of the oil-soaked beaches, where I joined a crew that was trying to remove the oil, and I photographed them as they worked.

After that, I got a boat ride back to shore and visited a fish hatchery in the town of Valdez. It had been converted to a rescue operation where volunteers tried to remove oil from seabirds. It was heart-wrenching to see the condition of those helpless birds. I rushed back to Denali during the night and got back in time to work my next shift. The following winter, I put together a slideshow on the oil spill and gave it many times in the communities around Joshua Tree.

When some of my Alaskan friends from Denali visited me at Joshua Tree, I thought they would want to be shown around the park and see desert animals. But what they really wanted to do was to go to Disneyland. So that was where I took them.

I made several trips overseas while I was working at Joshua Tree, including to England, Scotland, and Ireland. I visited the Tower of London, where they keep a small number of ravens in semi-captivity. Since medieval times, there has been a legend that as long as there are ravens at the Tower, England will not fall.

On one of those trips, I visited a remote glen in the Scottish Highlands where some of my MacIntyre ancestors were from. The landscape there is much like Lamar Valley in Yellowstone where I later studied wolves. A friend who teaches Gaelic languages told me that our clan name can be translated as "son of the land." That phrase was also a poetic name for wolves in Scotland.

Every winter, as visitor numbers dropped off in Joshua Tree in January and February, I was furloughed for about six weeks, but I was allowed to stay in my Park Service housing. I used that time off to work on writing projects. They included the books *Denali National Park: An Island in Time* and *Grizzly Cub: Five Years in the Life of a Bear*, the book that told the story of the Denali grizzly bear known as Stony. I also began work on a book that eventually came out in 1993: *A Society of Wolves: National Parks and the Battle Over the Wolf.*

BACK IN THE late 1980s, I had gone on a tracking flight with wolf researcher Diane Boyd, who was studying Canadian wolves recolonizing an area on the west side of Glacier National Park in Montana, and we had flown over a local pack crossing a frozen lake. Those were the first wolves I had ever seen in the lower forty-eight. Now, after being around wolves for fifteen seasons in Denali, where they were well established, I wanted to switch to a park where wolves were beginning to reclaim territory that had once been theirs.

In the summers of 1991 and 1992, I was a seasonal naturalist in the Many Glaciers section on the eastern side of Glacier National Park. I worked out an exchange deal with a Canadian park ranger who was stationed at Waterton Lakes National Park just north of the border. I would drive there and do a show, and he would give a talk in my area. I would also drive to the other side of Glacier National Park to try to see the wolves, but I did not spot any.

I took the winter of 1992–93 off to work on writing projects. In the spring of 1993, I was invited to do some talks in Alaska for the Bering Strait School District. I flew to

Anchorage, then to Nome, and from there took bush plane flights to small Native villages. I brought my slideshows on wolves and on ravens and both were big hits with the Native kids. I also brought a raven puppet. All the students wanted one, so I took orders, bought a lot of puppets, and shipped them to those schools. I also took trips to the Mojave desert and the Camp Pendleton Marine Base on the California coast to study and photograph nesting ravens.

In the summer of 1993, the small population of Montana wolves was still living in the northwest corner of Glacier. As there were no Park Service naturalist jobs in that section of the park, I volunteered for a grizzly bear nonprofit organization called Brown Bear Resources. My job there was to help local people and park visitors stay safe around grizzly bears. I also organized a weekly lecture series where researchers gave talks on grizzlies, wolves, and other wildlife. I was allowed to stay in a Park Service cabin near Polebridge, the only town in the area.

When I was in Polebridge, I occasionally helped Diane practice with her telemetry equipment. She would give me a wolf radio collar that transmitted a radio signal and have me hide it. When that was done, she would turn on her receiver and use a handheld antenna to pinpoint the direction of the signal, then move that way until she found the collar. Diane recently wrote a great book about her experiences with wolves in the Glacier area called *A Woman Among Wolves.*

The northwestern part of Glacier National Park is mostly forested, so it is challenging to find wolves there. Most of my sightings were of single wolves running out of the forest on one side of a road and into the trees on the other side. I did a lot of hiking and occasionally would see a pack in a meadow. By the end of the summer, I felt good about the sightings I had.

In his later years, Edward Abbey worked as a lookout at a fire tower in Glacier, in the western section of the park. The ranger who later staffed that fire tower allowed people to climb up to see the view and to look at the log with Abbey's handwritten notes and observations. Late one day when he was tidying the lookout, he realized someone had stolen that logbook. He felt terrible that his hospitality had resulted in the theft of a historic park document.

Sometime after that, the park got a package in the mail. Inside was the stolen Abbey logbook. In a note with it, an anonymous person said they had visited a friend who bragged about stealing the book. Incensed at that action, the Good Samaritan had stolen the book back and mailed it to the park.

That year I was contacted by the nonprofit organization the Wolf Education and Research Center in Idaho about contributing to a fundraising project. They were putting together a cookbook that would be called *Famous Friends of the Wolf Cookbook.* The idea was to have all of us submit a favorite personal recipe. The big-name celebrities who had already agreed to contribute to the project included Francis Ford Coppola, Clint Eastwood, Jane Fonda, Paul Newman, Linda McCartney, Dolly Parton, Brad Pitt, Arnold Schwarzenegger, and Elizabeth Taylor. My contribution was called Denali Five Minute Pasta, as that was one of the few things I knew how to cook.

After taking a break from Joshua Tree in the winter of 1992–93, I felt it was time to move on to a new winter park. I contacted Chief Naturalist Dennis Vásquez at Big Bend National Park, who I had worked with at Joshua Tree. I started there in the fall of 1993. When Dennis greeted me and the other new naturalist, he told us he considered us "hired guns" because we had both worked in so many other parks.

THE BIG BEND area was set aside as a National Park in 1944 and is 801,000 acres in size. The Rio Grande flows for 118 miles through the park and forms the border between Texas and Mexico. The river is about 1,800 feet above sea level. The highest point in the park, Emory Peak, is 7,832 feet above sea level. Big Bend is considered to be the most remote and least visited National Park in the lower forty-eight states.

As with the other parks I worked in, newly arrived naturalists had several days of training, including being driven around the park to see the main features. Within two weeks of arriving, I was doing nature walks and evening slideshows. I also staffed the park's three visitor centers, where I answered questions from visitors and suggested where to go to see more of the park.

For me, one of the big attractions to working at Big Bend was the chance to see mountain lions in the forested Chisos Mountains in the middle of the park. I often saw lions in the early morning, crossing the park road when I was driving to staff the visitor center up there. When I was at that visitor center one day, two people came back from a hike to report seeing a lion hiding in some bushes off a trail. My shift was almost over, so when it ended I rushed down that trail and saw the lion exactly where they had said it was. It looked like it was waiting to ambush a deer.

It was far more common to see javelinas in the Big Bend desert habitats. They look like pigs with hairy coats. Javelinas grow to be about twenty-four inches high and three to four feet long. They live in herds. Back then I got television reception from a small satellite dish I placed on the ground in front of my government apartment. On a regular basis, the screen would go black on and off for a minute or so when herds of javelinas walked in front of it.

The busiest times of our winter tourist season were always the college break weeks. We would set up a large room where several of us would issue backcountry camping permits. Anyone who wanted a permit would take a number from a display and we would call out which number could next come up to the permit desk.

One day when I was working in that permit room, I finished up with the folks I was helping, then called out the next number. A college-age man and woman came over to my desk and I asked where they wanted to hike and camp. They said they had just come back from their trip and wanted to report finding a dead person on a remote trail. That stopped me in my tracks. When I recovered, I told them that the next time they needed to report a fatality, they could bypass the numbering system and go to the front of the line.

I worked in Big Bend during an era when crossing the Rio Grande to the small villages of Boquillas and Santa Elena on the Mexican side was a common occurrence. There were no official border crossings or border patrol agents. If you stood on the north bank across from either village, someone would row over and take you across the river for a small fee. Both towns had restaurants that had limited items on the menu. When a chicken dish was ordered, you often would hear someone go out to the backyard and kill a chicken.

At the start of one of my winter seasons at Big Bend, we did a float trip down the Rio Grande. Halfway through the trip, we camped out on a sandy beach on the American side. There had been some reports of gunshots from the Mexican side toward parties on the river, but we did not have any trouble on our trip.

I really enjoyed getting to know the local culture in West Texas. Part of it was the expectation that you would be friendly to everyone you met. When driving long distances between small towns, you would do a West Texas wave at all drivers in the opposite lane. To properly do that, your right hand needs to be on the top of the steering wheel. Then you lift several fingers up to make a friendly gesture while holding the wheel with the rest of your hand.

The nearest supermarket was a hundred miles to the north of Big Bend, in the small town of Alpine. When in a store like that, you would look everyone in the eye who came down the aisle toward you, and nod in a friendly manner to acknowledge them.

While working in Big Bend, I went to New York City to do a program on wolves at the American Museum of Natural History. Without realizing it, I stayed in my West Texas cultural mode. When walking down a sidewalk in Manhattan, I looked every person coming toward me in the eye and nodded. That created a situation where all those people swerved well around me in fear that I was a maniac.

I got to be friends with Manuel Iron Cloud, a Native American man who was working in a maintenance position at Big Bend. We did a guided nature walk together for park visitors, taking them to a pictograph site that had images of desert animals. At the site, Manuel would talk about the meaning of the symbols to Native people. At that time, I was working on my anthology *War Against the Wolf: America's Campaign to Exterminate the Wolf.* Manuel graciously agreed to write an essay for the book on how Native Americans revere wolves. It was an outstanding piece of writing.

I had my first experience with a federal government shutdown when Congress failed to pass a budget bill in December 1995. Law enforcement rangers had to be stationed at the two entrances to the park to turn people back. One was my friend Jim Unruh, who I had worked with in Denali and Death Valley. Jim was the epitome of a friendly park ranger. He told me that stopping people from coming into the National Park was the worst assignment of his ranger career.

II

Yellowstone National Park

MY YEARS WATCHING wolves in Alaska had enabled me to start studying their lives and behavior. But I was only there for five months per year because the park road in Denali was not plowed in winter. There were times when I wondered if I might someday get in a situation where I could watch and study wolves year-round.

I first visited Yellowstone in late summer 1974, twenty-one years before the 1995 wolf reintroduction. I found plenty of elk, but bears, the animals I especially wanted to spot, were not commonly seen back then. After I got my summer job in Denali in 1976, I usually spent a week in Yellowstone on my way south from Alaska to winter jobs in desert parks.

In 1988, I left Alaska earlier than usual so I could get to Yellowstone to see the fires that were burning through large sections of the park. It had been an especially dry summer, and the fires had been set off by lightning strikes. The first fire started on June 14 and things got progressively worse through early September. Rain and snow fell on September 11, which allowed crews to control the burns.

Dean Clark, the crew leader from my 1975 firefighting job at Sequoia and Kings Canyon National Parks, was a fire boss on one of the bigger blazes in Yellowstone. I linked up with him and he got me on a plane flight over the fires. Later, Dean took me along when he did a helicopter flight to monitor some of the more remote fires.

After that, I drove around the park to see what the fires had done. Many forests were totally burned, but lodgepole pine, the most common tree in the park, is well adapted to fires, and the seeds from those trees were soon sprouting. Burned-over meadows had new grass shoots coming up by late September, and herds of elk were flocking to those areas to feed on the grass.

Although I was visiting Yellowstone every fall, I had never considered working there. Then everything changed when, in the early 1990s, park staff began planning a wolf reintroduction program to restore that lost species to Yellowstone.

I had done a lot of research on the history of wolves in Yellowstone for my book *A Society of Wolves*. Wolves were native to the area for thousands of years before the establishment of the world's first national park there in 1872. Most of the early Yellowstone rangers were former soldiers who were hired to control poaching in the park. Like most people in the country back then, they did not like wolves, partly because wolves preyed on the park's elk population. The park rangers mounted a wolf extermination program, and the last two Yellowstone wolves were killed near Lamar Valley in 1926.

During my 1993–94 winter season in Big Bend, I contacted the Yellowstone staff and arranged to get a summer job as the wolf interpreter in the park's Naturalist Division. All my talks and programs would be on the proposed wolf reintroduction. A week later, I got a call. The funding for my position had not come through and the park had to rescind the job offer. I had gotten a call from Rocky Mountain National Park, offering me a job, so I had that to fall back on. But I really wanted to be involved in the Yellowstone wolf reintroduction.

When someone puts a barrier in front of me, I like to take a good look to see if I can find a way around it. After thinking about the situation for a day, I called them back. I asked if I could raise the money for the job and was told that could work. The donations to fund my position could be made to the Yellowstone Association, the park's nonprofit partner, which would later be renamed Yellowstone Forever. Earlier in my life, I had done fundraising for a nonprofit, so I had experience in that area. It was a challenge, but I did raise the funding I needed.

In the spring of 1994, I packed up my belongings at Big Bend and drove 1,566 miles north to Yellowstone, where I started doing programs for park visitors on the planned wolf reintroduction. I was the wolf interpreter in the Naturalist Division for four summers; then, in 1998, I switched to working for the Wolf Project, the staff that studies the wolves. My official job title was biological technician. That meant I worked in the field rather than in an office. After that first summer, my position with the Wolf Project became year-round. I stayed in that job through early 2018, when I retired to write books. I raised my own funding for the twenty-four years I worked in the park (1994 to 2018). I think I was the only federal employee that did that.

For the first five years that I was employed in Yellowstone, I continued to work in Big Bend in the winter, so I was not in Yellowstone on January 12, 1995, when the first two packs arrived from Alberta, Canada. Each family was placed in its own acclimation pen for two months to give the wolves time to get used to their new home. Then they were set free.

One group became known as the Crystal Creek pack and the other was called the Rose Creek pack. The Crystal family had an adult pair (male 4 and female 5) and four male pups (wolves 2, 3, 6, and 8). Rose Creek consisted of a mother wolf, wolf 9, and her female pup, wolf 7. To make the small group a functioning breeding pack, a big unrelated male, wolf 10, was also placed in the pen. Both packs were released into the park in late March.

I arrived back in Yellowstone in early May 1995 and on my first full day out in Lamar Valley I saw all six Crystal Creek wolves. We had not expected the wolves to be very visible, so seeing them was tremendously exciting. Here are my field notes on that first wolf sighting.

May 13, 1995

At 0720 I spot the six Crystal Creek wolves (four blacks and two grays) across the Lamar River, about 250 yards to the south. They are moving east. The pack is led by the alpha female, wolf 5, to an old elk carcass near the south bank of the river. She feeds on it along with two of the four yearlings. The other three pack members, including the alpha male, wolf 4, do not eat but walk around the site and look at us on the road.

The pack then moves further east, still led by the alpha female. Two of the black yearlings catch up with her and run ahead. All of them are moving toward another old elk carcass, about 150 yards from the first one. Although the two yearlings are in front of the alpha female, it seems like she set the direction for the pack and those yearlings are just going the way she chose.

A large number of ravens are at that carcass. They fly off or hop away as the wolves approach. The two black yearlings arrive at the site first, sniff the carcass, then walk on and sniff the ground around the carcass. The alpha female walks by the carcass, then sniffs the area just past the site. She walks back to the carcass and does a squat urination scent mark and ground scratch next to it. On finishing, she walks off to the southeast.

Wolf 4, the alpha male, also walks past the carcass, sniffs around, then goes to the carcass and does a raised-leg urination and ground scratch at the same spot marked by the female. When he finishes, he follows after the alpha female to the southeast.

The wolves, led by the alpha female, continue to slowly travel to the southeast. A herd of bison is southwest of their position. Some of them are bedded while others are up and grazing. Several bison look toward the wolves but show no concern over their close presence. The majority of the bison do not even look at the wolves.

The alpha pair continues to the southeast and ignores the bison.

The bison are now moving west.

Two of the black yearlings stop, look at the last bison bull in the line, then move toward him. As they travel, they frequently stop to look back at the other pack members to the east. That last bull continues to slowly walk toward the main herd and the two blacks follow him. The gray, wolf 8, then the third black, join the first two yearlings. The lead black is now only about 15 meters from the lone bull. The bull stops and looks back at the yearlings. As soon as he stops, the four young wolves also stop and look like they are hesitating. Then two of the blacks and the gray go a little closer to the bison.

The bull continues on to the west and joins the rest of the bison. The three yearlings are now spread out and walking side by side toward the herd. A number of bison look back at the wolves. The yearlings stop, sniff the ground, and mill around. It looks like they do not want to approach the bison when they are looking back at the wolves.

The alpha pair is watching all this from a position about 200 yards to the southeast of the yearlings.

The herd now starts walking east toward the yearlings. Then the bison charge. The young wolves run off, clearly intimidated by the aggressive bison.

The four yearlings catch up with the alphas and the pack continues east across the valley. They spot a herd of about 150 elk and slowly walk toward them. The elk run a short distance toward the forest to the southwest. The wolves move toward the elk but are not running. The elk stop in front of the forest, about 100 yards from the wolves, and look back at them.

Then the herd trots to the east, traveling perpendicularly to the wolves, rather than away from them. Perhaps they are trying to keep the pack in sight so that they will not be ambushed. They come closer to the wolves and are now only 50 yards away.

The six wolves are watching the elk but are not moving toward them.

The elk turn around and run back to the west. Two of the black yearlings chase after them. The alphas stay put. Those yearlings run at only about a third of their top speed and do not seem to be seriously trying to catch the elk. Their gait looks like the playful gallop used when they chase each other.

One of the blacks stops but the other one continues after the elk alone. The herd splits into two subgroups and the black pursues one of them. That group of elk ends up between the bison herd and the wolves. The elk and the black yearling stop and look at each other.

The alphas had been watching the chase, but they soon lose interest and move off to the south, away from the younger wolves and the elk herd. The black yearling gives up on the elk and follows the alphas in that direction.

The pack disappears into the forest across the valley at 0800.

The gray yearling, wolf 8, was the smallest of the fourteen wolves brought down from Canada. The rangers guarding the Crystal Creek pen told me his three siblings continually picked on him. He was usually the last pack member to eat.

On June 27, I saw an incident involving him that greatly impressed me. Wolf 8 was out that evening with two of his black brothers. As they traveled, they played and chased each other. Suddenly, all three ran into a nearby forest. I got glimpses of animals running back and forth among the trees, then a black yearling sped out of the forest with part of an elk calf carcass in his mouth.

Wolf 8 and the other black reappeared, and all three brothers ran east, with 8 last in line. A fourth animal then charged out of the trees: a big grizzly bear. It was the one that had killed the calf. The bear gained on 8. As the bear was about to reach him, the wolf stopped, turned around, and confronted the grizzly. They were face to face, just a few feet apart.

The bear seemed confused. I felt that was partly because it could no longer see the wolf that had the calf and partly because it did not understand why a much smaller animal was defying him. Soon 8 casually turned around and followed his brothers, who, by now, were out of sight to the east. His bravery in that incident correctly indicated 8 was destined to accomplish great things in his life.

I saw the Crystal Creek family most days through July 5, then they moved up the Lamar River to the south and spent much of the summer in the remote area known as Pelican Valley. There were more elk there than in Lamar Valley, so that was the attraction.

The Rose Creek pack and the Crystal Creek wolves were released about the same time, in March 1995. Wolf 10, the Rose Creek alpha male, had bred alpha female wolf 9 while they were in the pen. After they were set free, the pack traveled east, and the mother wolf chose a den site slightly outside Yellowstone. Wolf 10 went out hunting for his mate and was illegally shot and killed.

Because of the tragic death of the alpha male, it was unlikely any of the eight pups born to wolf 9 would survive. A Park Service crew captured the mother wolf and her pups and brought them back to the acclimation pen in Lamar Valley where 9 and 10 had lived for two months before release.

I had helped carry meat to the Rose Creek wolves on two occasions. We would hike up to the pen, unlock the gate, go a short distance into the enclosure, drop off the meat, and leave right away. The mother and pups would run to the far side of the pen when we arrived. We were pleased to see that, because it indicated they had a natural fear of being near people.

I played a small role in bringing justice to the killer of wolf 10. It began when I was in the small town of Cooke City, a few miles east of the Northeast Entrance to the park. People there mentioned that a man had come into Miners Saloon and bragged about killing a wolf just east of the park. He was wearing a T-shirt that said something like Wolf Extermination Squad. The locals got his name and several of them agreed to talk to our law enforcement rangers. I contacted the park's chief ranger, and that information led to the man's arrest and conviction for killing an endangered species. He was sentenced to six months in prison and fined $10,000.

In early July, I showed the Crystal wolves to a group of people. One was a beautiful blond woman named Cindy, who stayed back to talk to me after the others left. I was surprised that she showed any interest in me. She lived in Arizona and her job required a lot of travel. We ended up in a long-distance relationship for many years.

After I finished my Yellowstone job that fall, I was invited to do a lecture tour in Japan. Wolves had been native there, but as in America, they had all been killed off. Now people in Japan were looking into doing a reintroduction. I went around the country giving a slideshow on how we had brought wolves back to Yellowstone.

Cindy joined me in Hawaii on my way back from Japan, and we met up with some ranger friends of mine from Denali who were working in Hawaiian parks. I did talks on the Yellowstone wolves in Hawaii Volcanoes and Haleakalā National Parks. We got to see flowing lava close-up at the volcano park.

That experience matched the time I stood in front of a surging glacier in Denali. I had joined some researchers and fellow rangers on a helicopter flight to a glacier on the north side of Denali that was surging forward at its lower end. We landed, walked to the site, and saw the terminal wall of ice creeping forward over the tundra vegetation. Arctic ground squirrels were running around looking for seeds to eat, oblivious to the coming destruction of their homes. I felt privileged to have witnessed the dynamics of nature in both fire and ice.

Another four packs of wolves were captured in British Columbia, and they arrived in Yellowstone in late January 1996. I had flown up from my winter job at Big Bend to take a class at the Yellowstone Institute in Lamar Valley. Cindy joined me, and we happened to be there when the wolves destined to form the Druid Peak pack arrived.

The crew that brought them down from Canada allowed us to look into the trailer at the individual cages that had held the wolves. One member of the crew told us that on the trip to the park they had stopped to check on the wolves. They found that wolf 38, a big male, had broken out of his steel cage and was walking around inside the trailer. They jabbed him with a tranquilizer dart and put him in another cage for the rest of the trip. The other wolves in the trailer were adult female wolf 39 and her three young daughters: pups 40, 41, and 42. 38 was captured as a lone wolf, so he was not related to the other wolves, but he bonded with the four females while in an acclimation pen.

Soon after they were released from their pen that spring, the Druids attacked the Crystal Creek wolves, who by that time were denning in Lamar Valley, and killed Crystal alpha male 4. Because of the fight, none of the newborn Crystal Creek pups survived. The pack now had only two members: alpha female 5 and a young male known as wolf 6. Those two Crystal Creek survivors abandoned Lamar Valley and went south to Pelican Valley, where they thrived. In 2000, they were renamed the Mollies pack after Mollie Beattie, who was the head of the US Fish and Wildlife Service during the reintroduction and had helped carry the pack members into the acclimation pen in early 1995. Mollie died at an early age from cancer. That family, the Mollies, is the only one of the original seven reintroduced packs still in business thirty years later.

AS A PARK naturalist, I devoted many hours to what the Park Service calls roving interpretation. That means you put on your ranger uniform, go to where park visitors are, and talk to them informally. I would drive out to Lamar Valley about an hour before sunrise, use a spotting scope to find the Crystal wolves, then invite visitors over to see them through the scope. As they took turns watching the wolves, I would tell the visitors the story of the reintroduction.

In the evenings, I did slideshows on the wolves in several of the park campgrounds. Before the show, I would walk around the campground, go to every site, and invite people to my talk. One evening at the Tower Fall Campground, I noticed several law enforcement rangers acting like something was up. They told me a license plate at one site matched that of a wanted felon, and he was known to have guns in the camper unit on the back of his pickup. The man was in that camper, and they needed to arrest him.

The rangers were discussing what to do if the man had a gun in his hand when he opened the camper door. His history indicated he might shoot any officers who pulled guns and tried to arrest him. I offered to help because as a park naturalist, I was not armed. I went to the site, knocked on the camper door, then stepped back a few paces. I made sure the man could see that my hands were empty and there was no gun on my belt. When he appeared at the door, he was not holding a gun. I told him I would be doing a wolf talk in a few minutes if he wanted to come. He thanked me and closed the door. I went back to the other rangers and told them what had happened. They went to the site, knocked on the door, and arrested him. Not many people know that Yellowstone has its own judge and courtroom, as well as holding cells. We now get five million visitors per year, and some of those people cause trouble.

As mentioned earlier, in 1998 I switched from my seasonal position in the park's Naturalist Division to a position as a biological technician with the park's Wolf Project. I would still be wearing a park ranger uniform with a badge, but in addition to helping people see wolves, I would now be involved in one of the most detailed studies of a large carnivore in the world. It also meant that starting in the spring of 1999, I would no longer be traveling to desert parks for the winter. I would be working in Yellowstone year-round.

One consequence of working for the Park Service all year was that our uniform rules required me to wear a tie in the winter. I was given a clip-on tie with a National Park Service gold pin to hold it in place. I was probably the only wolf researcher in the world who wore a tie in the field. I still have that tie in case I am invited to speak at a formal affair.

Although my job was technically five days a week, I would go out on my days off (not dressed in my park ranger uniform) so I could continue to study wolves and keep track of what the packs were doing. My habit was to get up before dawn, summer or winter, rain or shine, search for the wolf packs, and record their behavior. I would also help park visitors see the wolves and tell them about the park's reintroduction project. I would then go home for a nap and return in the evening. This was a pattern I had gotten into during my college days, and it served me well in Yellowstone because wolves are most active in the early morning and evening.

Those of us involved in Yellowstone's Wolf Reintroduction Project did not expect that the wolves would be very visible after they were released. But it turned out that we see wolves nearly every day. Being able to see wild wolves and observe pack interactions resulted in a huge increase in tourism to the park. The visitors who repeatedly returned to the park to see wolves became known as wolf watchers.

Most wolf researchers work in remote areas with only one or two other people as coworkers. When I studied the East

Fork wolves in Denali, I hiked off the road and only occasionally had someone with me. But today in Yellowstone I am often with dozens of other people when I watch wolves. That would be a mixture of wolf watchers, local wildlife guides with their clients, and park visitors. The wolf watchers come from every possible political, religious, and financial background.

Usually, showing people wolves is a simple process. I look for wolves from one of the parking lots along the park road. If I find them, I let people see them through my high-powered spotting scope. Sometimes I need to walk uphill to find wolves that are not visible from lower levels. In those cases, people along the road come up and join me.

One day a man in a wheelchair was in one of the parking lots when I arrived. He told me that his dream was to see wild wolves. We could not find any wolves from that site, so I hiked up the slope to the north and soon found a pack. The problem was that the man would have to come up to my location on the hill to see them. I went back to the road and asked several of the longtime wolf watchers to help me out. We pushed the wheelchair uphill, and as the man locked it in place, I set up my scope in front of him. The wolves were still there, and he got to see them.

In addition to being helpful and friendly, new and veteran wolf watchers assist me in my research. They spot wolves for me and pass on details of significant wolf behavior they see when I am not around. They also model proper behavior when wolves are visible from the road, keeping their distance and not approaching the wolves to take photos.

Of all the wolf watchers, the one that most stands out is a woman named Carla Rae. She and her husband, Matt, started coming to the park to watch wolves in 2021. Carla Rae later had a serious accident that injured her brain and affected her memory. She courageously fought through a long and difficult recovery. During that period, she memorized sections from my wolf books. Her doctor was impressed by how the stories of the main wolf characters inspired and motivated her to get well. Carla Rae did get better, and she and Matt continued to come to the park every spring to watch 907, the longtime alpha of the Junction Butte pack, and her family at their Slough Creek den.

My strongest memories of Carla Rae are about how much she loved to laugh. I think her delight in living and her focus on the funny side of things were big factors in how well she dealt with her health issues.

A few days before I wrote this section, Matt contacted me to say his wife had died. He added that the Yellowstone wolves had brought so much joy to her during her health challenges. I will always equate Carla Rae with our great alpha females, and most importantly with 907. All of them went through difficult times but somehow retained a positive spirit. Carla Rae took their stories and applied them to her life, and it helped her heal.

As word spread about how people could see wild wolves in Lamar Valley and other sections of the park, visitation greatly increased. Wolves were such a draw that research by University of Montana professor John Duffield and his colleagues found that by 2022 wolf tourism was adding about $82.7 million to the local economy. It also created a lot of well-paid guiding jobs. By 2024, nearly five million people were visiting the park every year, and an estimated

8,560 local jobs were dependent on tourists coming to the park.

I recently checked the Montana Department of Fish, Wildlife and Parks website and saw that a state resident could legally shoot up to ten wolves. A license required to kill ten cost $140. That meant the state was placing a value of $14 on each wolf taken. There is another way to estimate the value of a wolf. Since Yellowstone tends to have an average of a hundred wolves and the wolves bring in $82.7 million to the local communities, you could say each park wolf is worth $827,000. Wolves are far more valuable to the local economy alive than dead.

IN MY EARLY years in Yellowstone, I continued to do wildlife photography, but I was gradually losing interest in being behind a camera. I wanted to concentrate on watching and taking notes on wolf behavior. The opportunity to study the lives of wild wolves and witness and document their stories day after day and year after year easily won out and I stopped taking pictures.

There were a couple of incidents that reinforced for me that I had made the right decision. The first one happened in 2016 when I was watching wolves from the side of the road in Lamar Valley. A man joined me. Before I could point out the wolves to him, he started taking photographs of me from different angles. I told him a wolf pack was in view to the south, but he was not interested. He just kept taking photographs. I was getting annoyed and he finally sensed that. The man said he thought I knew he was doing a *National Geographic* magazine story about the park wolves and he needed to get photos of the wolf researchers. After that experience, I had a better understanding of what it might be like for wildlife when people approach them for photographs and interrupt their activities and movements.

The second incident happened when I was checking on a wolf pack near Mammoth Hot Springs. It was a workday, so I was in my ranger uniform. As I approached the area in my car, I saw an alpha female wolf run across the road and continue south at top speed. Then I saw a well-known professional wildlife photographer run after her as he frantically tried to get more photographs. I slowed down and yelled at him to leave the wolf alone. He stopped and I could tell from his expression that he knew he had done something wrong.

Once I freed myself from photography, I could totally concentrate on recording wolf behavior. I used a handheld voice recorder out in the field, and every evening I would type up my observations on my computer. In later years, research scientists who did not have the opportunity to spend as much time with the packs as I did would consult me about certain aspects of wolf behavior. I was always happy to share my notes with them, and I ended up with my name on a number of scientific papers.

I have arranged to donate all my wolf and Park Service material to Yellowstone National Park's Heritage and Research Center, including over 13,400 single-spaced typed pages of field notes about the park wolves.

I BOUGHT A small cabin in Silver Gate, Montana, in the spring of 2003, and I still live there. My cabin is just a mile from the Northeast Entrance to the park. Lamar Valley is about fifteen miles from my cabin and accessible by a road that is plowed year-round.

During the twenty years I worked for the Wolf Project, I averaged around two hundred talks a year out in Lamar Valley, many of them to school field classes and tour groups. I had great work partners: Tom Zieber, Erin Cleere, Elena West, Dan Graf, Emily Almberg, Erin Albers, Kira Cassidy, Colby Anton, Hans Martin, Pete Mumford, and Lizzie Cato. Our jobs were split between researching wolf behavior, helping park visitors see wolves, telling visitors about the wolf reintroduction, and managing the big crowds of people that came to see wolves. Erin Albers and Kira have been full-time employees of the Wolf Project for many years now. Kira is an exceptionally talented artist and does the maps and illustrations for my wolf books.

Not all my time in Yellowstone was focused on wolves. Sometimes I had the opportunity to help solve problems for people. One day I was hiking and searching for wolves in the west end of Lamar Valley when I spotted a stone plaque with a woman's name carved on it along with a brief summary of her life. She had been killed by terrorists while working for a humanitarian group oversees. The Park Service does not allow such memorials in National Parks, but I figured no one other than me would ever see the plaque, so I did not report it.

A few weeks later, a strictly-by-the-book law enforcement ranger spotted the plaque, removed it, and placed it in storage. Soon after that, a middle-aged man approached me when I was on duty and asked if I knew what had happened to the plaque. The man explained that, as a friend of the woman and her family, he had commissioned the plaque and had placed it there because Yellowstone was her favorite place in the world. I took the man to the ranger so he could explain. The ranger was sympathetic but would not agree to bend the park rules. I came up with an idea. The west side of my cabin faced the park, so I suggested we put the plaque there. Both men agreed, and the plaque is there to this day.

On another occasion, a photographer set up a trail camera and left food on the ground to attract animals. That is strictly forbidden in National Parks. The camera was found and turned over to the rangers. The man had forgotten that he had turned on the motion detector, so there were dozens of shots of him leaving the food there. It was an easy conviction because of the self-portraits.

During the years I worked in the park, Doug Smith was the lead biologist and head of the Wolf Project. He was the perfect guy for that position. Doug was an outstanding scientist who could plan out and lead various research projects. He could communicate information about wolves in scientific papers as well as in talks to regular people. But beyond that, he was a good guy who we all loved. I had dozens of other supervisors in my Park Service career but none were as admired by their staff as Doug Smith was.

When Doug retired in the fall of 2022, Dan Stahler took over leadership of the Wolf Project. Dan started working for the project in 1997. He completed a PhD on wolf genetics at UCLA in 2011. In addition to his wolf research, Dan supervises research on cougars and elk in the park, as well as research on threatened and endangered species. Like Doug, Dan has an easygoing personality that makes him a very well-liked leader.

I am now retired but I still go out into the park to look for wolves every day. The current Wolf Project biologists I am around the most in the field are Jeremy SunderRaj and Taylor Rabe.

Jeremy came to the park for the first time in 2007, traveling from Colorado with his parents when he was eleven years old. On that trip, he saw wolves from the Slough Creek pack kill two black bear yearlings. Starting in 2012, when he was sixteen, he worked in Silver Gate and went out early every morning to watch and study the wolves. After doing that for three summers, he went to the University of Montana and got a wildlife biology degree. Jeremy worked with wolves for the Montana Department of Fish, Wildlife and Parks for three summers during his college years. After college he returned to Yellowstone, worked as a wildlife guide, then got a job with the Wolf Project in the spring of 2019, the year after I retired.

Taylor first visited the park in 2012. She later worked as a wildlife guide in the park, from 2019 to 2022. During those years, she volunteered for the Wolf Project and usually partnered with Jeremy. In 2022 she was hired by the project. Jeremy and Taylor spend their workdays out in the park studying wolves, helping people see them, and doing talks on wolves for school field trips and wildlife tour groups.

Taylor and Jeremy use their vacation weeks every year to travel around the world and spend time with local biologists who study endangered animals. This has enabled them to explore the Himalayan mountains, see the elusive "gray ghost," more commonly known as the snow leopard, follow a pack of Tibetan wolves, and spend time watching Asiatic lions and photographing Bengal tigers. All of that was in India.

They then traveled to the African countries of Tanzania, Botswana, and Zambia. Both of them canoed across the Okavango Delta, trekked with African lions, and watched rare African painted dogs take down prey. Just recently they spent some time in Brazil, where they saw a jaguar in the Pantanal and helped a yellow anaconda cross a busy highway. Taylor and Jeremy have continued to expand their knowledge through learning about other ecosystems, while sharing the importance of wolf conservation and education with people all over the globe. That is what wildlife biologists do on their vacations.

Both Jeremy and Taylor are people of color in a field of wildlife research that has traditionally been dominated by white males. Their positions with the Wolf Project are partially funded by a nonprofit organization called Conservation Nation, which works to encourage people from nontraditional backgrounds to go into wildlife-related jobs, something I fully support.

After my last day with the Wolf Project in early 2018, I turned in my badge along with my uniform shirts, jackets, and hats so new rangers could make use of them. I am proud to say that during my forty-four years of working in the National Parks system, I never had a government office, a government desk, a government computer, or a government phone.

WHEN YOU ARE a park ranger, you never know what the next phone call might bring. One afternoon, while typing up my wolf observations from the morning, I got a phone call from Scotland Yard in London. For a moment, I thought I was in trouble, but it turned out the officer calling wanted my help.

A former British prime minister and his family were in the States and were heading to Yellowstone. He wanted to see wolves, so I was asked to spend the morning with him, his wife, and his kids.

I always say yes to anyone who asks for my help, so I agreed. We worked out the details on where and when to meet.

When that morning came, the party seemed like any other family visiting Yellowstone except that two men in plain clothes were with the parents and kids. They were the Scotland Yard bodyguards for the PM. I noticed that each of them had an unobtrusive pouch on the side of his belt, a pouch that any tourist might have to hold binoculars or other items. I figured each man had a small handgun in those pouches.

The PM had the same last name as some of my Scottish ancestors, so we talked about the possibility that we might be distantly related. If so, his side of the family turned out to be the wealthy one, while my side was poorer.

Over the years, I was often asked to take out well-known people to see Yellowstone wolves. They included actors Matthew McConaughey, Mel Gibson, Jane Fonda, Cameron Diaz, and Rebecca Romijn, as well as Melissa Mathison (writer of the movie *E.T.*); Ted Turner of Turner Broadcasting; *60 Minutes* correspondents Anderson Cooper and Ed Bradley; Montana Senator Max Baucus; and several other politicians. All of them were just as excited about seeing wolves as regular park visitors. I also noticed that everyone dressed and acted like normal people. When I was with the actors, no one recognized them. I stayed in touch with Melissa for some time after her visit and later spoke on wolves at her daughter's school in New York City.

Life Lessons From Wolves
Leadership

Throughout my career, I have been privileged to work for many great bosses. While watching the Yellowstone wolves, I have noted a number of characteristics that I admire and that human and wolf leaders share. One of the greatest wolf leaders of all was the wolf we called the 06 Female.

Named after the year of her birth, 2006, the 06 Female was famed Druid alpha male 21's granddaughter. When she grew up, we could see that she was much like her famous ancestor. She was big, fearless, and exceptionally smart. Later in life, 06 had to deal with a deadly rival: the alpha female of the much larger Mollies pack. Their conflict climaxed one spring when the Mollies alpha female led an assault on 06's den right after 06 had given birth. The two brothers 06 had chosen to help her form a pack heroically stood their ground against an entire pack of invading wolves. Their action, and 06's foresight in picking a den site that foiled the enemy's efforts to dig out the pups and kill them, resulted in a total victory for her side. 06 excelled at planning ahead and at picking allies who would risk their lives to support her. Those leadership qualities made her one of Yellowstone's greatest alphas.

Over the years, a number of young people have stood out to me as having these leadership qualities as well as good social skills when interacting with the public. I recommended that three of them be hired by the Wolf Project. I am proud that today these young people (Jeremy SunderRaj, Taylor Rabe, and Claire Lacey) have become tremendously accomplished Wolf Project biologists.

I tell the 06 Female's story in *The Alpha Female Wolf: The Fierce Legacy of Yellowstone's 06*.

12

907's Early Years

EVEN THOUGH I am retired, I still go out early every morning to watch wolves and study their behavior, something I have done for more than thirty years now in Yellowstone. These days, however, I do not go back out later in the day, as I did for over two decades. Instead, in the afternoons and evenings I work on my writing.

I have written a series of books based on my field notes to document the story of the Yellowstone packs from the time of reintroduction in 1995 to the present. The first book in the series, *The Rise of Wolf 8*, focused on the Rose Creek pack and was published in 2019. The next one, *The Reign of Wolf 21*, came out in the fall of 2020 and was mostly about the Druid Peak pack. After that, I wrote *The Redemption of Wolf 302* (2021), *The Alpha Female Wolf* (2022), and *Thinking Like a Wolf* (2024). A major character in that last book was wolf 907 of the Junction Butte pack.

The Junction Butte pack could be described as a merger of three prominent wolf genetic lines from the original wolf reintroduction to Yellowstone: the Rose Creek, the Druid Peak, and the Crystal Creek packs. Crystal Creek was later renamed Mollies pack.

The descendants of those three packs had a history of fighting with one another. But in early 2012, young females from the Mollies pack met up with some males descended from the Rose Creek and Druid lines and formed a new group that became known as the Junction Butte wolf pack.

In the spring of 2012, the Junctions denned near Antelope Creek, south of Tower Junction. The following year, they denned two miles west of Slough Creek in an area known as the Trough. 907 and her twin sister 969 were born at the Trough in April 2013. Based on our records and genetic studies, they were part of the fifth generation of wolves since the 1995 reintroduction.

I first saw 907 and 969 on August 1, 2013, when they were about three and a half months old. They were with two other gray pups and a yearling male. The family later moved a few miles east to Slough Creek, an area where 907 was destined to live the rest of her long life.

That was the same place where the famous 06 Female started a pack and denned in 2010. She and her two male partners raised four pups at the site that year. Her family was known as the Lamar Canyon pack. The 06 Female had rock star status among wolf watchers because of her personality and fierce character. I remember watching her defend her pups from a mother grizzly who was approaching 06's den with her two yearling cubs. 06 spotted the approaching bears and over the next four and a half hours mounted a harassment campaign that lured the bear family farther and farther away from the den and pups. She did that by getting the mother grizzly to chase her in the opposite direction of the den fifty-two times. 907's choice to be based at Slough Creek, her leadership skills, and her fierce commitment to her family demonstrated to me that she was an alpha female that was very like 06.

In the spring of 2016, the Junction pack's alpha female, wolf 970, died, and that set off an intense rivalry for the pack's alpha female position between 907 and her sister 969. That year, both denned at Slough Creek in an area that is highly visible from Slough Creek Campground Road. Hundreds of people gathered every morning and evening to watch the wolf family raise their pups. Three-year-old 907 emerged as the victor in that round and took over the alpha female position.

The following spring, 907 had her pups several miles south of the Slough Creek den. While 907 struggled to keep her pups alive, her sister 969, who did not have pups that year, took over as leader of the pack. Unfortunately, 907 got little help from other pack members and none of her pups survived. By the time 907 rejoined the other adults, they were used to having 969 as the alpha female, and 907 was demoted to a lower rank. I suspected that 969 had deliberately stayed away from her sister's den that spring so she could take over the pack.

In 2018 both sisters once again denned at Slough Creek, as did 969's adult daughter wolf 1382. 907 formed an alliance with her niece and the two of them worked together to overthrow 969, who was hindered by having an injured leg.

That put 907 in the alpha position for a second time. After that, all three mothers cooperated to raise their three litters of pups.

The following year, there was a reversal of allies as 969 and her daughter 1382 banded together against 907. Then, in an unexpected turn of events, young 1382 turned on her mother and seized the alpha female title for herself. That 2018–19 era in the Junction pack seemed like an episode of *Game of Thrones*, full of infighting and betrayal of allies.

From the spring of 2019 through the start of the 2022 denning season, 1382 reigned as alpha female. During that time, 969 died. Four Junction females were pregnant in the spring of 2022. Two of them, 907 and 1276, denned south of the road near Crystal Creek. Alpha female 1382 and another female, 1386, denned at the traditional Slough Creek site. 1386 later moved her pups to 907's southern site, and we eventually counted fifteen pups at that site.

During that time, 907 and 1382 got into a fight and the younger female won. 907 had previously lost her left eye and was at a disadvantage if her opponent came at her from that side. That defeat seemed to end any hope of 907 regaining the alpha position. But that turned out to be a wrong assessment, because the other Junction wolves sided with 907. With their support, she got a third term as the pack's alpha female. 1276, who was now the second-ranking female, began acting like 907's enforcer. That allowed the older wolf to concentrate on leading the pack. It was now 1382's turn to be relegated to a lowly position in the pack.

In early December, I saw 1276 walking around the other wolves with a raised tail. That troubled me because it might be a sign that she would someday challenge 907 for the leadership position. But she continued to act in a subordinate manner whenever she was close to 907.

At the end of 2022, the Junction pack numbered twenty-five wolves—ten adults and fifteen pups. The next biggest pack in Yellowstone had only fifteen members. The Junction Butte pack under the leadership of 907 and her mate, Black Male, now ruled Lamar Valley.

EARLY ON THE first day of 2023, I went out my front door to start my car. It was so dark I did not see a huge two-thousand-pound bull bison walking on the far side of my car until he had passed me. If I had been a few steps farther ahead, I would have startled him and likely would have been headbutted by the bull and sent sailing through the air or trampled.

The snow in the park was very deep that winter. One day I saw the Junctions traveling single file through snow up to the shoulders of the adults. The lead wolf had to bound up and down to make any progress. Before a new wolf could relieve that leader, the pack spotted a mule deer and ran after it along the trail broken by the deer. That gave the wolves an advantage, and they easily pulled it down.

In late March, I saw 1276 approach 907 with a low wagging tail. 907 raised her tail and pinned her young ally. That confirmed that 907 was still the undisputed highest-ranking female in the pack. By April, 907 looked pregnant. This would be her ninth litter. As far as we knew, 907 had produced more litters of pups than any other Yellowstone female. She was now ten years old, the oldest known wolf in Yellowstone. Her second in command, 1276, was also pregnant.

In mid-April, I saw signs of fresh diggings at both dens at Slough Creek. We determined that 907 was using the upper den, which we called the Natal Den, and 1276 was based at the lower one, known as the Sage Den. On April 26, 907 went into 1276's den, likely to see if that other female had had her pups yet. 907 was noticeably thinner now, and when she came out, she went to a nearby spring and drank from it for some time, a sign she was nursing pups and needed water for her milk production. Two days after that, 1276 was also slimmer, suggesting she too had given birth.

Black Male, the family's alpha male, returned to the area where both dens were located later that morning. 907 ran out of her den and greeted him. He regurgitated a big pile of meat to her and 907 ate all of it. After that, he followed her to her den and she went inside. He looked into the den for some time. Younger pack members came over and wagged their tails when they also peered in the den entrance. Soon after that, we saw little pups come out of both dens. We counted a total of seven pups between the two litters.

There was a major event at the den area on the morning of May 7. It started when low-ranking 1382 approached 907's den. Something about 1382 set off 907 and she charged at the other female, who ran east, toward the Sage Den. Other wolves joined 907 in chasing 1382.

At that moment, 1276 came out of her den and saw those wolves running in her direction at top speed. I think she mistakenly thought they were going to attack her and her pups. 1276 reacted by charging forward. She pounced on a big gray wolf, pinned it, and viciously began biting her. That was 907.

My friend Melba Coleman filmed the incident, and I later studied her footage. I saw that both 1382 and 1276 were biting 907, who had rolled on her back so she could defend herself. She tried to bite her attackers but that did not deter them. Then something happened that I had missed when watching the event. 907's longtime mate, Black Male, ran in, jumped on the back of 1276, and bit her repeatedly. I had never before seen a male wolf intervene when females were fighting. His efforts were not working, however, as 1276 was in such a frenzy that she ignored his bites and continued her assault on 907.

Finally, the attack ended. 1276 walked off and 907 got up. She licked her wounds, especially one on her leg. In the following days, 907 and 1276 seemed to move on from their fight. On May 10, 907 went in and out of 1276's den, and the following morning both bedded together. However, 907 did not dispute that 1276 was the pack's new alpha female. She had beaten 907 in the fight and the issue was settled. 907's third reign as alpha was over. The pack's alpha male, Black Male, continued to support 907, coming back from a hunt with a big piece of meat in his mouth. Ignoring 1276, he gave all the meat to 907.

That month, former Junction male 1048 came back to the pack's den for a visit and 907 rushed over to lick his face. I had seen the two of them mate in 907's younger years, so it was touching to see them together again. 1048 stayed with the Junctions for a day before wandering off, as was his custom in his senior years.

That summer, the Wolf Project hosted a group of young cancer survivors from Texas Children's Hospital in Dallas. They got to see the Junction pack, and I told the kids stories of 907, mainly ones about her overcoming setbacks and challenges in her life. Because so many people have helped me over the years, I have been donating all the income from my Yellowstone wolf books to good causes. That includes Texas Children's Hospital, St. Jude Children's Research Hospital, Make-A-Wish, the Red Cross, Yellowstone Forever (the nonprofit arm of the National Park), and organizations that help wolves, such as the International Wolf Center and Wolves of the Rockies.

In early June, the two mother wolves moved the pack's two surviving pups from the Slough Creek den area to a rendezvous site on Jasper Bench on the south side of Lamar Valley. This was a place where the pups could hang out and play while the pack went out to hunt. By late July, we reluctantly concluded that only one Junction pup was still alive. It was a black female who later was collared and became known as wolf 1479. The adults gave her special attention and played with her a lot. That helped make up for 1479 not having other pups to play with. We joked that the adult wolves were spoiling her rotten. We never knew why the pack had such a low pup survival rate that year.

I noticed that 907 and the pup often bedded together. That suggested she was the mother, and later genetic testing confirmed it. It was a touching sight: the pack's oldest wolf spending a lot of time with the pack's youngest wolf. To me, it was like seeing a queen mentoring a princess.

I saw Black Male return from a hunt carrying a big piece of meat. He went directly to 907 and his daughter and dropped the meat in front of them. After regurgitating another big pile of meat, he bedded down beside them. 1276 regularly approached 907 with a raised tail, and the older female would respond by lowering her tail submissively. At times, the younger wolf would aggressively pin the elderly 907.

Around that time, I saw six Junction adults interacting with the pup. They played chasing games and wrestled with her. She seemed to like rough play and repeatedly ran back to engage the older wolves.

By August pup 1479 had learned how to hunt small mouselike rodents known as voles. She would chase one, pounce on it with both front paws, then eat it. The young pup also caught and ate grasshoppers. She learned to locate adult wolves by howling and listening for their answering calls. 1479 could also find the adults by following scent trails. One morning I saw mother wolf 907 lick the pup's neck, throat, face, and head for some time. This intimate action releases oxytocin in mother and pup and would be a pleasurable bonding experience for them.

That summer Doug Smith and I had a contest to see how many references to rock songs we could fit into our talks on wolves at a conference. I won, mainly thanks to wolf 302. In his early days, when he got females pregnant and then abandoned them, I said he was on a "Highway to Hell" (AC/DC). But late in life, when he became a proper alpha male and died saving his pups, you could say he was on a "Stairway to Heaven" (Led Zeppelin).

WOLF 1382, THE female who fought with 907 over the alpha female position, died that September. A crew hiked to the spot where her radio collar was sending out a mortality signal and found that she had been killed by a kick from a bison or elk.

Black Male regularly brought meat to 907 and her young daughter, and the adults continued to sleep next to each other while their daughter napped a few feet away.

There was a major event in the Junction pack later that September involving alpha female 1276. She continued to aggressively pin 907 through the nineteenth to show her dominance. We did not see her in the following days. On the twenty-fourth, someone took a photo of her. She was a shocking sight. Her lower jaw was hanging straight down, an injury so severe that we figured it soon would be fatal. We guessed she might have been shot in the jaw while out of the park or kicked in the mouth by an elk or bison.

The following morning, we saw that 907 was once again acting like the pack's alpha female. When Black Male did a scent mark on a bush, 907 went right over to the spot and marked over it. That day we saw 1276 wade into the Lamar River and lower her face into the current. That allowed water to flow into her mouth. She came out of the river and moved away when she saw the Junction pack traveling in her direction. I took that to mean she knew she could not defend herself if a rival female challenged her.

On a later day, 1276 joined a few other Junction wolves at a big bison carcass. I thought that there would be no way for her to feed. But 1276 used a technique where she scraped some meat off the bison with her upper canines, then swallowed that small bit of food. 907 was also at the carcass and at one point she fed next to 1276. 907 did not do anything to harm the severely injured rival wolf who had previously attacked and dethroned her.

A video of 1276 was taken on October 6. It was hard to watch, for by then her lower jaw was gone. She was extremely thin and her stomach looked empty. We never saw her again after that day and assumed she had died of starvation. Later, we got a report that a man had shot a wolf just north of the park a few weeks earlier. The bullet did not kill the wolf and it got away. If the bullet had hit her lower jaw, that would explain what had happened to 1276. The pack now numbered fourteen adults and one pup.

The death of 1276 meant that 907 had outlived all of her rivals. She was now in her fourth term as the Junction alpha female. I had never heard of a male or female wolf that had accomplished that. People saw her get an elk calf by herself that fall, even though she was limping badly on her left front leg and missing one eye.

I continued to be impressed by female pup 1479. In November I saw the six-month-old confidently leading the pack as they traveled. On another day, I noticed that 907 was the last wolf in line. I figured her injured leg was especially painful that day, but she caught up to the other wolves when they stopped to rest. The pup continued to bed next to her mother. I took that to be confirmation that mother and daughter had a strong bond.

The first three wolf packs were brought down from Canada in early 1995 and placed in pens to help them get used to living in Yellowstone. This is the Crystal Creek pack. Wolf 8, the main character in my first Yellowstone wolf book, *The Rise of Wolf 8*, is the gray wolf on the far left. **NPS/Jim Peaco**

In the 1990s, I led weekly hikes to the acclimation pen where the Crystal Creek pack lived during their first two months in Yellowstone before being released into the park in March 1995. A young wolf from that pack, wolf 8, grew up to be a superstar alpha male. He was the main character in my first Yellowstone wolf book, *The Rise of Wolf 8*. **NPS/David Gray**

My first sighting of 907 and the three other pups in her litter at Slough Creek on August 1, 2012. 907 was to spend all her life in this area. She lived to be eleven and a half years old, the fifth-oldest wolf ever recorded in Yellowstone, and had more litters of pups (ten) than any other female wolf in the park. **Jeremy SunderRaj**

A November 2024 night-vision photograph of 907 taken toward the end of her life. Despite losing an eye at age four, 907 was the four-time alpha female of the Junction Butte pack. She died in late December 2024 after single-handedly fighting a rival pack that had invaded her territory. **NPS/Jeremy SunderRaj**

A 2020 shot of twenty-one Junction Butte wolves. Alpha female 907 is the gray wolf standing in the upper left. That year, the pack had sixteen adults and eighteen pups, making it the second-largest pack in Yellowstone history. **NPS/ Jeremy SunderRaj**

In recent years, six Junction Butte males have joined the Mollies pack and at least three of them are sons of 907, including alpha male 1339. He is likely the father of the gray pup in this 2025 photograph. That means it is 907's grandpup. **Kira Cassidy**

I retired in 2018, but I still go out and watch wolves and talk to visitors every day. My hope is that every person who hears the wolves' stories will be on their side for the rest of their lives. **David G. Bluth**

Young biologists Taylor Rabe (left) and Jeremy SunderRaj (right) are among the new generation pushing the boundaries of wolf research for the future. This photograph is from a field trip they took to Brazil in 2023 to learn about jaguars. **Taylor Rabe**

13

The End of an Era for the Junction Butte Pack

AT THE START of 2024, the Junction Butte pack varied from ten to twelve wolves, with one pup. To the west, the Rescue Creek pack had eight adults and seven pups. To the south, the Mollies pack had nine adults. Both the Rescue and Mollies packs counted former Junction wolves among their members, including alpha males that had been born in the Junction pack.

On January 4, the Mollies turned up near Slough Creek. The Mollies usually stayed in Pelican Valley, but I heard that few elk were in the Mollies' territory, so that is probably why they came north. There was some chasing back and forth when the Mollies and Junction packs ended up near each other, but it was a nonaggressive interaction. Old male 1048, who had been in the Junction pack for many years before he joined the Mollies, seemed to have a moderating influence on the interactions that day.

One morning in mid-January, temperatures in our section of the park went down to minus 47 Fahrenheit (-44 Celsius). I was wearing fourteen layers of clothing, but I still was freezing. The wolves, unfazed by the cold, went about their lives as usual.

In mid-January, a big bison died in Lamar Valley. After most of the carcass had been consumed, I saw the Junction pup carry off a section of the hide. An adult wolf came over and the two of them had a tug-of-war. The pup won and ran off with her prize. I suspected the adult had let her win.

I saw the first wolf mating of the year on February 8. The Rescue Creek pack's alpha female was in a mating tie with a gray who was not the pack's alpha male. When the black alpha male saw what was happening, he ran over, jumped on the back of the gray male, and bit him several times, but as the wolves were already in a mating tie, it was too late to stop them. That incident showed that an alpha female mates with whoever she wants to, not just the alpha male.

A week later, that female mated with the alpha male. We have had cases where pups from one litter were sired by more than one male. A female's choice to mate with two males could be a hedge against the possibility that one of them was sterile. Years earlier I had seen an alpha female mate with three males: two from her own pack and an outsider.

Later in February, a new black male came into the Junction territory. He was 1407 from the Willow Creek pack, which was based in the eastern section of Yellowstone. 1407 was drawn to Junction female 1386. She and an uncollared Junction gray female ended up running off with him, and the three wolves set up a territory in the Hellroaring Creek area.

No one saw 907 and Black Male mate that February, but by March I had noticed that she was often last in line when the pack traveled at a fast pace. At one point, she bedded as the other wolves continued on. After a rest, she got up and followed their route. I guessed her pregnancy was beginning to hinder her. She still had a limp on her left front leg and was now also limping on her left hind leg. Later, I saw her bed and lick her left front paw.

On a later day that month, the Junctions came across an old bull bison in the Hellroaring Creek area. A detailed video of the successful hunt showed the wolves attacking the bull from the side rather than from the front or rear. That was a smart strategy, as a bison can seriously injure a wolf by kicking backward or by charging forward and headbutting it. The bull eventually collapsed and the wolves finished him off. Junction pup 1479 wisely stayed clear of the bison during the attack. She occupied herself by chasing ravens that were landing in anticipation of getting plenty of meals after the wolves killed the bull.

On March 13, 907 split off from the pack and visited her den site at Slough Creek. She bedded down there and did a lot of howling. I felt she was trying to get the other wolves to come to her. Soon she got up and moved off toward the pack.

Two days later, I saw the Junctions chase a herd of elk. The herd easily outran the wolves, but one cow lagged behind. A gray wolf caught up with the cow and bit into her hindquarters. Other Junctions ran in and helped finish off the cow.

That cow elk and the bull bison had physical issues, and in both cases the Junction wolves picked out vulnerable animals from large numbers of healthier and more fit bison and elk.

In some cases, wolves identify the most susceptible elk or bison by seeing it limp or noticing that it is slower than other members of the herd. In other cases, wolves use their extraordinary sense of smell to detect an animal that has an infection or a disease. I often read news stories of how easily dogs can be trained to detect illnesses in people. That ability comes from their wolf ancestors.

I looked at the Slough den area on April 1 and saw that the Junction wolves were there. 907 went to the lower of the two den sites, the Sage Den. She did a scent mark there, then looked into the den entrance. She did another scent mark and her mate, Black Male, came right over and marked over her site. They then walked off and bedded beside each other.

Soon after that, a grizzly came into the den area. Black Male got up and walked toward it. He bedded between the bear and 907, a position that guarded her if the grizzly approached any farther. The bear also lay down. The big male wolf got up, circled around behind the grizzly, then darted in and nipped it on the rear end. The grizzly charged the wolf and tried to swat him with a front paw. Black Male turned to face the bear, then casually walked off toward the bedded 907, who had been watching the interaction. After that, the grizzly moved off. The alpha male wolf followed until the bear was well away from the den. That day he functioned as 907's personal bodyguard.

In mid-April, the Mollies wolves returned to Lamar Valley from their territory to the south. Their gray alpha male,

1339, had been born to 907 at the Slough Creek den in 2020. Jeremy told me that six of the nine wolves in the Mollies pack that year came from the Junction family. All were males. That included male 1048, who had developed a unique bison-hunting technique.

When the Mollies chased a cow bison to the south bank of the Lamar River in early May, 1048 got in front of her, lunged forward, and bit into her nose. That held her in place as other wolves attacked her from different angles. When the bison fell into the river, the wolves gave up on her and ran off in search of other prey. I stayed with the cow and saw that she eventually drowned. Her body caught on something in a spot where the river was shallow enough to allow the Mollies wolves to later wade out and feed.

907 STILL LOOKED pregnant on April 26. She was now eleven years old, the oldest known wolf in the park. Her mate, Black Male, was nine. That day 907 looked into the Sage Den, then went into it. She came back out an hour later. In the following days, I noticed that she often went down to a nearby spring and drank a lot of water, a sign she was nursing pups.

Other pack members frequently went to the den, looked in, and wagged their tails. Black Male was faithfully performing the responsibilities of an alpha male and frequently brought food to 907.

As of early May, there were seven adults in the Junction pack. Later in the month, we saw several young Junction males that had been traveling with the Mollies wolves hanging out at the Slough den. It seemed they had come home to see the new additions to the family. Some of them went back and forth from the Mollies to the Junctions in the following weeks.

As in past springs, there were often hundreds of people watching the den from Slough Creek Campground Road about a mile away.

On May 18, gray adult female 1478, a daughter of 907, went into the Sage Den and soon came out with a tiny black pup in her mouth. She carried it off. 907 had left the den to get a drink at the spring. She saw what was happening and ran back. On reaching 1478, 907 grabbed one end of the pup. Then both adults jointly carried the pup back toward the den. As they reached the entrance, 1478 let go of the pup and mother wolf 907 took it down into the den. I later suspected that 1478 had carried off the pup so she could play with it.

The following morning, 907, 1478, and yearling 1479 were at the entrance to the Sage Den. Both of the younger females were daughters of 907, so they were older sisters to the new pups. Under the three adult wolves, we saw two black pups and a gray pup. The adults had lowered their heads so they could interact with the pups. One of the adults bedded and a pup climbed up on her back.

I thought about how exciting it must be for 1479 to be with the new pups. She was the only surviving pup from her litter the previous year and had missed out on playing with littermates. Now she could make up for that with the new pups.

The pups went to 907, who was sitting up, and nursed on her. This was 907's tenth litter, a record for a Yellowstone wolf. On the following morning, father wolf Black Male went to the den entrance and looked down into it to check on the pups. Jeremy SunderRaj reviewed our observations at the Slough Creek den and estimated that the pups were born on April 28. Our first sighting of all three pups out of the den was twenty-one days later.

In late May, another grizzly came into the den area. Black Male followed the bear and got in front of it when it veered toward the den. 907 and two other adult wolves ran over and also got between the grizzly and the den site. The bear changed direction, and Black Male darted forward and bit it on the rear end. After suffering that indignity, the bear left.

By late May, the pups had become adept at walking and were exploring the area around the den entrance. One morning 1479 returned to the den and regurgitated two piles of meat to her mother, 907. One of the pups came over and fed alongside its mother. Later, the three pups followed their older sister 1479 around the den area. The pups were still nursing on 907 on the last day of May.

On the morning of June 1, I saw the three pups walking around the den area. Some of the adults had traveled off to the north. 907 nursed one of the pups, then followed the route the other wolves had taken to the north. I guessed they were going to a carcass. That was the first time I had seen 907 leave the den area since she had had her pups.

I looked back at the den area and saw a two-year-old uncollared black male go partway into the den. We think it was one of the Junction wolves who had been living in the Mollies pack. He came out with one of the two black pups in his mouth. As the adult walked off, the pup acted like it was struggling to be let go. Then the pup fell out of the male's mouth to the ground. The male reached down, aggressively grabbed the pup by the head, and resumed carrying it.

From that point on, the pup hung limply out of the adult's mouth. After carrying it uphill, the male dropped the pup and walked off. I think that when the wolf had grabbed the pup, he had accidentally used too much pressure and killed it. It was a terrible incident to witness. Now only two of 907's three pups were alive. She soon returned to the den. The two surviving pups ran to her and all three bedded together.

I saw a turkey vulture flying into the area. It must have spotted the dead pup, as it circled several times before landing and spreading out its huge wings over the pup's body. That blocked our view, but we were sure the vulture was eating the pup.

I looked back at the den and saw the two remaining pups nursing on 907. I left the area around that time. I later got a report from a woman who continued to watch the site. She saw 907 leave the den and go to where the young male had dropped the dead pup. 907 must have followed his scent trail. The mother wolf sniffed around, then found what was left of the pup's body. She picked it up but soon dropped the pup, likely when she realized it was dead. For any mother, human or wolf, that would be a devastating experience. After that, 907 went back to her den.

IN MID-JUNE, THE two Junction Butte pups saw several cow elk and a calf coming into the den area. This may have been the first time those pups saw elk that close. They reacted by running off and hiding in the den. An hour or so later, 907 went to the den. The pups came out and nursed on her for two minutes. After that, they bedded down with their mother. Her presence must have reassured them that the elk were not a threat.

A black bear came into the den area in mid-June. Black Male and several other wolves charged toward it and the bear climbed up a nearby tree. The wolves bedded nearby. When the bear came down, the wolves charged at it a second time, and the bear climbed up a new tree. That happened two more times. After chasing the bear up four different trees, the wolves lost interest in it and bedded down.

A friend saw yearling 1479 catch a trout in the Lamar River. She dropped it and walked off without eating it. Apparently, the young wolf had never seen a fish before and did not understand that it was edible. A few days later, she caught another trout in that area and that time she ate it. The incident indicated to me that 1479 was a fast learner.

I drive west into the park in the dark from my cabin in Silver Gate early every day. One morning a huge herd of bison was walking east, toward me, on the park road. My headlights were reflected back at me by their eyes. I felt like I was in the zombie show *The Walking Dead.*

The last time I saw the pups try to nurse on 907 was July 3. The attempt was brief and the mother wolf snapped at them. It seemed her milk was drying up. The pups were now a little over two months old. That evening she regurgitated meat to her pups instead of nursing them, and the pups ate the meat. We determined that the gray pup was a female and the black pup was a male.

Jeremy told me about some recent Wolf Project research findings. The majority of cow elk in the park are around two years old, which is very young. But the average age of cow elk killed by wolves is fourteen to sixteen. That means wolves are predominantly killing the oldest and likely least fit individuals.

Going back to 1995, Wolf Project biologists have necropsied 5,981 carcasses of elk of all ages. They found that grizzlies and black bears, not wolves, are the main predators of elk calves in the park.

Yearling female 1479 frequently played with the two pups, usually in chasing games. She would also wrestle with them. The pups often licked her face. By mid-July, the pups were howling back when they heard adult pack members howling from a distance.

A big development took place on the evening of July 18. A black female adult wolf, a gray female adult, and three black pups showed up at the Junction den. The following morning, I saw those new wolves. We figured out that the black adult was former Junction female 1386. She had paired off with male 1407 the previous winter and I had seen them mating. They later denned west of the Slough den.

We all assumed that 1386's mate had died and that this was why she had returned to her parents with her pups. But it turned out we were wrong. The Wolf Project staff found that 1407 had gone back to the Willow Creek pack in the eastern section of the park. I do not know of any other cases in Yellowstone where a male wolf deserted his mate and their pups in the way that 1407 did. 907 fully accepted the three pups into her family and helped raise them along with her own two pups.

Jeremy later told me that the last time he got signals from 1407 was on June 25. That meant that before bringing her pups to the Slough den, 1386 had tried to support them for twenty-three days without any help from the male that sired her litter. Soon we could not tell which black pup had 907 as their mother and which ones belonged to 1386.

Black Male played with all five pups and did not treat the new ones any differently from the two pups he had sired. He was probably the grandfather of 1386's litter. 1479 also played with the five pups a lot. Eventually, we determined that one black pup was female and the other three blacks were males. The gray pup was a female.

IN JULY THE Junctions killed a bison that seemed to be dying in Lamar Valley. They fed on it for several days, and later, when the meat had been all eaten, I saw one of the pack members pluck fur from the hide, then eat the hide. That would be like a person eating shoe leather.

In late July, a big bull bison died east of Slough Creek Campground Road. The following morning, a grizzly and some of the Junction wolves fed on the carcass. Later, a mother grizzly and her three yearling cubs controlled the carcass site. Junction wolves still managed to slip in and feed despite the presence of the bear family.

On a later day, a black bear fed on the carcass. Yearling 1479 arrived at the site alone and chased off the bear, even though it was much larger than she was. Her confident attitude continued to impress me. Many of the Junction adults who fed on the bison carried pieces of meat back to the den and gave them to the pups. They also regurgitated meat to the pups. The Wolf Project staff recently determined that the park wolves are now eating more bison meat than elk meat. That is probably partly due to a significant increase in bison numbers in recent years.

By that time, we were calling the young black male who had accidentally killed the pup Dark Black. Dark Black behaved very subordinately to Black Male, who frequently chased him away from the Junction den area. On a later day when the young male was playing too roughly with a pup, 907 came over and bared her teeth at him.

We heard that a new group, the Bliss Pass pack, formed by 907's daughter 1341 with Hawk's Rest male 1437, had a litter of five pups in the upper Slough Creek area. 1341 later disappeared and another Junction female, 1477, took over the alpha female position. A second male from Hawk's Rest eventually joined the pack.

In early August, I noticed that yearling female 1479 was still spending much of her time either watching the pups play or playing with them. She often followed the pups around, looking like she was supervising them. By that time, the pups were catching and eating grasshoppers and voles.

The adults were still regurgitating meat to the pups in late August. Four bull bison had died in the Junction territory, so the pack had access to a lot of free meat. We figured that the carcasses kept them going for about six weeks.

The last day we had pups at the Slough den area was September 2. The following day, the pups and adults were based about a mile south of the den in a meadow along Slough Creek. There was an abandoned coyote den there that the pups liked to investigate.

Three days later, the pups traveled a few miles west with the adults. September 6 was the first day we did not see any

Junctions in the Slough Creek area. I had watched wolves at Slough Creek every day from April 19 through September 5, a period of four and a half months (109 days).

IN SEPTEMBER, PROBABLY after losing a fight with another bull, an additional bison died at Slough Creek. The following morning, the Junctions were back. The bison carcass was close to Slough Creek Campground Road, and large numbers of people gathered there in hopes of seeing wolves and grizzlies.

Most of the Junction wolves stayed a mile or two away from the carcass during the day because of the crowds, but they likely fed on it during the night. I saw 1479 come back to the pups from that carcass and regurgitate bison meat to them. That was how the adults had fed her the previous year, when she was a pup.

On September 14, three unknown blacks approached Slough Creek from the west, but backed off, probably because they realized that the Junctions were just east of them. Middle-aged Junction female 1386 followed them and socialized with the three strangers, so the blacks were likely all males.

The black wolves were too far away for us to see if they had radio collars, but Jeremy later confirmed they were from the Rescue Creek pack, which had denned about sixteen miles west of the Slough den site. At that time, there were three Junction-born adult males in the Rescue pack, including alpha male 1393, who was four years old. He had been born to 907's sister wolf 969, so 1393 was 907's nephew.

By October 2024, I noticed 907 was having a hard time getting up from a bedded position. In human years, she was around ninety years old and she had many physical issues that were making life more difficult and painful for her.

At that time, Montana allowed legal wolf hunting along the northern border of Yellowstone. One hunting unit was known as 313, and it allowed only three wolves to be shot in the fall and winter wolf-hunting season. The Junctions sometimes traveled to this unit to look for elk. The limit of three wolves was reached on October 26, and we thought that the Junctions would now be safe from hunters.

In late October, I left the park for a week to promote my new book *Thinking Like a Wolf*. I did talks in Colorado and Utah, including one at the Sundance Resort. I also spoke at several elementary schools about a children's book I had put out earlier in the year, *The Unlikely Hero*, which was the story of one of the first wolves to be reintroduced to the park: wolf 8.

The most unusual personal event of 2024 involved wolf 8. I was contacted by a professor at Rutgers University in New Jersey. She teaches a class at a nearby maximum-security prison and uses stories from my adult book *The Rise of Wolf 8* to spark discussions among the inmates about dealing with challenging life issues. One inmate wrote to me and said that wolf 8's story meant a lot to him because he was bullied when young, just as 8 had been by his bigger brothers. The professor sent me a photo of the men in her class. They all looked like tough guys from the TV series *The Sopranos*.

MY FIRST FULL day back in Yellowstone was November 4. That morning, I saw the Junction Butte pack and got a full count of fifteen wolves: ten adults and the pack's five pups. Two days later, the low was 11 Fahrenheit (–12 Celsius), and the nine-member Mollies pack had come back to Lamar Valley. Six Junction males were still in the pack. The other three were Mollies females.

In mid-November, the Mollies wolves were on the south side of the valley and the Junctions were on the north side. After the packs howled at each other, the Junctions moved off farther north and 1339 led the Mollies away from the Junctions to the south. I wondered if the Junction wolves in the two packs recognized each other's howls and chose to avoid any conflict by leaving the area.

There was a major event on November 23. We spotted fourteen Junction wolves going north at Slough Creek. Black Male, the alpha, spotted a lone cow bison and ran at her. She stood her ground and charged him. The male wolf tried to circle around behind her, but the cow turned to face him. 907 arrived and the cow charged her. Black Male went after the cow from the rear. She kicked back with a hind leg but missed him.

After that, 907 charged in from behind the cow. The cow kicked out and hit 907 with such force that she went sailing backward in the air, then crashed to the ground. All that was several miles from our position, so it was hard to record all the details. Most of the pack members were too afraid of the cow to help the alphas attack her. Deciding the cow bison was too much for them, the pack moved off to the north and we soon lost sight of them.

A friend named John Wood, who is a golf analyst for NBC Sports, videotaped the interaction. I later looked at the sequence, which showed what happened in far more detail than what I had seen through my scope. When 907 approached the bison from behind, the bison kicked out with both hind legs and hit 907 hard in the chest. The wolf literally flew backward through the air, then landed hard. But amazingly, 907 got right up and went after the cow again from the rear. This time, when the cow kicked out with both hind legs, she hit 907 in the face. The wolf staggered backward. Jeremy also filmed the attack, and his footage showed that at one point the cow kicked backward and hit Black Male in the face. The wolf ignored the blow and went right back at her.

It was dreadful to see how hard 907 was kicked those two times, especially considering how elderly she was. That incident, especially the moment when she went right back at the bison after the first kick, forever defined 907's courage and character for me.

Because that cow bison weighed around a thousand pounds, her kick would create about two thousand pounds of force on impact. You could compare it to a human getting kicked by a horse.

I feared those kicks had done real damage to 907's head and chest. When I told Jeremy about the failed attempt to get the cow bison, he said wolves getting kicked by prey animals is the second leading cause of death for wolves in the park. Wolves killing wolves is the top cause of death. That is mostly in territorial disputes.

The morning after the failed attack on the bison, the Junctions were traveling west, and 907 was lagging much farther behind than usual. On a later day, I saw Black Male stop and wait for 907 to catch up. Once she joined him, they continued on together. It was a touching scene to witness, for it summed up their relationship and care for each other. By that time, they had known each other for eight years and had grown old together.

WE SAW A skirmish between six Junction wolves and eight members of Mollies pack on December 1. No wolves were harmed in the encounter, which was mainly just the wolves chasing one another back and forth. All the adult males in the Mollies had grown up in the Junction pack, which probably explains the lack of aggression.

907 and a few other Junctions were back at Slough Creek during the encounter. When I saw 907 a few days later, she was still lagging behind as the pack searched for prey animals to hunt. It occurred to me that this was the only life 907 had ever known, and only death would stop her from hunting with her packmates.

We did not know it at the time, but the Junctions traveled through Unit 313 in mid-December, then continued into a larger wolf-hunting area known as Region Three. The quota there was fifty-two wolves. The Junctions had never gone that far north before.

Soon the Wolf Project got word that two young, uncollared wolves had been shot in Region Three: a black male and a gray female. GPS data from Junction gray female 1478 put her in that area, so the two dead wolves were probably from the Junction Butte pack. After that, a third wolf was shot in the same area, but I did not get any information on age or color. Black Male and several other Junction wolves were missing, and I was worried about them.

On December 20, signals from 907 and Junction females 1385, 1478, and 1479 indicated they had returned safely to

Lamar. We spotted a new bison carcass about two miles west of Slough Creek that morning, and early that afternoon, two black pups, likely Junction wolves, were feeding on it.

On December 22, the day I describe in the introduction to this book, six Junction wolves were bedded west of the creek, including 907. We were concerned about the missing pack members, especially the alpha male. He was extremely loyal to 907, so I worried that he had gotten shot and died in a place where he had not yet been found.

Suddenly, nineteen Rescue Creek wolves came running in from the west. The Junctions jumped up and ran north. A gray Junction wolf lagged behind and the Rescue wolves pulled it down. After biting it a few times, they ran off in pursuit of other wolves. The Junction wolf got up and did not seem to be seriously injured.

I spotted 907 to the north. She had stopped and was looking back at the Rescue wolves, who were now milling around. Then she bedded and calmly monitored the invading wolves. The Rescue wolves went north to the Junction den area before running off. By that time, 907 had slipped away.

Late that day, people saw the nineteen Rescue wolves on the bison carcass west of Slough Creek. After feeding for a while, they chased a lone gray canine that was approaching the carcass from the south. They caught and attacked it, then went back to the carcass to feed. The wolf watchers were not sure if the animal they had attacked was a wolf or a coyote. I worried it was 907. She was in poor shape after being kicked in the chest and the face by the cow bison a few weeks earlier and could not outrun a pack of wolves.

The following morning, December 23, we searched for 907 and other Junction wolves but could not spot any of them. The Rescue Creek wolves were still feeding on the bison carcass. They were back in their territory ten miles to the west the next morning.

Around that time, we heard reports that forty wolves had been shot in Region Three. Eventually, the quota of fifty-two was reached, and that closed the hunt for the year. We feared that more Junctions had been taken. We reluctantly concluded that 907's mate Black Male was one of them. Jeremy later gave me some very bad news: Black Male was illegally shot in that northern area on Christmas Day. We got some satisfaction when we heard that the man responsible was caught. He was fined and lost his hunting privileges.

TAYLOR RABE OF the Wolf Project got normal signals from 907's radio collar in the Slough Creek area on the morning of the twenty-fourth. If instruments in the collar do not detect motion for a period of twelve hours, the beeps per minute in the radio transmitter double. That is called the mortality signal. We hoped the signals meant 907 was still alive that morning.

Taylor was off on Christmas Day, then went back out early on the twenty-sixth. She got 907, but the signal from her collar was in mortality mode. Taylor, her husband, Jack, and their friend Michael got ready to head out to locate 907's body.

A few hours later, I returned to Slough Creek in time to see Taylor and her crew bringing 907 back in a plastic sled. A big crowd had gathered and everyone was in a sober mood. Taylor let everyone come over and have some final moments with 907.

In her prime, the Junction alpha had weighed 121 pounds, which is huge for a female wolf. Although she had lost weight as she aged, 907 was still a very big wolf. The most striking thing about her was the size of her paws. I touched her side. Her body was muscular with no hint of fat.

The crew found 907 a half mile or so east of where people had seen the Rescue wolves attack the gray canine that we now knew had been 907. That implied she had survived the fight, which had been late in the day on the twenty-second. To get there, she would have traveled east into an area we call Aspen Drainage. She was positioned partway on a route to her den where she could have hidden from the other wolves. 907 died there from her wounds. The site of her death was about a mile west of her den and two miles east of where she had been born in the spring of 2013. She had spent her entire life in that territory.

I first saw 907 on August 1, 2013, when she was a three-and-a-half-month-old pup, and last saw her alive on December 22, 2024, when she was eleven and three-quarters years old. 907 lived nearly four times the average lifespan of park wolves, and as far as we knew, she was the second-oldest wolf to have lived in the park since the reintroduction in 1995.

907 was the only known Junction wolf wounded or killed that day, despite the Rescue wolves having been in the core of the Junction territory. I recalled how similar the death of 907 was to the final minutes of her father's life, wolf 911, a longtime Junction Butte pack alpha male. In the fall of 2016, he killed an elk in the Lamar River. A rival pack of wolves arrived and charged at 911. He stood his ground, one wolf versus a pack, and died during the battle. No other wolves in his family were harmed that day.

It had been hard for me to deal with the death of 911 and it was just as difficult to accept the loss of his daughter, but if I had to choose between 907 being shot by someone who hated wolves or dying after fighting alone against nineteen rival wolves, I would pick the latter.

I pictured 907 standing her ground and growling as the wolves that had encircled and attacked her turned around and left. Only then did she leave the scene of the battle and walk to the secluded site where she lay down to lick her wounds and rest. For her entire life of nearly twelve years, she had been a fierce warrior who fought with prey animals many times her size, fought with rival females in her pack, and fought with neighboring wolf packs who had invaded her territory. I was thankful that 907 had lived so long and accomplished so much. I think it is fair to say any soldier who has served in combat would agree that 907 had a good death.

In the days after her passing, I thought about 907's advanced age and her many health issues. I also thought about how her longtime mate, Black Male, had been killed in the recent hunt. 907 was related to all the other males in the pack. As wolves do not mate with close relatives, this meant it was unlikely she would have any more pups. All that added up to me thinking it had been time for 907's story to be completed and time for a younger pack member to take over.

JEREMY TOLD ME they had brought 907 to a cold-storage area at Park Headquarters. Male wolf 1048, a longtime member of the Junction pack who 907 knew well, died of natural causes linked to old age, around that time. I had seen the two wolves mate in 2017, when 907 was nearly four years old. Jeremy placed 1048 next to 907 in the Wolf Project's freezer, an action that greatly pleased me. Both wolves would later be examined, and their conditions and injuries would be recorded in Park Service records.

There is one more thing to say about 907 that helps me cope with her death. A year ago, my Native American friend John Potter, who lives near Yellowstone and often performs wolf blessing ceremonies in the park, told me: "When wolves die in the park, they do not really die. They live on in a different form up in the mountains." That means 907 has reunited with her mate Black Male, her parents 911 and Ragged Tail, and other relatives in that spirit realm.

After Taylor and her crew drove off with the body of 907 on December 26, I went out to look at the bison carcass and saw ten wolves at the site. They were still there the next morning. At first I thought that meant more surviving Junction wolves had returned from north of the park, but on talking to Jeremy and Taylor, I found out the group included several Rescue wolves: black male 1392, gray male 1484, black male 1489, two uncollared black males, and a gray uncollared yearling male.

When things settled out, we had a new blended family in the park: six Rescue males, three Junction females (1385, 1478, and 1479), and two black pups, which was about the average size of a Yellowstone pack. After the Rescue males joined the Junction females, the other Rescue wolves mostly stayed out of the Junction territory.

I had watched and studied the Junction pack nearly every day since the pack formed in 2012. The arrival of the Rescue males changed the sad story of 907's death and the loss of many other Junction wolves into a miraculous reinvigoration of the thirteen-year-old pack. It reminded me of how 907, in her first term as alpha female, accepted four males into the family that came from the pack that killed her father, wolf 911. The Junction pack had been close to falling apart, but in accepting the Rescue males into their family, they had come back from the brink.

Jeremy and Taylor soon concluded that two-and-a-half-year-old black Junction female 1385 was the new Junction alpha female. She had been born in 2022 to female 1382, a niece of 907's. That made her a grandniece to 907. Gray female 1478, who looks just like her mother 907, is bigger than 1385, so she may later try to seize the alpha female position.

AT THE BEGINNING of 2025, there were nine wolf packs in Yellowstone. Four of them had Junction wolves in alpha positions: Junction Butte, Mollies, Rescue Creek, and Bliss Pass.

We saw two matings in the Junction pack in February 2025. New alpha male 1392 mated with alpha female 1385. Later, an uncollared, gray Rescue male also tied with 1385. I saw one of 907's sons who had dispersed to Mollies pack mate with a young female in that family.

We began to get glimpses of little pups coming out of the Natal Den at Slough Creek on May 9. Soon after that, we got a count of six black pups. By that time, they were about the size of young kittens. They all seemed healthy and vigorously nursed on 1385.

Then there was a surprise: a photo taken of two-year-old 1479 clearly showed that she had distended nipples, proof that she had also given birth. Soon, we saw 1479 nursing a group of pups. Eventually, we got glimpses of pups that were smaller than the six born to 1385 and figured they had 1479 for a mother. As that was taking place, it looked like Junction gray female 1478 was denning behind Jasper Bench in Lamar Valley, close to one of the Junction pack's main rendezvous sites. Both 1478 and 1479 were daughters of 907, so their pups would be her grandchildren. Meanwhile, the Mollies were denning a few miles to the east in Lamar Valley. The sire of those Mollies pups was likely 1339, a son of 907.

As I recorded my sightings of the new generation of wolves, I took comfort in the fact that 907 is still here, in the sense that her genes are so strongly represented in the Junction and Mollies packs. That is a good measurement of the impact of the life of a wolf. The Junction Butte pack is once again a powerful enterprise. 907 served as a model of how an alpha female should lead her pack. It is up to the next generation to ensure the pack survives.

I have been studying wolves for over thirty years in Yellowstone and written books on the lives of our most prominent alpha wolves: 8, 21 and 42, 302, the 06 Female, and 907. All of these wolves were legendary during their lifetimes, but none of them were lone wolves, and their success was only possible because their packs supported them.

An analogy would be a professional sports team that has a star player. The star will score a lot of points and perhaps make the game-winning play, but they need teammates to pass the ball to them and block opponents. When a star player retires, their team continues on and there will be new most-valuable players.

The story of the Yellowstone wolves lies not in individual wolves but in the longevity of the packs in which they live, play, and reproduce. The Crystal Creek genetic line in Yellowstone is now thirty years old, and that dynasty, represented by the Mollies, Junction Butte, Rescue Creek, and Bliss Pass packs, dominates the park.

Life Lessons From Wolves

Perseverance

The wolves I have observed over the years have had a great impact on my life and inspire me to do all that I can to help protect them. As Yellowstone's Junction Butte alpha male 911 got older, he had several physical challenges that slowed him down. But he still went out every day to hunt large prey animals and stood his ground when an entire wolf pack was about to attack him.

I am also getting older, but I still go out into the park early every day regardless of rain, snow, cold temperatures, or the steep ridges I have to climb to study wolves. If I start thinking of slacking off, I motivate myself by asking, "What would 911 do?" He would press on, and that is what I end up doing too.

I tell wolf 911's story in *Thinking Like a Wolf: Lessons From the Yellowstone Packs.*

14

The Power of Stories

ON MAY 19, 2025, I got up at 4 a.m., left my cabin at 5:12, and drove twenty-four miles to Slough Creek Campground Road. I focused my spotting scope on the Junction den and saw nine adult wolves and three black pups.

That was a fairly normal morning for me, but it also happened to be my ten thousandth day of looking for wolves and watching packs in Yellowstone National Park, going back to May 12, 1995. Ten thousand days divided by 365 equals 27.4 years. That includes a fifteen-year period (2000 to 2015) when I was out in the field every day without a break.

I have had a total of 126,372 wolf sightings in those ten thousand days. To define terms, if I watch a pack of ten wolves, I count that as ten wolf sightings. The last time I figured out the percentage of days when I saw wolves, it was around 93 percent, a success rate that was unimaginable when I first arrived in the park. I have seen wolves make 217 kills and witnessed 147 matings during my years in Yellowstone. I have never tried to add up the number of people I helped see wolves or talked to about wolves over my three decades in Yellowstone, but I guess it would be several multiples above my count of 126,372 wolf sightings.

But there is something more important than those numbers. Most of the time when I spot wolves, park visitors pull over and ask what I am seeing. I am always happy to share my wolf sightings with anyone who approaches me. As I tell them about the wolves they are viewing, I invite them to look through my spotting scope. Often it takes a few moments for people to adjust to using a high-powered scope. Then there is the magic moment when they excitedly blurt out something like "I see them, I see them! They are absolutely gorgeous!"

Doug Smith, longtime head of the Wolf Project, once said: "Facts don't change people, but stories do." Although many people call me a wildlife biologist, I think of myself primarily as a storyteller. I am well aware that wolves are controversial and that many people dislike them. That is why I tell wolf stories in my books and talks and why I am optimistic about changing people's attitudes toward wolves. I have had the privilege of witnessing the stories of the wolves and it is my responsibility to tell those stories to as many people as possible.

Late 2024, when so many Junction wolves were shot and killed north of the park, was a depressing time for us who knew those wolves so well. Months later, when I was watching the new, revitalized version of the Junction pack raising six pups, a woman and her husband approached me. She told me how much she enjoyed reading my wolf books. Then she mentioned that she got her husband to read some of the books. She added that he had previously killed many wolves. He spoke up at that point and said, "Yes, I used to hunt and kill wolves, but I don't do that anymore."

That is the best example I have ever come across that proves the power of stories to change people.

ACKNOWLEDGMENTS

Many people have helped during my years in Yellowstone, most especially Doug Smith (former head of the Wolf Project), Jeremy SunderRaj, Taylor Rabe, Dan Stahler, and Matt Metz; my Wolf Project work partners Tom Zieber, Erin Cleere, Elena West, Dan Graf, Emily Almberg, Erin Albers, Colby Anton, Hans Martin, Pete Mumford, Lizzie Cato, and Kira Cassidy; friends Laurie Lyman, John Kerr, Tom Murphy, Jeff Adams, and Doug McLaughlin; Lisa Diekmann and her staff at Yellowstone Forever; Nathan and Linda Varley and all the other wildlife tour guides who work in Yellowstone; and the hundreds of good people collectively known as Yellowstone's wolf watchers.

A special thanks to Tom Tankersley, who hired me for my first Yellowstone job as the wolf interpreter in 1994. Thanks to other supervisors who hired me before Yellowstone: Bud Getty in Anza-Borrego Desert State Park, Bill Truesdell in Denali National Park and Joshua Tree National Monument, Virgil Olson in Death Valley National Monument, Dennis Vásquez in Big Bend National Park, and before all that, Dean Clark, boss of our fire crew at Sequoia and Kings Canyon National Parks.

And, as always, a big thank-you to all the people at my publisher, Greystone Books, in Vancouver, British Columbia: my longtime editor, Jane Billinghurst; copy editor Brian Lynch; proofreader Meg Yamamoto; publisher Jen Gauthier; designer Fiona Siu; marketing director Megan Jones; founding publisher Rob Sanders; and all the other members of the Greystone team who make sure my books get into the hands of readers.

REFERENCES

Books and Articles

Abbey, Edward. 1968. *Desert Solitaire: A Season in the Wilderness.* New York: McGraw-Hill.

Ballard, Warren, et al. 1981. "Causes of Neonatal Moose Calf Mortality in South Central Alaska." *Journal of Wildlife Management* 45(2): 335–342.

Ballard, Warren B. 1983. "The Case of the Disappearing Moose." *Alaska*, January, February, and March 1983 issues.

Boyd, Diane K. 2024. *A Woman Among Wolves.* Vancouver: Greystone Books.

Bugliosi, Vincent, and Curt Gentry. 1974. *Helter Skelter: The True Story of the Manson Murders.* New York: W. W. Norton & Company.

Busiek, Julia. 2019. "A Mystery in Death Valley." *National Parks*, fall issue.

Cole, Martin. 1983. *Journey to Caribou Land.* Whittier, CA: Cole Revocable Trust.

Dawe, Albert R., and Wilma A. Spurrier. 1969. "Hibernation Induced in Ground Squirrels by Blood Transfusion." *Science* 163: 298–299.

Fatsis, Stefan. 2016. "'No Viet Cong Ever Called Me [the N Word]': The Story Behind the Famous Quote That Muhammad Ali Probably Never Said." *Slate*, June 8, 2016.

Follmann, Erich. 1982. "Physiological Studies of Arctic Carnivores." Office of Naval Research, Report NR 207-287.

Gebhard, James. 1982. "Annual Activities and Behavior of a Grizzly Bear (*Ursus arctos*) Family in Northern Alaska." Master's thesis, University of Alaska.

Haber, Gordon, and Marybeth Holleman. 2013. *Among Wolves*. Fairbanks, AK: University of Alaska Press.

Heacox, Kim. 2016. *The National Parks: An Illustrated History—100 Years of American Splendor*. Washington, DC: National Geographic.

"How Bill Keys Was Freed by the Court of Last Resort." 2023. Desert Way with Jaylyn and John, www.thedesertway.com/bill-keys/.

Manly, William L. 1894. *Death Valley in '49*. San Jose, CA: Pacific Tree and Vine.

McIntyre, Rick. 1986. *Denali National Park: An Island in Time*. Sequoia Communications.

McIntyre, Rick. 1990. *Grizzly Cub: Five Years in the Life of a Bear*. Anchorage, AK: Alaska Northwest.

McIntyre, Rick. 1993. *A Society of Wolves: National Parks and the Battle Over the Wolf*. Stillwater, MN: Voyageur Press.

McIntyre, Rick. 1995. *War Against the Wolf: America's Campaign to Exterminate the Wolf*. Stillwater, MN: Voyageur Press.

McIntyre, Rick. 2019. *The Rise of Wolf 8: Witnessing the Triumph of Yellowstone's Underdog.* Vancouver: Greystone Books.

McIntyre, Rick. 2020. *The Reign of Wolf 21: The Saga of Yellowstone's Legendary Druid Pack.* Vancouver: Greystone Books.

McIntyre, Rick. 2021. *The Redemption of Wolf 302: From Renegade to Yellowstone Alpha Male.* Vancouver: Greystone Books.

McIntyre, Rick. 2022. *The Alpha Female Wolf: The Fierce Legacy of Yellowstone's 06.* Vancouver: Greystone Books.

McIntyre, Rick. 2024. *Thinking Like a Wolf: Lessons From the Yellowstone Packs.* Vancouver: Greystone Books.

McIntyre, Rick, and David A. Poulsen. 2025. *The Unlikely Hero: The Story of Wolf 8.* Vancouver: Greystone Books.

Moore, Terris. 1967. *Mt. McKinley: The Pioneer Climbs.* Fairbanks, AK: University of Alaska Press.

Murie, Adolph. 1944. *The Wolves of Mount McKinley.* Washington, DC: United States Government Printing Office.

Murie, Adolph. 1961. *A Naturalist in Alaska.* New York: Devin-Adair.

Murphy, Bob. 1993. *Desert Shadows: A True Story of the Charles Manson Family in Death Valley.* Morongo Valley, CA: Sagebrush Press.

National Geographic. 2016. "Yellowstone: The Battle for the American West" (single issue).

Neher, Chris, et al. 2022. "Economic Impact of Wolf-Related Visitation to Yellowstone National Park: An Update of 2005

Estimates." *Greater Yellowstone Wildlife-Related Activity Valuation Study*. Boulder, CO: RRC Associates.

Pearson, Arthur M. 1975. "The Northern Interior Grizzly Bear *Ursus arctos*." Canadian Wildlife Service Report Series no. 34. Ottawa: Canadian Wildlife Service.

Rawson, Timothy. 2001. *Changing Tracks: Predators and Politics in Mt. McKinley National Park*. Fairbanks, AK: University of Alaska Press.

Reid, Nancy, and Shiela Liermann. 1996. *Famous Friends of the Wolf Cookbook: Benefiting Wolf Recovery in the West*. Avon, MA: Adams Media Corporation.

Reynolds, Harry V., and John L. Hechtel. 1980. "Structure, Status, Reproductive Biology, Movement, Distribution, and Habitat Utilization of a Grizzly Bear Population." In "North Slope Grizzly Bear Studies" by Harry Reynolds. Project Progress Report, July 1, 1978, to June 30, 1979. Alaska Department of Fish and Game.

Reynolds, Harry V., and John L. Hechtel. 1984. "Population Structure, Reproductive Biology and Movement Patterns of Grizzly Bears in North Central Alaska Range." Project Progress Report, July 1, 1982, to June 30, 1983. Alaska Department of Fish and Game.

Seton, Ernest Thompson. 1898. *Wild Animals I Have Known*. New York: Charles Scribner's Sons.

Sherwonit, Bill. 2015. "Gordon Haber's Final Days." *Anchorage Daily News*, September 27, 2015.

Spurrier, Wilma, et al. 1976. "Induction of summer hibernation in the 13-lined ground squirrel shown by comparative serum transfusions from Arctic mammals." *Cryobiology* 13(3): 368–374.

Steinhorn, Leonard. 2006. *The Greater Generation: In Defense of the Baby Boom Legacy*. New York: Thomas Dunne Books.

Thesz, Lou. 2001. *Hooker: An Authentic Wrestler's Adventures Inside the Bizarre World of Professional Wrestling*. Seattle, WA: Wrestling Channel Press.

VanderMolen, Tyler. 2021. "When Stars Wars Came to Death Valley National Park." *Backpacker*, May 4, 2021.

Watts, P. D., and Charles Jonkel. 1988. "Energetic Cost of Winter Dormancy in Grizzly Bear." *Journal of Wildlife Management* 52(4): 654–656.

Documentaries

WILDFIRE! True Story of Firefighters vs. Out of Control Forest Fire. Posted in 2013 by Bright Enlightenment on YouTube, www.youtube.com/watch?v=HfZw31FKZoo.

"The Wolf That Changed America." *Nature* (PBS), 2009.

INDEX

Illustrations, maps, and photographs indicated by page numbers in italics